—— KILLING THE PRESIDENT ——

– KILLING THE PRESIDENT –

Assassinations, Attempts, and Rumored Attempts on U.S. Commanders-in-Chief

Willard M. Oliver
and Nancy E. Marion

 PRAEGER

AN IMPRINT OF ABC-CLIO, LLC
Santa Barbara, California • Denver, Colorado • Oxford, England

Library of Congress Cataloging-in-Publication Data

Oliver, Willard M.
   Killing the president : assassinations, attempts, and rumored attempts on U.S. commanders-in-chief / Willard M. Oliver and Nancy E. Marion.
      p. cm.
   Includes bibliographical references and index.
   ISBN 978-0-313-36474-7 (hard copy : alk. paper) — ISBN 978-0-313-36475-4 (ebook)
1. Presidents—Assassination—United States—History. 2. Presidents—Assassination
attempts—United States—History. 3. Presidents—United States–Biography.
4. Assassins—United States—Biography. I. Marion, Nancy E. II. Title.
   E176.1.O45 2010
   364.152′4—dc22   2010011871

ISBN: 978-0-313-36474-7
EISBN: 978-0-313-36475-4

14   13   12   11   10   1   2   3   4   5

This book is also available on the World Wide Web as an eBook.
Visit www.abc-clio.com for details.

Praeger
An Imprint of ABC-CLIO, LLC

ABC-CLIO, LLC
130 Cremona Drive, P.O. Box 1911
Santa Barbara, California 93116-1911

This book is printed on acid-free paper ∞

Manufactured in the United States of America

To my biggest fan, my mom, Carol R. Oliver, with love.
W.M.O.

To my biggest fans, Vince, Jacob, and Anthony, and Mom and Dad.
N.E.M.

Contents

Illustrations

Preface

Article II of the U.S. Constitution states very explicitly that the "executive Power shall be vested in a President of the United States of America." The Office of the President, since the establishment of this American governmental institution under President George Washington, has been the most visible and widely known office in American government. While the power and prestige of both the U.S. Congress and the Supreme Court cannot be dismissed, the powers that the Constitution gives to the president of the United States are vast. The president is the commander-in-chief of the military, he can grant reprieves and pardons, and he is empowered with a cabinet. He is also given the power to enter into treaties and appoint ambassadors and federal justices (including those on the U.S. Supreme Court), all with the "advice and consent" of the U.S. Senate. These are, however, only his formal powers, those specified in the U.S. Constitution. The president also has what are called *implied powers*, and these relate to his ability to issue executive orders, give speeches, and hold press conferences. Taken together, these powers have helped to establish the American president as the most prominent and visible member, both nationally and internationally, of the American government. In a sense, the person who holds the office of the president is often perceived, by those outside of the United States and U.S. citizens alike, as the sole representative of our American government.

As a result of being America's most prominent leader, the president is often the focus of the public's attention. There are many who listen to the president in order to understand the policies of the U.S. government. There are many who agree with the president and his position on public policies, and these people often become his ardent supporters. However, in a democratic electorate there are often those who disagree with the president's policies, and they can often be as vocal as his supporters. Many of these people speak out against the president's policy positions and his political party, and sometimes they criticize the president himself. Many will often vent both their frustrations and anger toward the American government by focusing their derision on the president. In most cases, these disagreements arise in the form of letters to the editor, political interest groups, and civic protests over a president's policy position or actions on the part of government. In a few rare cases, the president becomes the target of an assassin because the disgruntled, the deranged, and the psychotic often fixate on high-profile individuals. There are also those who believe that killing the president will right some perceived wrong or change the course of history for the better.

At the time of the writing of this book, forty-four men have served in the Office of the President. Of those forty-four, eight have died in office while serving as president. Four died by an assassin's bullet (Lincoln, Garfield, McKinley, and Kennedy), and four died of natural causes (Harrison, Taylor, Harding, and Franklin D. Roosevelt). Two other presidents were targets of assassins and were struck by a bullet but survived (Theodore Roosevelt and Reagan). Four other presidents were in immediate danger of assassination, but were neither struck nor injured in the attempts (Jackson, Franklin D. Roosevelt, Truman, and Ford twice).

There have also been assassination attempts on the presidents' lives in which they were not in imminent danger but were in proximity to the attempt. Two of these occurred while the president was actually still the president-elect (Lincoln and Obama), nine occurred while the president was serving in office (Nixon, Carter, Clinton, George W. Bush, and Obama), and one occurred after the president's term had ended (George H. W. Bush)—a total of twelve separate incidents. It should be noted that there are often threats against the president's life by people whose actions could be perceived as threatening (e.g., hopping over the White House fence), but these are not classified as assassination attempts. Finally, while there is no conclusive evidence, rumors have always circulated that two of the presidents who died by natural causes (Taylor and Harding) actually died at the hands of assassins.

Although some of these assassinations and attempts have been detailed in other books, they have not always received the same level of treatment. The assassinations of Presidents Abraham Lincoln and John F. Kennedy have received the lion's share of books. The other two presidents who died by assassin's bullets, Garfield and McKinley, have received far less coverage. The rest of the assassination attempts have had limited coverage, some having received none at all.

There have been a number of compilations about assassinations and attempts, some in encyclopedic format, often including all of the assassinations—presidential and otherwise—that have occurred in the United States.[1] Two of these books certainly stand out. One provides descriptions of the many assassinations in America but is plagued by a running commentary on the events and people involved.[2] The second is a study that attempts to categorize the psychological mind-set of the assassins.[3] While each of these books conveys many of the lesser-known events related to the assassinations, they stray from presidential assassinations and include many nonpresidential assassinations as well. Finally, because they were published before the Reagan attempt assassination, they are somewhat dated. Distinct from these older efforts, this book aims to provide the details of presidential assassinations, attempted assassinations, and rumored assassinations in a narrative format.

The first ten chapters will depict either the assassination or attempted assassination of a president by opening with a brief introduction to the actual assassination or attempt. The chapter will then provide short biographies of the president and of the assassin, followed by a detailed description of the assassination or attempted assassination and the aftermath, with particular focus on the outcome of the president, the outcome of the assassin, and whether or not the security of the president changed in the wake of the event. The last two chapters are formatted in a different way: chapter 11 details all of the other assassination attempts in shorter sections, and chapter 12 details the two rumored assassinations of U.S. Presidents Taylor and Harding in a split-chapter format.

The development of this book arose out of the research interest of both authors in regard to the Office of the Presidency, specifically as it relates to crime and crime-control policy. While most of our research has focused on the president and his role in shaping crime policy in America, we both thought that the ultimate intersection between presidents and crime was the assassination of a president. Thus, our strong interest in presidents and crime resulted in the book you now hold.

The authors would like to first thank our institutions for their assistance and cooperation in the research of this book: Sam Houston State University (Huntsville, Texas) and the University of Akron (Akron, Ohio). In addition, we would like to thank the archivists who work for the National Archives and Records Administration (NARA) at the various presidential libraries, as well as those at the Library of Congress; their assistance proved invaluable for providing various facts, settling disputes amongst the written record, and securing photographs to complement the chapters in this book.

—— 1 ——

Andrew Jackson

INTRODUCTION

As the funeral of Representative Warren R. Davis of South Carolina, held at the U.S. Capitol, came to an end, congressmen, Supreme Court justices, and President of the United States Andrew Jackson began to process by the funeral bier. President Jackson walked slowly, clearly showing signs of age and his hard years in the military. He leaned on his treasury secretary for support with one hand while balancing himself with a cane in the other. They passed slowly under the rotunda and down to the east porch in order to exit the Capitol.

A short slender man of no great distinction stepped out from behind a column. He was less than ten feet away from the president when he pulled a pistol from beneath his cape and pointed it at President Jackson.

Jackson, the seventh president of the United States, was accustomed to violence after a life in the military. It is unlikely that he expected, however, to be the first president of the United Sates to experience an assassination attempt.

ANDREW JACKSON

Andrew Jackson was born on March 15, 1767, in the Waxhaw area along the border of North Carolina and South Carolina to his immigrant parents Andrew (Hugh) and Elizabeth (Betty) Jackson.[1] Unfortunately, several days before Andrew Jackson's birth, Hugh was attempting to move a heavy log, strained his heart, and collapsed. He died before his namesake was born.

Jackson grew up with two older brothers. At the local one-room schoolhouse, young Andrew enjoyed the first of the three Rs but was poor in the second and a failure in the third. He could read by age five, and by age nine had become a public reader, but he did poorly at his studies. His real joys were riding horses, roaming the woods, and learning to be independent.

When Andrew was thirteen years old the American Revolution was underway, and he joined a local regiment and served as a courier. Andrew and one of his brothers, Robert, were captured on a courier run and imprisoned. It was here that Jackson experienced his first true brush with violence. A British officer demanded that Andrew clean his boots. Andrew refused, and the irate officer slashed at Andrew with his sword. Andrew suffered cuts to both his left hand and head, the first wounds he ever received in anger toward him, but most certainly not the last.

The prison conditions were poor, and both Andrew and his brother were close to starvation. They also contracted smallpox and suffered greatly from the disease. At this time, their mother, Betty, managed to gain their release and brought them home. Robert, however, died of smallpox a few days later. Andrew recovered.

Betty Jackson decided to try to help other sick and injured American soldiers by working on the prison ships docked in Charleston Harbor. Given the unsanitary conditions on board, diseases were rampant on the ships. Betty contracted a disease and died, leaving Andrew, now age fourteen, an orphan.

Andrew left Waxhaw and for a short time worked in a saddle maker's shop before moving to Salisbury, North Carolina, where he began to read law. In 1787 he was admitted to the bar and became a practicing lawyer. He moved to Jonesboro, the Western District of North Carolina, which would later become Tennessee, to begin his practice. The following year, he was appointed solicitor of the district. When the territory of Tennessee was created in 1791, Jackson held the same position with the new territorial government.

Jackson became involved in politics in 1796 as a delegate to the Tennessee Constitutional Convention. Then, when Tennessee gained statehood in 1796, Jackson was elected to Congress as a member of the U.S. House of Representatives. The next year he was elected to the U.S. Senate, where he served one year before resigning to serve as a judge on the Tennessee Supreme Court, a position he held until 1804.

In that year Jackson also acquired "The Hermitage," a 640-acre farm located outside of Nashville, Tennessee. He would later expand the farm by purchasing an additional 360 acres, and his primary crop was cotton. Jackson owned nine slaves when he started the farm and had forty-four by 1820.

Although Jackson was attracted to both the legal and political professions, he also was enamored with all things martial. Utilizing his political and legal connections, he received an appointment as the commander of the Tennessee militia in 1801 and was befitted with the rank of colonel. In a sense, this was largely a political position unto itself, for the country was not at war. However, all that would change with the War of 1812.

When Tecumseh incited the "Red Stick" Indians to attack white settlements, 400 settlers were killed in the Fort Mims massacre. This triggered the Creek

War, and Jackson was made commander of not only the Tennessee militia but also all American forces. Jackson fought the Red Stick Indians at the Battle of Horseshoe Bend in 1814, and for his victory was promoted to major general.

Flush with success, Jackson was called upon to defend New Orleans as British forces were beginning to threaten the city on the Gulf Coast. Jackson maneuvered his 5,000 soldiers against Britain's 7,500 and won the Battle of New Orleans on January 8, 1815 (one month after the war was technically over). The British suffered over 2,000 casualties in the battle, while Jackson's forces suffered thirteen killed and fifty-eight wounded or missing.[2]

Jackson earned the nickname "Old Hickory" for being as "tough as old hickory," and also received a gold medal from Congress. Perhaps even more important, he earned the respect of an entire nation and was hailed as the first military hero since General George Washington.

Two years later, President James Monroe called upon Jackson to deal with the Seminole and Creek Indians in Georgia and to prevent Florida from becoming a refuge for runaway slaves. Jackson ruthlessly attacked the Seminole and Creek Indians and he ventured into Florida, then owned by Spain, creating an international maelstrom. In the end, Jackson's forces caused the Seminole and Creek Indians to cease their attacks on behalf of Spain and the United Kingdom, and Spain ceded Florida to the United States. Jackson was then made the military governor of Florida, serving most of 1821.

Jackson had become the preeminent military officer in the United States. His reputation led to his run for the presidency in 1824. Against a slate of high-quality candidates including Treasury Secretary William H. Crawford, Secretary of State John Quincy Adams, and Speaker of the House Henry Clay, Jackson received the most popular votes. The electoral votes were split, however, with Jackson holding the plurality, and the election was decided by the House of Representatives. Adams became president. Many, including Jackson, felt he had been robbed of the presidency.

Jackson used this argument to his advantage four years later, when he once again received the nomination for president. In this election, Jackson created the Democratic Party, mobilized the nation, and handily defeated Adams to become the seventh president of the United States. What should have been the happiest of times for Jackson, though, turned into a nightmare when his wife, Rachel, died on December 22, 1828, just prior to his inauguration.

Jackson's first term as president proved to be both highly successful and highly controversial. He proposed and signed into law the Indian Removal Act, which forced Indian tribes to trade their lands in the east for lands out west or be forcefully removed. He also dealt with the belief of some states, particularly southern ones, that they could nullify tariff legislation passed by the federal government. Jackson threatened to send in military troops to prevent this secession, and South Carolina bowed to the pressure.

In 1832, Jackson ran for a second term as president with Martin Van Buren as his vice president. He won easily. He then made it his goal to destroy the

Second Bank of the United States. The Second Bank was a private bank that held the government's money and was authorized in 1816 under President James Madison. The bank's federal charter was for twenty years, to be renewed in 1836. Jackson worked to rescind the charter on the grounds that the bank concentrated the financial strength of America into a single institution, it served simply to make the rich richer, it threatened America's sovereignty due to potential control by foreign interests, it had too much control over members of Congress, and it favored the northeastern states over those in the South and West. In 1833, Jackson succeeded in destroying the charter and ordered the funds withdrawn from the bank. The secretary of the treasury refused, so Jackson fired him. In September 1833, the new secretary of the treasury withdrew the funds. Despite receiving a censure from the U.S. Senate on March 28, 1834, Jackson had won his victory and now had to find ways of managing the money in other banks and preventing the collapse of not only the new banks but also the entire U.S. economy.

At the time that Jackson was dealing with this issue, Representative Warren Davis of South Carolina died, and his funeral was to be held in the U.S. Capitol on January 30, 1835.

RICHARD LAWRENCE

Richard Lawrence, Jackson's would-be assassin, was born in England, not in the United States as many had believed. His birth date is unknown, but it is believed that he was born in either 1800 or 1801.[3] When Lawrence was twelve years old, his parents left England for America and settled in the Washington, D.C., area. Lawrence grew up there and attended school for a short time. He was of a very slight build and approximately five feet seven inches tall. Apparently, Richard's life was very simple, uneventful, and by all accounts "normal." At his trial, a number of relatives and acquaintances testified as to Lawrence's demeanor. One stated that he was "a remarkable fine boy . . . reserved in his manner; but industrious and of good moral habits."[4] He was not a religious man, but he did occasionally read the Bible and attend church. In his teenage years, he began painting houses for money and continued to do so until he entered his early thirties. He typically worked in the Georgetown area of Washington, D.C., and managed to make a living. This was Richard Lawrence's life until the winter of 1832.

In November of that year, Lawrence announced that he was returning to England.[5] He was gone for only a month before returning. He had made it as far as Philadelphia, Pennsylvania. He explained that he had decided not to take the trip to England because the weather there was too cold. He remained home for several months and everything appeared to return to normal until Lawrence once again "left for England," this time intending to study landscape painting. He went to Philadelphia to catch a passenger ship to England, but once again he returned, offering only the explanation that "people" would not allow him to travel to his destination. He also believed that the government was not inclined to let him travel. When asked for evidence, he explained that it was all made clear to him when he reached Philadelphia, for it was there that all the newspapers had made attacks on both his character and his plans for traveling. He summarily decided he would return to Washington, D.C., save up his money, then hire his own ship with captain and crew in order to make the journey to his country of birth.

Lawrence was clearly becoming mentally unstable. He was beginning to exhibit the signs of mental illness that others in his family had exhibited. His father had been institutionalized at one point for mental problems, and one of his aunts died insane. Thus it was at this point in his life that things began to unravel.[6] He quit painting houses and spoke of his various delusions to friends and family. When asked how he would support himself, he told his sister and her husband that he would soon come into money. When asked how, he further explained that he had made claims before the U.S. Congress and that they would soon issue him large sums of money as he was, in fact, King Richard III of England, and as royalty he had the rights to several estates for which the U.S. government would have to pay him.

As time went by, he began to see President Jackson as his enemy. Lawrence felt that Jackson's fight against the national bank would jeopardize the settlement of his claims. Removing Jackson through assassination was the only way to ensure that he would receive his rightful inheritance. Once Jackson was out of the way, Vice President Martin Van Buren would clearly see that Lawrence's claim was justified and demand that Congress pay him and pay him quickly. Lawrence would then be free to travel to England.

Lawrence's behavior began to change in other ways as well. He became very fashion conscious during this time, and began buying and wearing extravagant clothing, dressing like an "English dandy." He grew a mustache to complete the look. He also became interested in women, to whom he had not seemed particularly inclined before, and was often seen riding horses with women of "loose character."[7] Lawrence was also suspicious of everyone who surrounded him, believing they were government agents spying on him. Moreover, he began to have episodes of rage and violence—on one occasion he threatened a black maid, and it was reported by his sisters that he had threatened and shook one of them violently and had struck the other several times. He was reported to be having fits of uncontrollable laughter and cursing, he would hold incoherent conversations with himself, and he would make odd gestures with his hands or sit motionless for long periods of time.[8]

In the final weeks before his attack, one witness stated that Lawrence would sit in his old paint shop for hours on end, talking to himself. In one such conversation he was overheard saying, "Damn him, he does not know his enemy; I will put a pistol. . . . Erect a gallows. . . . Damn General Jackson! Who's General Jackson?"[9] Because he had not worked for years, numerous bills were coming due, and Lawrence was becoming more violent and confrontational. When his landlord asked how he was doing, Lawrence responded with "Go to hell! What's that to you?"[10] The landlord, a brave soul (or a fool), tried to explain to Lawrence that he owed him back rent. Lawrence said in an icy cold voice, "You mean to warrant me for it, I suppose? If you do, I will put a ball through your head."[11]

Finally, one witness claimed to have seen Lawrence on the morning of the assassination attempt in his old paint shop, sitting atop a chest, holding a book, and laughing out loud. Suddenly he dropped the book, left the shop, and while chuckling stated, "I'll be damned if I don't do it."[12]

THE ASSASSINATION ATTEMPT

The attempted assassination of President Andrew Jackson marked the first time in American history that an individual, with the intent to kill, openly and purposefully attacked the president. The nation had come through six presidents in slightly more than forty years with no such attempt, but it is perhaps fitting that Jackson was the first. Andrew Jackson had an abrasive personality and had managed to make a number of enemies in his lifetime. As historian Robert V. Remini explained, Jackson "was just a little too strong, too controversial, too dominant a character, and therefore an obvious target for the demented in society."[13] While Jackson's personality does perhaps share some of the blame for Richard Lawrence's distaste for the president, equally to blame is what American society had wrought in the nineteenth century: its own form of societal dementia.

American society had changed vastly between the presidencies of George Washington and Andrew Jackson. The country had more than doubled in size, and a mass migration west had occurred. The number of newly arrived immigrants continued to rise and cities grew rapidly as the American industrial revolution progressed. While this revolution created jobs and much in the way of economic prosperity, it also brought with it a growing disparity in wealth. It increased poverty, created an unprecedented focus on materialism, and led to rising crime, violence, and numerous riots. Many believed that America had taken a wrong turn somewhere along the way and was greatly in need of reform. This is why, when remarking about the presidential assassination attempt, the *New York Evening Post* considered it merely "a sign of the times."[14]

Another of the signs was the spread of threats against the president. On May 6, 1833, while aboard a steamboat traveling from Alexandria to Fredericksburg, Virginia, a disgruntled young man by the name of Robert B. Randolph had shoved his hand into Jackson's face, leaving it bloodied.[15] Randolph had been a naval officer, but was drummed out of the service for allegedly misappropriating funds.[16] Jackson was unharmed; he had been seated behind a table, which made it difficult for Randolph to reach his quarry. Jackson's nephew, Andrew Donelson, who was present that day, later wrote, "The object of the attack was no doubt assassination, but the ruffian was unnerved by the countenance of Uncle and he could do no more than display his intention."[17]

Randolph was quickly taken into custody and turned over to local authorities, but the incident demonstrated the potential threats Jackson faced as president. There was a rumor circulating in Washington, D.C., that a conspiracy was forming in Baltimore with the plan to raise 5,000 soldiers to destroy the president. When told of the potential danger to his life, Jackson replied in typical fashion—he threatened to hang all 5,000 participants. He also began receiving death threats in the White House mail. One that came in February 1834 began, "Damn your soul, remove them deposits back again, and recharter the Bank, or you will certainly be shot in less than two weeks, and that by myself!!!"[18] He received similar threats in April and October of that year, raising the specter that someone might actually carry out a threat. Someone would, early the next year, but not entirely over discomfiture with Jackson's changes to the banking system.

The assassination attempt on President Jackson's life took place on January 30, 1835. The day was very damp and misty. Several days earlier, Representative Warren R. Davis of South Carolina had died and his funeral services were being held in the House chamber at the U.S. Capitol.[19] It was a large funeral with every politician still in Washington, D.C., attending, including members of the House and Senate, the president and his staff, and all of the cabinet members. The services were long and drawn out, and the chaplain gave a very long eulogy that pontificated on the notion that "life is uncertain, particularly for the aged."[20] The president sat stoically listening to the droning of the chaplain, and Harriet Martineau, an English socialite in attendance, observed, "There sat the gray-haired president, looking scarcely able to go through the ceremonial."[21] Yet although he looked somewhat feeble, he still struck a commanding figure as he sat in front at the place of honor.

Once the funeral rites were complete, the congregation lined up to pass the funeral bier to pay their last respects. The members of the House passed first, since Davis was one of their own; they were then followed by the Senate, and finally the president. They descended to the Rotunda and moved toward the exit on the east porch of the Capitol building. The congressmen began to mill about, waiting for the president to exit in order to pay their respects. As Jackson approached the east portico entrance to the Rotunda, a slender man with a thick black beard stepped in front of him, only six feet away. He drew a pistol from his pocket, and pointed the weapon directly at Jackson's heart.

Lawrence squeezed the trigger and the movement of his finger was associated with a large explosion that someone said sounded as loud as the crack of a rifle. Another eyewitness, Senator John Tyler, who had stepped out of the processional line to wait for President Jackson, described the sound as that of an "ordinary cracker."[22] Thomas Benton gave a more detailed description when he later explained that "the explosion of the cap was so loud that many persons thought the pistol had fired,"[23] although in fact only the cap had exploded. He remembered that he had "heard it at the foot of the steps, far from the place, and a great crowd between."[24]

There are varying accounts as to what happened next, but most agreed that, unlike some of those in attendance who ducked or froze upon hearing the noise, Jackson headed straight for his assailant with raised cane ready to strike Lawrence.[25] Lawrence, in the meantime, dropped the pistol and immediately pulled a second pistol of the exact same make and design out of his other pocket with his left hand. He cocked the gun, aimed it directly at Jackson's heart, and pulled the trigger.

Although a number of those witnessing the events had comprehended what was going on and, like Jackson, were trying to respond, they were all too slow. The second gunshot exploded, echoing through the Rotunda. Lawrence had squeezed off the second shot before Jackson reached him and then, as the walking cane was about to strike him, he managed to duck and avoid the wrath of the president. The second shot had resounded like the first shot, but again, only the cap exploded. Jackson was still alive, spared by the fortune of two guns misfiring. Jackson was also as feisty as ever—despite his old age and poor health, he reportedly yelled at Lawrence, "Let me alone! Let me alone! I know where this came from."[26] It is believed that Jackson immediately suspected the underhanded workings of his most recent enemy, Senator George Poindexter.

Meanwhile, Levi Woodbury, Jackson's secretary of the treasury, also reacted by aiming a blow at the assailant. He was a little slower than Jackson, but just behind Jackson's walking cane. He too missed as Lawrence twisted away. It was finally Lieutenant Thomas R. Gedney of the U.S. Navy who knocked Lawrence to the ground. At that point, a number of those in attendance pressed forward to ensure that the president's assailant was subdued. These included Senator Davy Crockett of Tennessee, who later said of the incident, "I wanted to see the d-mnd-st villain in the world—and now I have seen him."[27] Even the president himself participated in the final subduing of the assassin. The daily papers remarked the next day, "The President pressed after him until he saw he was secured."[28]

The throng immediately began to press forward to either see for themselves the would-be assassin or find out what all the commotion was about. It is said that Jackson was boiling with rage and kept trying to thrash the young man with his cane. As others realized the danger of the situation, they began to usher the president quickly toward his carriage and, once he was loaded onboard, it sped away to the White House. As the carriage proceeded, Jackson said nothing and no longer seemed agitated, nor did he show any outward signs regarding the excitement of what had just happened. In fact, once he arrived at the White House, he acted as if nothing had happened at all. When Vice President Martin Van Buren arrived at the White House from the scene, he had expected Jackson to be in a rage. Rather, he was stupefied to find the president sitting with one of Major Donelson's children on his lap and conversing with Major General Winfield Scott about another matter. The vice president remarked that Jackson was "apparently the least disturbed person in the room."[29] Another, Meriwether

Lewis Randolph, the grandson of Thomas Jefferson, explained, "I went over to the old man, about an hour after the occurrence of the affair, and found him as cool, calm, and collected, as though nothing had happened."[30]

A thunderstorm broke outside the White House and brought a heavy downpour, lightning, and pealing thunder. Another thunderstorm had been averted, for had Jackson been killed he would have been the first president to have been assassinated. As it was, Jackson had just become the first president to face an assassination attempt in American history—a point of notoriety, if not distinction.

THE AFTERMATH

Richard Lawrence was quickly taken into custody by the House sergeant-at-arms, who turned him over to the civil authorities, but not before asking him why he had attempted the assassination. Lawrence gave what would be the first of nearly a dozen reasons for his actions, this time saying that Jackson had killed his father three years previously. He was then removed to the yard of the Capitol and then on to City Hall, where he was incarcerated in the local Washington, D.C., jail. At this point he identified himself as Richard Lawrence, a painter. Again he was asked why he had attempted the assassination, and this time he muttered that he was the legitimate heir to the British throne and that Jackson had impeded his natural succession. Both explanations were obviously and dramatically false, and it was quickly proven that Lawrence's father had in fact died in 1823, twelve years before the assassination attempt, and had never lived in America.[31] "There is nothing but madness in all this" was the summation of John Tyler.[32]

Lawrence's interrogators called in several physicians to assist in the examination. The doctors inquired about Lawrence's physical and mental health, and in their interviews the doctors stated that Lawrence "replied that it had been uniformly good, and that he had never labored under any mental alienation . . . nor did he admit the existence of any of those symptoms of physical derangement which usually attend mental alienation."[33]

The physicians then inquired as to the motive behind Lawrence's behavior, reporting that he "had been told that the president had caused his loss of occupation, and the consequent want of money. . . . He believed that to put him out of the way was the only remedy for evil."[34] Lawrence, however, could not remember who told him this, but when asked why he wanted to kill Jackson, he replied, "Because he was a tyrant."[35] Questioned as to who had told him this particular notion, "He answered, it was a common talk with the people, and that he had read it in all the papers."[36] Queried if he saw any personal benefit in killing the president, Lawrence claimed that "he could not rise unless the president fell" and that "he expected thereby to recover his liberty, and that the mechanics would all be benefited; that the mechanics would have plenty of money; and that the money would be more plenty."[37] When asked why there would be "plenty" of money, Lawrence stated that it would more easily be "obtained from the bank,"[38] and when the name of the bank was requested, he stated, "The Bank of the United States."[39] Questioned further, Lawrence asserted that he was the rightful heir to the British throne and that Jackson stood in his way of gaining that throne. The doctors declared Lawrence to be insane.

The sergeant-at-arms at the Capitol, in the meantime, had recovered both pistols and found that they appeared to have been properly loaded. In fact, they were found to have been loaded with the "finest powder," or, more specifically, "with fine glazed dueling powder and ball."[40] Meriwether Lewis Randolph also commented on the pistols, finding them loaded with "the powder of the best quality, & the balls rammed tight," but "the percussion caps exploded without igniting the powder."[41] Not to mention they were fired nearly at point-blank range. Jack Donelson recapped the pistols and tested the weapons to see if they would fire.[42] They did, perfectly. In a letter to his son, Senator Tyler stated it best when he explained, "It is almost a miracle that they did not go off."[43] In fact, an "expert on small arms" determined the odds of two successive misfires of perfectly loaded pistols with high-quality powder to be about 125,000 to 1.[44]

As people began to discuss what had happened, different perspectives, opinions, and politics began to play heavily throughout Washington, D.C. There were many Democrats, including Andrew Jackson, who believed that Lawrence was in reality a political assassin for the Whig Party. When Harriet Martineau visited Jackson several days after the assassination attempt, she commented about the insanity of Lawrence. Jackson was quick to rebuke her comment. Martineau later explained, "He protested, in the presence of many strangers, that there was no insanity in the case" and "that there was a plot, and that the man was a tool."[45] There was never any actual proof, only proof as conceived of by a president who had become so paranoid by the numerous attacks on his character that he had difficulty separating fact from fiction.

The proof, according to Jackson, was found in the very statements by Lawrence to his interrogator. When Lawrence began to speak of his hatred for Jackson and repeatedly argued that Jackson should not be president, one of his interrogators asked him who he thought *should* be president. Lawrence answered, "Mr. Clay, Mr. Webster, Mr. Calhoun," all three staunch Whigs and haters of Jackson. "It seems he has been a furious politician of the opposition party," wrote Francis Scott Key, "& is represented by some as a very weak man, easily duped or excited."[46] Jackson himself actually suspected that the instigator of the plot was Senator Poindexter of Mississippi, for he and Jackson had been feuding for several years, despite the fact that Poindexter had been with him in New Orleans and had defended Jackson for his actions in the Seminole War affair.[47] The allegation that Poindexter was involved in the plot to kill the president was leaked to the press, and he immediately called for a Senate investigation to clear his name. He was granted the investigation, which, not surprisingly, cleared him of all charges and declared that the allegations "proved to rest upon the most frivolous and untrustworthy assertions, no one of which would bear the slightest examination, and some of which were distinctly false."[48]

Those who surrounded Jackson also saw conspiracy plots wherever they looked. Francis P. Blair of the *Washington Globe* suspected that Lawrence was involved in a plot, publicly stating that "a secret conspiracy had prompted the perpetration of the horrible deed."[49] This speculation was further fueled by Judge William Cranch, the chief justice of the district and a Whig, who set the bail for Lawrence at a meager $1,500. Roger B. Taney, later to become the chief justice of the U.S. Supreme Court, inquired into the small sum and was told that "there is much excitement among our friends on account of the smallness of the sum required."[50] The conspiratorial discussion over the bail quickly died away when it was found in the next several days that Lawrence did not have the means by which to post bail.

The rhetoric changed dramatically over the next several weeks, largely because of Jackson's reaction to the assassination attempt. The language shifted from talk of backdoor conspiratorial plots to intervention by the very hand of God himself. When the king of England sent a letter to express his concern over the attempt on Jackson's life, Old Hickory responded by acknowledging that "a kind of providence" had managed "to shield me."[51] Word of Jackson's response leaked out, and many quickly agreed with his belief in divine Providence. Senator Thomas Benton, who was a witness to the assassination attempt, explained,

The circumstance made a deep impression upon the public feeling and irresistibly carried many minds to the belief in a superintending Providence, manifested in the extraordinary case of two pistols in succession—so well loaded, so coolly handled, and which afterwards fired with such readiness, force, and precision—missing fire, each in its turn, when leveled eight feet at the President's heart.[52]

"Were I inclined to superstition," Meriwether Lewis Randolph pondered, "the conviction that the President's life was protected by the hand of a special providence would be irresistible."[53] Even editorials in the newspapers, such as one written by Blair of the *Washington Globe*, echoed these sentiments: "Providence has ever guarded the life of the man who has been destined to preserve and raise his country's glory and maintain the cause of the people."[54]

All of this not only would translate into political support from those inside Washington, D.C., but also managed to have a major impact on the public. Mass public opinion held that Jackson's escape from death could only have come from the intervention of God and, therefore, God had something in mind for Jackson. Since Jackson had some form of "special interposition of Providence,"[55] then whatever Jackson did must have the support of God. Jackson had been spared by God to lead the country, so while Jackson's controversial policies had been treated with suspicion before the assassination, they were now the divine policies of Providence and Jackson was the messenger.

Interestingly, in the month following the assassination attempt, George Endicott of New York would publish a lithograph titled "The Attempted Assassination, of the President of the United States, Jan. 30, 1835" (see Figure 1.1). The lithograph was said to have been "drawn from a sketch by an eye witness," depicting Lawrence firing the second pistol at Jackson with the first pistol lying on the ground. Unlike most lithographic pictures of the day, this one was neither a caricature nor satirical in nature, but was rather an attempt at straightforward news. While the depiction of the event is largely inaccurate, the details of those in attendance were rather refined. The lithograph shows Lieutenant Gedney in full naval uniform lunging at Lawrence, followed by President Jackson, Levi Woodbury, and, again, Lawrence firing the second shot.[56]

Lawrence, in the meantime, sat in jail awaiting his trial, which began on April 11, 1835. The prosecuting attorney was Francis Scott Key. Lawrence came to the trial "dressed in gray shooting jacket; black cravet [*sic*] and vest, and brown pantaloons,"[57] attempting to look every bit the part of English royalty. In fact, when the judge entered the courtroom, Lawrence stood up immediately and cried out, "What means this personal indignity? Is it decreed

Figure 1.1.   Lithograph of Richard Lawrence (right) firing the second pistol at President Andrew Jackson (center-left) with cane. Standing next to President Jackson is Levi Woodbury (center-right) and lunging at the assassin in full naval uniform is Lieutenant Gedney (left). Note the first pistol lying on the ground at Lawrence's feet. (Courtesy of the Library of Congress.)

that I am to be brought here, and for what?" The judge told him to take a seat, but Lawrence pressed the issue by saying, "I desire to know if I, who claim the Crown of the United States, likewise the Crown of Great Britain, and who am superior to this court, am to be treated thus?"[58] The trial itself did not last long, but it was made somewhat longer by these repeated interruptions and orations.[59] When the trial was finished and the jury was given its instructions, Lawrence issued one last perfunctory utterance: "It is for me, gentlemen, to pass upon you, and not you upon me."[60]

The jury took less than five minutes to deliberate and they returned with their verdict, finding Lawrence "not guilty" as he was "under the influence of insanity."[61] In more modern terms, Lawrence was found to have demonstrated "symptoms of the extreme and irrational suspicion and hostility that characterize the paranoid schizophrenic."[62] He was thus remanded to the newly opened Washington, D.C., insane asylum, the blandly titled Government Hospital, where he remained for the rest of his life. He died on June 13, 1861.

CONCLUSION

President Andrew Jackson was the last U.S. president to have been a veteran of the American Revolution and the second president to have been a prisoner of war. He was the first and only president to ever fight a duel and the second general to become president. And he has the distinct honor of having been the first president to have faced an assassination attempt.

Richard Lawrence, a Washington, D.C., house painter of little note who became mentally unstable in his early thirties, believed he was the rightful heir to the English throne. He saw Jackson's breakup of the Second Bank of the United States as a threat to his ability to gain his monetary claim against the U.S. government, and so he decided to remove this threat. He loaded two pistols; presented himself at the funeral of Representative Warren Davis at the U.S. Capitol on January 30, 1835; and waited for Jackson to leave. As Jackson walked under the Rotunda toward the east porch, Lawrence pulled one pistol and fired. Seeing it had misfired, he pulled his second pistol, pointed, and fired, only to have it misfire as well. He was taken into custody, put on trial, and found not guilty by reason of insanity.

Lawrence would remain in the Government Hospital, later renamed St. Elizabeth's, until his death on June 13, 1861. Jackson would gain a greater respect by the people, who believed that the hand of Providence had intervened to save his life. He finished out his second term and enjoyed eight years in retirement before dying on June 8, 1845, of chronic tuberculosis, dropsy, and heart failure. The entire era in which he served as president and until his death would become known as the "Jacksonian Era."[63] Richard Lawrence, in contrast, died in obscurity.

The attack on the president, interestingly, yielded little in the way of changes to how presidents were protected. Earlier, James Monroe had instructed workers to set up an iron fence with a series of heavily locked gates around the White House. In the wake of Lawrence's attempt on Jackson's life, the only change was to install a "watch box" at the gate that leads to the presidential garden, located on the south side of the White House. The box was to be manned by a lone sentry.[64] After Jackson left office, the box was manned infrequently. There seemed little concern for future assassination attempts, much less an actual assassination.

2

Abraham Lincoln

INTRODUCTION

President Abraham Lincoln, at six feet four inches, towered over most Americans in the mid-1800s. He was a man of great physical strength, but had a warm and tender heart.[1] He thoroughly enjoyed attending the theater, where he could escape from the pressures of leading the country during a tumultuous and stressful time. On the night of April 14, 1865, President Lincoln and his wife, Mary, decided to attend a production of *Our American Cousin*, a popular comedy of the time, at Ford's Theater in Washington, DC. They arrived midway through the opening act to cheers and an ovation from the audience, many of whom attended the play that night simply to see Lincoln.

President Lincoln was fifty-six years old, and had completed the tasks of ending slavery and keeping the country united—accomplishments that did not sit well with all Americans. John Wilkes Booth, a well-known actor of the time, had entered the building at some point. He was a familiar face, so no one stopped him or questioned his presence in the theater. Booth was not an admirer of President Lincoln. Even more, he was armed, motivated, and had access to the president's suite upstairs in the theater. With Booth in place, the Lincolns' choice to attend the theater that night would for all time be described as "fateful." Booth made his way to the suite and awaited his cue.

ABRAHAM LINCOLN

Lincoln, the sixteenth president of the United States, was born on February 12, 1809, in a one-room log cabin in Hardin County, Kentucky. When he was young, the family moved to Indiana, where his mother died. His father remarried, and Abraham's stepmother encouraged him to read and learn. The family joined a Baptist church that was opposed to slavery. Abraham became a sexton in the church and listened to many sermons against slavery.

As a young man, Abraham was asked to send a flatboat loaded with grain, meat, sugar, and tobacco down the Mississippi River to New Orleans. There, for the first time, Lincoln encountered large numbers of slaves and even witnessed slave auctions. He saw blacks who were chained and whipped. Abe's trips to New Orleans were instrumental in forming his opinions on slavery.[2]

Lincoln's first experience with government work was as the town's postmaster, a position to which he was appointed by President Andrew Jackson. Although the job only paid $30 a year, he enjoyed it.[3] When the new county surveyor, John Calhoun, asked Lincoln to become his assistant, he readily accepted. Abe had no training for the job, but he learned quickly. In this position, he was able to travel around the county and meet many people. Throughout his travels, Abe made it clear that he disliked violence, alcohol, and tobacco. He also disliked hunting and would not use a gun. Because of his strong moral convictions, his popularity grew and he was well liked in the community.

Lincoln first attempted to achieve public office when he was only twenty-three years old, when he ran for the Illinois State Legislature and lost. Despite the loss, it was a defining time for Lincoln. He became a member of the Whig Party, which supported governmental aid for improvements that included infrastructure such as railroads, bridges, canals, and navigation systems. He supported a national bank to create a uniform system of national investment and currency. Such programs, he thought, would help develop the West.[4]

In 1834, Lincoln ran again for the Illinois legislature and this time was successful. He relied on votes from people he met as a postmaster and surveyor.[5] With four consecutive victories, Lincoln served in the Illinois House for eight years. He was a popular member of the legislature, and was named chairman of the finance committee. He led the effort to move the capital to Springfield and supported the Internal Improvements Act, a measure designed to improve the railroad and canal systems in the state. While in office, he also made statements against slavery.[6]

A student of the law, Lincoln was admitted to the bar in 1836[7] and was offered a partnership in a law firm with John Todd Stuart the next year. Lincoln traveled to each county seat in Illinois to handle cases including divorce, custody, trespass, and criminal defense. In 1839 Lincoln met Mary Todd, the refined twenty-one-year-old daughter of a prominent plantation owner and slaveholder.[8] They were married in 1842 and had four boys, only one of whom survived into adulthood.

Lincoln did not seek reelection to the legislature when his term ended in 1841. Instead, he chose to concentrate on his law practice and save enough money to pay his debts. Party leaders encouraged him to run for governor in 1841 and 1844, but he declined.[9] But he did agree to campaign for the Whig Party's nominee, William Henry Harrison, in 1840, and to campaign in 1844 for Henry Clay. But in 1842, Lincoln returned to politics and sought the Whig nomination for the newly established Seventh District of central Illinois. Fellow attorney John Hardin got the nomination instead of Lincoln that year.[10]

Abe again tried to enter the political scene in 1843 when he threw his hat into the ring for the U.S. Congress, but he did not get the nomination. In 1846, Lincoln once again tried his hand at public office and was elected to Congress by an unprecedented majority.[11] He served in Congress from 1847 until 1849. There he supported a strong protective tariff and a national bank, while also opposing the war with Mexico. He argued that the president had no power to declare war under the Constitution because that was a power of Congress. Lincoln was disappointed to learn that some viewed his position on the war as unpatriotic.[12]

In the second year of his term, Lincoln was concerned about the issue of slavery. He made it clear that he opposed slavery, but at the same time was not an abolitionist. He believed that slavery in the states was protected by the Constitution and that Congress had no power to interfere with it.[13]

Lincoln served only one term in Congress, partly because of his unpopular stance on the war with Mexico, but he reentered politics again in 1848, challenging Stephen Douglas for the U.S. Senate. He lost the election but won the admiration of many who had heard him speak around the country. After losing the election, Lincoln returned to practicing law. His firm with William Herndon flourished, building a strong base across Illinois and the Midwest. He appeared before the U.S. Supreme Court in March 1849 concerning a case regarding property ownership. He also became an expert in patent cases, and by the mid-1850s, was perhaps the most respected attorney in Illinois.[14]

In 1854, a new law drew Lincoln back into politics. Senator Stephen Douglas proposed a bill called the Nebraska Bill, which would divide Nebraska into two states: Nebraska and Kansas. The choice as to whether they would be free states or slave states would be determined by popular vote. This upset Lincoln because he believed that new states entering the Union should be free states, and that slavery should be confined to the southern states in which it was already established.[15]

Lincoln presented his views against slavery in a major speech in Peoria in 1854. He described slavery as morally wrong, saying that "no man is good enough to govern another man, without that other's consent."[16] Many people were impressed with the speech and his passion. The speech helped Lincoln again achieve the Whig nomination for a seat in the state legislature, but when elected he resigned so that he could contest the nomination for the U.S. Senate in 1855. He lost that campaign.[17]

The issue of slavery was causing dissension in the Whig Party. Although Lincoln was loyal to the Whigs, he saw that the party might not recover from its split over the Kansas-Nebraska Act.[18] At a Whig convention in 1856, a small coalition of anti-Nebraska forces found itself agreeing with another group from the North who called themselves Republicans. It soon became apparent to Lincoln that he agreed with the ideas of the new organization. He joined the new Republican Party and brought many other Whigs with him.[19]

In 1858, state Republican leaders unanimously passed a resolution endorsing Lincoln as their candidate to oppose Senator Stephen Douglas, who was seeking reelection to the U.S. Senate. The centerpiece of the campaign was the Lincoln-Douglas debates. The two candidates agreed to travel around the state and debate issues of the day, including slavery. There were seven face-to-face debates, attended by thousands; the candidates also appeared separately in different cities and towns.

Throughout the debates, Douglas supported slavery. He argued that the country was "made by the white man for the benefit of the white man."[20] He believed that the country could endure with half slave and half free states, as it had existed for half a century. Lincoln, on the other hand, believed that all Americans, regardless of color, should be free to enjoy the fruits of their own labors.[21] He argued that slavery violated the promise of the Declaration of Independence because it negated liberty and equality. He believed African Americans were human beings and by "natural law" deserved to be treated with dignity and respect. However, Lincoln did not support full equality for blacks. He did not approve of interracial marriage and did not advocate black suffrage. He did not believe that blacks were the equal of whites on social levels.

Other than debating the issues, Lincoln did not take an overtly active part in the campaign. At that time, it was customary that candidates gave no interviews or speeches between the time of the nomination and the election, primarily because senators were not elected by popular vote but by a vote of the state legislatures. Instead, others close to the candidate spoke on his behalf. But in reality he was deeply engaged, analyzing campaign reports and discussing events with advisors. In the final balloting, Douglas received fifty-four votes, and Lincoln forty-six.[22]

Despite the loss, Lincoln continued to speak about slavery. He impressed enough people within the new Republican Party that during their Convention in 1860, Lincoln received the party's nomination for the presidency.[23] In the national vote, Lincoln had strong support in the Northeast and West, but he carried no southern states—in most places in the South, his name was not even allowed on the ballot. In the end, Lincoln won with less than 40 percent of the popular vote nationally. He had 1,866,452 to Douglas's 1,376,957 votes. In the Electoral College, Lincoln received 180 electoral votes, none of them from below the Mason-Dixon line.[24]

Many people did not know what to expect from Lincoln. Some described him as a clodhopper—timid, unsure, and unorganized.[25] Others were concerned that Lincoln had never held an executive office that required a broad range of administrative duties or action on a variety of issues, and that he was unprepared for the task before him.

The issue at the forefront of Lincoln's presidency was slavery. The divisions between the North and South over slavery had become very wide and deep.

Citizens in both the North and the South were distrustful and angry. To the southern states, slavery was their way of life; it was their right. But to those in the northern states, slavery was wrong, an evil.

Lincoln tried to make it clear to the South that he had neither the power nor the desire to abolish slavery in their states and that the federal government could not eradicate slavery in states where it already existed.[26] He tried to convince the South that as president, he would not take any action against them. Nonetheless, many southerners believed that he meant to end their slave system and destroy their traditional way of life. Upon news of Lincoln's victory, the southern states immediately started seceding from the Union. Even before all the votes were in, South Carolina called its state legislature into special session to authorize the formation of a southern confederacy. In December 1860, six weeks after Lincoln's election, they passed an ordinance of secession and sent commissioners to every slaveholding state to invite them to join. Six more states followed: Mississippi, Florida, Alabama, Georgia, Louisiana, and Texas.[27]

Lincoln believed that the secession of the southern states was an act of rebellion against the government. The situation was made worse when secessionists took control of federal forts and transferred monies from the U.S. Mint in New Orleans to the new government of the Confederate States of America. Lincoln knew that Fort Sumter in South Carolina was still under federal control and had to remain that way. He chose to supply Sumter only with provisions, but not soldiers or armaments. South Carolina considered this decision to be an act of aggression and fired on Fort Sumter on April 12, thus starting the Civil War.

To most, there was no doubt that Lincoln was dedicated to preserving the Union, and would even allow slavery to exist in southern states in order to do so. But he would not permit slavery to develop in the territories.[28] He made it clear that the territories must be kept free and that slavery should not extend beyond the states where it already existed. Like his fellow Republicans, Lincoln believed that if slavery could be confined to the southern states, it would eventually be exhausted. And he knew that when the free territories became states, the national political balance would shift toward freedom.

On January 1, 1863, Lincoln issued the Emancipation Proclamation. The document freed slaves and allowed black men to be accepted into the Union Army and Navy. It further ordered that Union officers had no duty to return slaves to their masters. Lincoln knew that freedom would provide the slaves with an incentive to fight for the Union.

Because Lincoln acted out of his war power authority in issuing the proclamation, the document applied only to states that were currently "in armed rebellion" against the government, or those that had seceded from the Union. That meant it applied only to the southern states. So in reality, the proclamation freed virtually no slaves.[29] However, it successfully created confusion in the South and deprived the Confederacy of vital manpower.

In the end, the proclamation was really just a political measure taken by Lincoln to weaken the South. Lincoln understood that the war gave the president authority that he never would have had in times of peace. Accordingly, some questioned the legality of the proclamation. Many thought Lincoln had far exceeded his presidential powers in issuing the order, and believed that he did not have the constitutional authority to do so.

The proclamation was immediately met with criticism and skepticism from southern slave owners. As expected, the South ignored Lincoln's order, since they did not consider themselves part of the Union and did not recognize Lincoln as their president. At the same time, abolitionists in the North believed the proclamation stopped far short of what it might have been. Nonetheless, the proclamation raised Lincoln's stature among abolitionists, even if it did not go to the lengths they desired.

While Lincoln was dealing with slavery and the Civil War, he was also facing serious personal problems. Not long after taking office, Lincoln began to receive an unusual number of letters about plots to kidnap or assassinate him, although most were anonymous and undocumented. One time, Lincoln received gifts of dried fruit that were found to be poisoned.[30] In February 1861, a plot to kill Lincoln in Baltimore as he was on his way to Washington to be inaugurated was uncovered and thwarted (see chapter 11).

Despite all the threats, Lincoln believed that in a democratic society the chief executive must not be screened from the public. He took few precautions to prevent any harm to himself. There was no military guard at the White House, even at the outbreak of the Civil War. Also, Lincoln chose to take long walks, alone, through the streets of Washington late at night or in the early morning.

Although there were calls to cancel or postpone the presidential election of 1864, Lincoln believed that free and regular elections were the foundation of a democracy, and he was determined that the 1864 election should proceed in an orderly fashion. Lincoln wanted to serve a second term and considered it his duty to finish the business of winning the war. But he was not a popular president. In the South, he was considered to be an ogre, but northerners also denounced him for exercising emergency powers during the war (e.g., he suspended habeas corpus and censored some newspapers). Many Americans viewed Lincoln as crude, coarse, and comical, and his presidency as the most damaging in the nation's history. An active, hostile party organization against the president emerged. Lincoln was unsure that he would win another term of office.

Once again, Lincoln did not actively campaign because tradition held that presidential candidates not engage in a direct appeal for votes. If Lincoln were to speak at Republican rallies, he faced heckling. As a president who appreciated the dignity of the office, he did not want to compromise that by publicly appealing for votes.[31] Instead, he spoke to returning Union regiments, visited hospitals, and attended charitable events.

Lincoln was reelected on November 8, 1864, by a landslide. He carried twenty-one states and received 55 percent of the popular vote. He won all the

Union states except Kentucky, Delaware, and New Jersey. The final electoral vote was 212 for Lincoln to 21 for George B. McClellan, former general-in-chief of the Union Army.[32] To Lincoln, his victory was a clear mandate that the war should continue until success was achieved, meaning a reunification of the Union and the elimination of slavery.

Lincoln's second inauguration took place on March 4, 1865. It was a cold, wet day, but the sun came out just as Lincoln rose to take the oath of office. Afterward, he gave a public reception at the White House, where he met with 5,000 people. As he began his second term, he was thin and pale. He was sleeping and eating poorly, and at times indicated a desire to escape from the burdens of the presidency. He even resorted to having a cabinet meeting at his bedside.[33]

Lincoln had periods of deep depression and was plagued with dreams about being assassinated. Soon after Appomattox, he told Mary that he dreamed the president had been assassinated. He was unable to shake his feelings of dread, telling author Harriet Beecher Stowe, "I shan't last long after the war is over."[34] He regularly received death threats and letters warning him against assassination, many of which he kept in his desk.[35]

But Lincoln continued to regard the threats as idle words and continued to deny any attempts at security measures. One guest to the White House wrote that a potential assassin could easily enter the president's office. Lincoln defended his open-door policy on the grounds that all citizens had a right to see the president and present their grievances or express their opinions. It allowed him to keep in touch with the people and to know what they were thinking.

During Lincoln's second term, the main subjects of debate were the Reconstruction of the South, restoring the rebel states to their former relations with the national government, and how they would be governed during the transition back to a unified nation. It was a difficult and unsolved issue, and there were many opinions as to what should be done.

Lincoln wanted Reconstruction of the South to take place gently, with a certain amount of forgiveness. He did not intend to punish the Confederates. Instead, he wanted reunification to occur quickly.[36] In December 1863, he issued the Proclamation of Amnesty and Reconstruction. He thought that the generous terms of the proclamation would encourage southern soldiers to lay down their arms. One proposal was called the Ten Percent Plan. Under the plan, when 10 percent of a state's citizens swore an oath of allegiance to the national government, the state could be readmitted to the Union. Those citizens who swore an oath of allegiance (excluding high-ranking Confederate officers and government officials) would be granted a full pardon. While many moderate Republicans supported the plan, radical Republicans did not. Instead, they wanted to punish the rebels for causing hundreds of thousands of deaths in an unnecessary war.

In the summer of 1864, Congress passed the Wade-Davis bill, its plan for Reconstruction. For southern states to rejoin the Union, the bill required that at least 50 percent of its voters take an "ironclad" oath of loyalty to the federal government and renounce the Confederacy. Additionally, that state had to guarantee the civil rights of freed slaves. The bill outlawed slave ownership, making it a federal crime punishable by imprisonment and fines. The president would appoint, and the Senate would confirm, provisional governors. The measure reflected the idea that it was necessary to punish the southern states. Lincoln vetoed the bill, arguing that such punishments might prevent Reconstruction efforts already underway in those sections of the South occupied by federal troops.[37]

Lincoln also wanted a constitutional amendment to end slavery for all time. Passing such an amendment was not an easy task, and Lincoln relied on his vast political skills to garner the votes needed. He invited members of Congress from both political parties to the White House for private conversations, offered federal jobs to congressmen and their family members, promised support to politicians whose seats were not considered to be "safe," and generally twisted arms and called in favors. The bill passed by 119 to 58, with 8 abstentions. Within a year the required three-quarters of the states had ratified it. The Thirteenth Amendment protected the work the Emancipation Proclamation had begun, and did so before any legal challenges could be made.

On April 9, Confederate General Robert E. Lee surrendered the Army of Northern Virginia. The next day Lincoln gave his final speech, which was a plea for speedy restoration of the rebel states to the Union.[38] On April 11, crowds spilled onto the White House lawn. That evening, after returning from a visit to Richmond, Lincoln addressed the crowd. He was focused on Reconstruction and on the proposed constitutional amendment to give citizenship and all legal rights to former slaves.[39]

The audience listening to the speech that night included John Wilkes Booth, an actor who often performed in local theaters. Lincoln had frequently seen Booth in plays at Ford's Theater and Grover's Theater. Lincoln had most recently seen Booth act in Washington in the tragedy *The Marble Heart*.[40] But as he gave his final speech that day, Lincoln was not aware of Booth's hatred of him or of Booth's plots to harm him.

JOHN WILKES BOOTH

John Wilkes Booth came from a Maryland family of actors. His father, Junius, was the country's most famous actor, but was also described as an alcoholic and mentally unstable. He left his wife and child in England and came to America in 1824 with his pregnant mistress, Mary Ann Holmes, to settle in Maryland.[41] Many years later, Junius's son (by his first wife) came to America and found his father living with Mary Ann and their ten children. The son returned to England to tell his mother, and she and Junius were divorced on April 18, 1851. Three weeks later, Junius and Mary Ann were married.

John Wilkes Booth's mother, Mary Ann Holmes, was a beautiful woman who was devoted to her children, all of whom were born out of wedlock, and six of whom survived into adulthood.[42] John was born on May 10, 1838, the ninth child and clearly his mother's favorite.

Booth grew up on the family farm near Bel Air, Maryland; in a log cabin, and in Baltimore. His father's death in 1852 forced John Wilkes to end his formal education at fourteen and become the man of the house while his older brothers were away. Prior to this, he had attended school erratically at several private schools in the vicinity. At the time that he attended the Milton School for Boys, the father of one of his classmates was killed by a runaway slave who resisted being returned to slavery.

Booth tried his hand at farming but was not successful, so he turned to acting. He made his debut at seventeen, in 1855, and after that he was almost constantly on the stage. He had no training, and his early performances were crude, but he kept improving.[43] Booth was a matinee idol before he was twenty-five and was particularly renowned for his athletic twelve-foot leaps onto stage and for duels so realistic that blood was shed. He was strikingly handsome, with thick dark hair and large, expressive eyes. By 1858, he was paid $11 a week in the Richmond Theatre in Richmond, Virginia, and at the height of his career, he earned $20,000 a year.[44] Although he was popular, Booth was never as good as his father at acting.

Booth chose to live in the North throughout the war, but was a Southerner at heart. He believed that he belonged to the southern gentry and he developed excellent manners that won him access to social circles in the Deep South from which he had been excluded in Maryland.

Booth feared the emancipation of the black man and believed that blacks and foreign-born whites were inferior. In his eyes, slavery was a blessing for both the slave and the master.

Booth believed that Lincoln was the cause of the country's woes, and hated him for it. He blamed Lincoln for threatening the system of slavery in Booth's native state of Maryland, and for refusing to allow the Confederate states to secede from the Union without a fight. Booth regularly voiced concern that Lincoln had his sights on overthrowing the Constitution and becoming "King of America."[45]

To prevent this from happening, Booth organized a group of Confederate sympathizers and devised a plan to kidnap Lincoln on the road as he went to see a play at a hospital near the Soldiers' Home. They planned to hold him for ransom—in exchange for the South's independence—or exchange him for thousands of southern prisoners who were being held in northern prisons. But Lincoln's carriage had failed to appear, so Booth set his group to kill Secretary of War Edwin Stanton and Secretary of State William Seward.[46]

Lincoln's speech on April 11, in which he called for citizenship for former slaves, changed Booth's plans. He now intended to assassinate the president rather than kidnap him. Booth was in the crowd when the president spoke of suffrage for blacks who were educated or had served in the Union armies. Booth was outraged when the president raised the idea of giving African American veterans the right to vote, and interpreted that statement as meaning citizenship for blacks.

The announcement three days later that Lincoln would be at Grover's Theater that evening gave Booth the opportunity to carry out his plan. He gathered three other conspirators and made final preparations to kill not only Lincoln but also Vice President Andrew Johnson and Secretary of State Seward. Booth knew that murdering these men would bring down the Republican Party and save the Confederacy. George A. Atzerodt was assigned to kill Johnson, Lewis Powell would attack Seward, and Booth would kill Lincoln. The attacks would be carried out simultaneously, beginning at ten o'clock. Afterward, the men would meet at the Navy Yard Bridge, then go to Surratt's Tavern in Maryland and cross into Virginia, where they would continue south to escape.[47]

The morning of the assassination, Booth went to the barbershop for a shave and haircut, then walked to Grover's Theater to inquire if the president would be attending the play that evening. He was told the president would not be there. Disappointed, Booth walked to Ford's Theater to pick up his mail and found out that the Lincolns would be attending a play there instead. Booth put his plan into action.

Booth perfected his getaway by riding his horse in circles several times in the alley outside of the theater. He stopped in at the adjacent Star Saloon to have several drinks with a stagehand. He walked around the theater, and entered the box where Lincoln would be sitting. He even drilled a small hole with his penknife in the door of the box to give him a view of the rocking chair which Lincoln would use that night. Later that day, Booth went to Mary Surratt's boardinghouse to hide some weapons.

THE ASSASSINATION

Friday, April 14, 1865, was Good Friday. Five days earlier, Robert E. Lee had surrendered his army, the Army of Northern Virginia, to Union General Ulysses S. Grant at Appomattox Court House, less than a week after the fall of the Confederate capital of Richmond to Union troops. On April 14, in South Carolina, Union forces reoccupied Fort Sumter and raised Old Glory over the same place where the war had begun.[48]

That day, Lincoln was happier than he had been in a long time. He arose around 7:00 A.M. and ate breakfast at 8:00 A.M. with his family, including his son Robert, who was just back from Grant's Army in Virginia.[49] Lincoln then took care of business, including meeting with Speaker of the House Schuyler Colfax and Representative Cornelius Cole. He gave some interviews, after which he visited the War Department. Lincoln asked Secretary of War Stanton and his wife to accompany him and Mary to the play that evening. Stanton declined because he was not a theatergoer, and also expressed concern about

Lincoln's plan to attend the theater. Stanton had countless times advised the president to stay out of theaters and to cut all public appearances to a minimum, but Lincoln didn't listen. Grant was also at the War Department, and Lincoln invited him to the play. Grant expressed his regrets for not being able to join the president for the show that night.[50]

Lincoln left the War Department. He signed the pardon of a soldier who had deserted and ordered the release of a Confederate spy who had been sentenced to death. At 11:00 he met with his cabinet for three hours. It was a heated meeting in which they discussed Reconstruction. When it ended, Lincoln ate lunch, met for twenty minutes with Vice President Johnson, and then met briefly with Ohio Congressman Samuel Shellabarger from Ohio.[51]

Later that afternoon, President Lincoln and his wife took a carriage ride to the Navy Yard, where they viewed three damaged ironclads and talked to some of the men. On the way, he and Mary discussed traveling to Europe and to California, and returning home to Illinois.

Back at the White House, Lincoln had a few more meetings, then ate dinner with Mary, Robert, and Tad. He took his usual after-dinner walk to the War Department to read the latest telegrams from the South, and when he returned, more callers were waiting to speak to him. At about 8:00 P.M., Mary broke into his conversation and asked, "Well, Mr. Lincoln, are you going to the theater with me or not?"[52] Mary wore a gray silk dress and a bonnet, and Lincoln his overcoat and white kid gloves. Lincoln grabbed his hat and coat and prepared to leave.

On the way to the theater, the Lincolns picked up their theater guests, Major Henry R. Rathbone and his fiancée, Clara Harris, the daughter of a New York senator. The newspapers had printed that the president and General Grant would be attending the play, so there were groups of citizens waiting for the president to arrive. Many of them had bought tickets to the play just to see Lincoln. Ford's Theater was on 19th Street, just six blocks from the White House. It did not take the president and his guests long to get there.

Lincoln's bodyguard for the evening was John F. Parker, a Metropolitan policeman who was assigned to protect the president. Parker had previously faced charges of being drunk, of using vile language to a superior, and of not patrolling his post.[53] He stood against the wall near the main entrance of the theater, waiting for the guests. When the president's carriage pulled up, Parker led the president and Mrs. Lincoln into the building. They walked through the lamplit lobby, climbed the staircase, and crossed the first balcony on the way to their box.

The play that night was *Our American Cousin*, featuring Laura Keene. The Lincolns arrived about 8:30 P.M., partway through the opening act. The orchestra interrupted the actors and played "Hail to the Chief." The audience rose and clapped, cheering wildly, and gave the president a standing ovation. Lincoln stepped to the railing of the box and bowed to the audience before taking his seat. Soon the audience also sat down and the actors resumed their performance.[54]

Miss Harris sat on one of two stuffed chairs at the right side of the box, nearest the stage, and Major Rathbone lounged on a sofa behind her. The president sat in his favorite Victorian rocker, made of black walnut upholstered in red damask. It was the manager's chair and had been taken out of storage and installed especially for the president's visit. The rocker was placed near the left wall of the box, so that Lincoln was partly concealed by the curtain around the box. Mrs. Lincoln sat on the other stuffed chair to Lincoln's right.[55] The box itself had been decorated with flags, patriotic bunting, and a framed portrait of George Washington.

The audience was in an upbeat mood. The play had many humorous lines. Lincoln had also been upbeat all day, relieved by the end of the war, and he appeared to be enjoying the play. While the Lincolns watched the performance, Booth, as mentioned, steadied his nerves with brandy at a tavern next door and kept his eye on the clock.

Booth was intimately familiar with the theater. He knew the layout and the employees. He also knew the back doors and hidden passageways. He had no trouble slipping upstairs during the performance. He climbed the staircase from the lobby to the dress circle and slid past the back row of spectators. Parker had left his post in the passageway to take a seat in the gallery to watch the play, leaving the president guarded only by Charles Forbes, a White House footman.[56] When Booth showed Forbes his calling card, he was admitted to the presidential box. Booth slipped behind Lincoln, who was leaning forward with his chin in his right hand and his arm on the railing.

It was not long after 10:00 P.M., and the third act was in progress. Booth had a perfect view of the back of Lincoln's rocking chair through the peephole he carved into the door earlier in the day. He pulled a .44-caliber derringer pistol and a nine-inch knife from under his black coat. As the audience laughed at a humorous line, Booth pointed his derringer at the back of Lincoln's head and fired a bullet into his brain behind the left ear.[57]

Before anyone could react, Booth pushed his way between the president and Mrs. Lincoln, dropped the pistol to the floor, and pulled out the knife. He raised the blade and swung it in a high arc in an effort to drive the blade into Rathbone's heart. Major Rathbone jumped off the sofa and began struggling with the assailant, who slashed his arm from the elbow nearly to the shoulder, cutting an artery, nerves, and veins.[58] Booth then leaped twelve feet from the box onto the stage. When he jumped, he caught his spur in the flag draped over the presidential box and fell onto the stage, breaking the fibula in his left leg. On stage, he yelled, "Sic semper tyrannis!"[59]

The dull sound of Booth's pistol firing was noticed by only a few people in the noisy theater.[60] Mrs. Lincoln saw the president's head tip forward on his chest as if he had fallen asleep. She was confused and tried to wake Mr. Lincoln from his nap but could not. She had to hold him upright so he wouldn't fall forward onto the floor. Major Rathbone and Miss Harris were both screaming at people to stop Booth, but no one stopped him. He escaped out the back door of the theater into an alley, mounted his waiting horse, and within minutes of shooting the president was galloping away into the night on his way to Virginia.

Figure 2.1.   Currier & Ives lithograph depiction of the assassination of President Abraham Lincoln at Ford's Theater by John Wilkes Booth on Good Friday, April 14, 1865. (Courtesy of the Library of Congress.)

The audience was confused, terrified, and outraged all at once. Some people yelled for ropes, water, or even a ladder. It all happened in a matter of seconds, and no one fully understood what had happened.

The first doctor to help Lincoln was an army surgeon only two months out of medical school, Charles Leale, who immediately came into the box to attend to the unconscious president.[61] At first he thought Lincoln was dead. Dr. Leale was quickly joined by more physicians, including Dr. Albert F. A. King, a Washington doctor who was sitting in the dress circle near the outer door to the box, and Dr. Charles Taft, who came onto the stage, announced he was a doctor, and was boosted up to the box.

They cut off Lincoln's collar and cut open his shirt and coat from his neck to his elbow. They found very little blood, since there was no knife wound or cut artery. They lifted one of Lincoln's eyelids and noted that the left eye was dilated, indicating neurological damage. They continued to look for a wound and found a small bullet hole behind Lincoln's left ear. The wound was plugged with a small clot of blood. They believed that the ball from the gun was lodged behind Lincoln's right eye. It became clear to them that nothing much could be done for the president. The wound was mortal.[62]

Fearful that Lincoln would die at once if he was placed upright, the doctors kept him horizontal. Laura Keene entered the box and wanted to hold the president's head in her lap. Those attending to the president decided to take him to the nearest bed, but agreed that it would be too dangerous to move the president to the White House since the streets were too rough. They wanted to move him out of the theater. Someone suggested they move him to Taltavul's saloon right next door, but agreed that it would not be right for the president to die in a saloon. Across Tenth Street from the theater was a boardinghouse, and one young boarder directed that Lincoln be brought into the house. The home belonged to William Peterson, a German tailor. The president was carefully carried to the boardinghouse, still alive but unconscious.[63] As they carried him across the street, blood and brain matter seeped out of his wound, and half of his clothes had been cut off.

Lincoln was taken to a small bedroom located at the far end of the narrow hallway on the first floor of the boardinghouse. It was a small room, only nine and a half feet wide by seventeen feet long, and had a small dresser and two chairs in addition to the bed. The front parlor served as a mourning room for those who came to visit Lincoln, and for the family.

The four-poster bed was too small to hold the president's long body so he was laid diagonally across it.[64] The bed was pulled away from the wall so that the doctors could move freely around three sides. Leale made the president as comfortable as possible. Lincoln's large bare feet were sticking out by the wall, his swelling, discolored head propped up on two large pillows.

Mary sat at his bedside near his head and pleaded with him to speak to her, but Lincoln lay comatose and unresponsive. Mary was frantic with grief, even delirious. She occasionally rested in the front parlor but returned every hour to her husband's side.[65] Mary believed that she must get their young son Taddie to come to Lincoln's bedside. She told people that Lincoln loved Taddie so much, Taddie's voice would revive him.

Other physicians came, including Lincoln's family doctor and the surgeon general of the United States. All agreed that the wound was fatal and that the president had only a few hours to live.[66] Crowds gathered in the street in front of the Peterson house. Lincoln's cabinet members, awakened during the night, hurried to the house, not knowing what to expect. All members of the cabinet except Seward, who had been attacked by Booth's co-conspirator, came to see Lincoln. Stanton arrived and for several hours assumed the role of acting president. The Reverend Phineas D. Gurley, pastor of the New York Avenue Presbyterian Church, which the Lincolns frequently attended, came to give spiritual comfort. It is estimated that ninety people came at one time or another.[67]

Lincoln's breathing grew fainter and fainter, and at 7:22 A.M. on April 15, it stopped. Surgeon General Joseph K. Barnes crossed Lincoln's hands across his chest. Robert Todd Lincoln cried uncontrollably. Reverend Gurley offered a brief prayer, and one of the physicians informed Mary, "The President is no more." Stanton, choking back tears, said quietly, "Now he belongs to the ages." Lincoln was fifty-six years old.[68] Nine hours had passed since the shooting, and he had never regained consciousness.

THE AFTERMATH

At the same time Booth was entering Lincoln's box at Ford's Theater, Lewis Powell was forcing his way into Secretary of State Seward's home. Seward's servant admitted Powell after he claimed to be delivering medicine from Seward's doctor for the secretary because he had been ill. Seward's son, Frederick, confronted Powell, who then agreed to leave the home. But as he left, Powell pulled out a gun and fired at Frederick. The gun misfired, so Powell beat Frederick with the gun, fracturing his skull. The attacker then ran up to Seward's bedroom, knocking the secretary's twenty-one-year-old daughter, Fanny, unconscious with a single punch. Powell threw aside an army nurse who was in the house to help the secretary as Powell jumped on the secretary's bed. Powell punched Seward multiple times, intending to slash his jugular vein with a knife. Luckily, Seward was wearing a brace that deflected several of the blows. Another of Seward's sons, Major Augustus Seward, pulled Powell off of Seward. In the end, five members of the Seward household were injured, three critically, but all five survived.[69]

News of Lincoln's assassination and the attack on Secretary Seward spread quickly through Washington, producing fears and rumors of more possible attacks. Stanton took charge and acted to secure the city and track down the assassins. He, Corporal James Tanner, and Chief Justice David Cartter of the U.S. District Court for the District of Columbia interviewed those who had witnessed the assassination. By dawn, they knew the identities of the attackers. They had enough evidence to arrest Booth, convict him, and hang him.[70] Stanton also learned that Seward had been attacked by Lewis Powell, issued an arrest warrant for Booth and Powell, and launched a massive search for the fugitives. He ordered that all bridges and roads leading out of the capital be closed.

After he shot Lincoln, Booth ran across the stage and out a door that led into an alley. There, "Peanuts John" Burroughs was watching Booth's horse. Booth quickly climbed aboard the horse and galloped down the alley. He rode to the Surratt tavern in Surrattsville, about thirteen miles away, where two more accomplices, tavern owner Mary Surratt and David Herold, waited. They retrieved some weapons, including two Spencer carbines, ammunition, and field glasses.[71]

Booth and Herold then rode for several hours in the rain to Dr. Samuel Alexander Mudd's home. Mudd was the Charles County, Maryland, physician and a southern sympathizer who sometimes helped to deliver mail for the Confederate underground. Booth had been at Mudd's home numerous times in the previous year, so they were not strangers. The doctor examined Booth's leg, set the bone, fitted it with a splint, and then gave him a special shoe and a pair of crutches. Booth slept at Mudd's home for the rest of the day.

A few days later, Mudd went into town to run some errands and heard that Booth had killed the president, not just abducted him, as Mudd had thought. This angered Mudd, because Booth was putting Mudd's entire family at risk. He returned home and demanded that Booth and his friends leave his property. After they left, Mudd told investigators about the stranger with the broken leg who had come to his house. At first he denied that it was Booth, and even claimed that he did not recognize Booth because he was wearing a false beard.

After he left Dr. Mudd's house, Booth and Herold spent many days arranging for a way to cross the Potomac River and enter Virginia. While they planned the trip, they were given shelter by Thomas A. Jones, the chief Confederate agent in the region. When the men got to Virginia, Booth was given shelter at the home of Richard Henry Garrett, who did not know who Booth was. During that time, Booth went by the alias James W. Boyd because he had *JWB* tattooed on his hand. After a few days, the Garretts became suspicious of Booth and Herold and asked them to leave. The Garretts arranged for the men to borrow a neighbor's wagon, but agreed to allow Booth and Herold to spend one more night inside their tobacco barn. The Garrett boys locked the men inside the barn for the night as a way to watch them.

On the morning of April 27, federal soldiers searching for Booth arrived at the Garrett farm at about 2:00 A.M. When told the identity of their visitors, Richard Garrett was stunned and told the search party that the men were in the tobacco shed. The shed was immediately surrounded by the soldiers, who demanded that the fugitives give up and come out of the barn. Herold surrendered, but Booth would not leave. Soldiers set fire to the barn to force Booth out, but it exploded into flames. Through the slats, the soldiers could see Booth leaning on his crutches with a gun in his hand.

All at once, a shot rang out. One of the soldiers, Sergeant Boston Corbett, had shot Booth. The bullet cut through the right side of Booth's neck, shattered several vertebrae, and cut his spinal cord, paralyzing him. The soldiers dragged him away from the fire and laid him on Garrett's porch. Booth was in and out of consciousness for two and a half hours. The soldiers sent for a doctor, but he could do nothing, and Booth died a few hours later on Garrett's front porch. Afterward, Corbett was rebuked by his superiors, who wanted the soldiers to bring Booth back alive.

Booth's body was identified through his distinctive tattoo, his personal effects, and his face—many people knew him from his acting career and were able to identify him. There was also an autopsy, with Booth's dentist and doctor testifying to certain telltale physical characteristics. Booth was secretly buried beneath the floor of the ammunition room of the Old Penitentiary building at the Washington arsenal. His body remained there for four years until it was released to relatives for burial in the Booth family plot in Baltimore.

Others who were involved in Lincoln's assassination were later arrested and charged with conspiracy. Andrew Johnson, now president, ordered that the accomplices stand trial before a military commission rather than a civil trial because Lincoln had been killed during a time of war. The trial began on

May 12, 1865, and more than 300 witnesses gave testimony.[72] On June 30, the military commission found all eight defendants guilty of conspiracy. Three of the defendants were sentenced to life imprisonment at hard labor, one received a sentence of six years at hard labor, and four received the death sentence. Because it was a military court, there were no appeals.

The executions were carried out on July 7, 1865. It was an extremely hot day, about 100 degrees, but more than 2,000 sightseers came to watch. Only 100 tickets were issued, so many did not get to see the accomplices put to death.

As the nation watched the fate of the accomplices, it also mourned the death of the president. Immediately after Lincoln died, there was an outpouring of grief not seen before or since in the nation's history. In cities and towns across the country, ordinary business came to a halt the day after the assassination as people gathered to express their grief. Offices and shops, in Washington and in many other towns and cities, were closed for the day, and flags flew at half mast. In Worcester, Massachusetts, church bells tolled at 3:00 A.M. to call the citizenry to prayers for the president. In Philadelphia, men and women wept openly in public, and Chestnut Street was draped in black within an hour of the news. The armies in the field, who liked the president because he often visited them in their camps and talked to them personally, were devastated. Easter Sunday turned into a day of mourning for the slain president. It would be remembered as Black Easter as churches were draped in black, and ministers laid aside their sermons celebrating the risen Christ. They told their congregations that Lincoln's work was done and so God had taken him to heaven.

The autopsy on Lincoln's body revealed that the bullet entered the back of his head, passed directly toward the center of the brain, and lodged there.[73]

At first, there was speculation that Lincoln would be buried in the vault under the dome of the Capitol, which was originally intended to receive George Washington's remains. But Mary Todd Lincoln and her son Robert decided that he should be buried in Springfield, where he had lived and risen to fame. They arranged for a train cortège to take Lincoln's body on a trip around the country.

On April 19, Lincoln's embalmed body was placed in a richly ornamented walnut coffin costing $1,500 and laid on a catafalque in the East Room of the White House. He wore the same suit he had worn for his inauguration in 1861. There, at noon, the first of many funeral rites for Lincoln took place. Only invited officials, their wives, diplomats, high-ranking army and navy officers, and delegations representing various city and state authorities were admitted to the White House ceremony. Mary Lincoln was too distraught to attend. General Grant sat at the head of the open coffin. Dr. Phineas D. Gurley of the New York Avenue Presbyterian Church preached the sermon.[74]

After the White House funeral, a procession formed and a fourteen-foot hearse, with a military escort, carried Lincoln's body down Pennsylvania Avenue to the Capitol. Lincoln's favorite horse accompanied the hearse, riderless, with his boots reversed in the stirrups. Following that was a carriage with Robert and Tad, and then General Grant and cabinet members, clergymen, marshals, and twenty-two honorary pallbearers. Military units with hundreds of convalescent soldiers followed. Four thousand African American residents of Washington, wearing high silk hats and white gloves, held hands and walked side by side to the Capitol.[75] Along the streets, tens of thousands of mourners gathered under a cloudless sky to pay their respects to the president.

In the Capitol, Lincoln's body lay in state in the Rotunda. The room was draped in black cloth, and the casket was mounted on a canopied catafalque in the center of the room. The casket was opened for almost two days while an estimated 25,000 people filed past to look at Lincoln's face and to pay their respects.

Early on the morning of April 21 (a week after he had been murdered), Lincoln's body, along with his son Willie's disinterred remains, was taken to the Baltimore and Ohio Train Station and placed on a train consisting of a specially outfitted mourning car, eight passenger cars, and an engine. The thirteen-day trip from Washington to Springfield, Illinois, covered more than 1,600 miles and stopped in twenty cities. The War Department designated the tracks over which the train traveled as military roads and cleared them of traffic. People stood by the tracks all along the route as the slow-moving train passed. Towns and cities prepared funeral displays and, when the train stopped, held services. Robert Lincoln was the only family member to accompany his father; Mary was too upset to travel, and Tad was too young to leave his mother.[76]

The first stop for Lincoln's train was Baltimore,[77] where a procession of thousands, headed by state and city dignitaries, escorted the coffin. On every street, crowds of African Americans watched the hearse pass by. The coffin was opened at the Merchants' Exchange Building. During the two hours allotted for the funeral, only about one-fifth of those who had waited, many since dawn, were able to view the body.

After that the train went to the Pennsylvania state capitol at Harrisburg. The coffin was again opened and a long line of people waited to pay their respects; again, many were not able to see the president's body.[78]

On April 23, the body lay in state in Philadelphia's Independence Hall all day and for four hours at night. The line of people extended for three miles. Early the next morning, it left for New York. Along the way, it stopped briefly in several New Jersey towns, including Trenton, but the casket remained in the car. At Jersey City, the coffin was placed on a mourning-draped ferry and crossed to New York. Thousands of people in Manhattan watched from buildings as the coffin was transferred to a hearse for the procession to City Hall. Half a million people viewed the body in the New York City Hall rotunda on April 24 and 25. By now the body was deteriorating quickly and had to be touched up frequently.[79]

The body continued to Albany, Syracuse, Batavia, and Buffalo, New York, then through Ohio and Indiana. Lincoln's body then lay in state in Chicago for two days, and on May 3, twenty days after the assassination, the funeral train made its last stop: Springfield, Illinois.[80]

Mary Lincoln vetoed the local committee's plan to bury Lincoln in a grove of trees in the city. Instead, his remains were interred outside of town in the Oak Ridge Cemetery. There, on May 4, a final, simple ceremony was conducted. A Methodist bishop, Matthew Simpson, delivered the burial sermon, and Reverend Gurley delivered the final benediction.[81]

More than 1 million Americans viewed the remains of Abraham Lincoln as he lay in state in various cities on the trip to Springfield. One in every four Americans came to see Lincoln or watch his funeral train pass by—sometimes in the wee hours of the morning.[82] Those who were not able to participate grieved in their own fashion, through prayers or by buying black-edged cards to put in the family album. Many citizens wore mourning ribbons, some with the president's likeness on them.

Across the world, people were in shock over the assassination. England was filled with grief and indignation. Memorials were held throughout Britain, and the House of Lords took the unprecedented action of expressing its outrage and sympathy to the American people. The French were shocked, as were citizens of Canada and Latin America.

The feeling of outrage following Lincoln's death had never been experienced in America before this. Lincoln was the first American leader to be assassinated. Many citizens believed a crime like this could not occur in America, where there was liberty and self-government. Even though many southerners privately applauded the assassination of the northern "tyrant" and were glad Lincoln had been shot, others feared the possibility of revenge and that Reconstruction would be made more difficult. Some southern Unionists organized public meetings in Raleigh, North Carolina, and other southern towns to adopt resolutions expressing "abhorrence of the atrocious deed."

Vice President Johnson assumed the presidency on April 15 at 10:00 A.M., two and a half hours after Lincoln had died.[83] He proclaimed a national day of fasting and prayer on June 1. On May 2, the new president issued a proclamation for the arrest of Confederate President Jefferson Davis and several other "rebels and traitors" for inciting the assassination of Lincoln and the attempt on Seward's life. A reward of $100,000 was offered for Davis. He was eventually arrested, imprisoned, and indicted, but never tried.

Mary Lincoln spent five weeks in the White House before she was emotionally and physically able to leave. Most days she was bedridden. After her husband died, Mary worried about finances, even though Lincoln's estate was ample enough to pay off her debts and she was given a pension by Congress. Ten years after the death of her husband, Mary was certified as a "lunatic" in Cook County, Illinois. She was committed to a private sanitarium but was released after a second trial a year later and spent the last months of her life in a dark room dressed in widow's clothes.

Lincoln's death has long fascinated people, and even today, conspiracy theories abound about the reason Booth killed the president. One theory revolves around the idea that Booth acted as a puppet for others, especially Jefferson Davis and the Confederate high command. Another holds that the man captured in the Virginia barn and killed by soldiers was not Booth but an innocent bystander who was substituted for Lincoln's killer. In support of that theory were sightings of Booth in Europe, Mexico, and South America.

Eleven years after his assassination, Lincoln would become the target of one more conspiracy.[84] In 1876, a group of Chicago counterfeiters plotted to steal Lincoln's body and hold it for ransom. They planned to demand a $200,000 ransom, along with the release of the gang's master engraver, who was in prison in Illinois. The Secret Service infiltrated the gang and prevented the theft. This would set in motion a plan to provide security for the president's body until the casket was buried and encased in concrete.

CONCLUSION

Lincoln was born into a poor family and rose to become a surveyor, businessman, politician, lawyer, and president. He was a loving and tolerant father to his four sons.[85] He was a compassionate friend, often representing clients in court without charge simply because he sympathized with their situation or because he wanted to help out. But he was also a masterful and fiercely ambitious politician. He was not perfect, but he was a good man, kind and honest, and simple in his tastes.

As president, Lincoln led the country through the Civil War and saved the Union. He believed that all Americans should have the opportunity to prove themselves and to fulfill their own potential, as he had done. To that end, he ended slavery and provided for the fulfillment of the national promise of equality for all Americans regardless of color. Today, Lincoln is revered as our greatest president by amateur and professional historians alike.

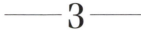

3

James A. Garfield

INTRODUCTION

On the morning of July 2, 1881, President James Garfield ate breakfast with his close friend and advisor, Secretary of State James Blaine. The president was relaxed and lighthearted and looking forward to taking a much-needed vacation in New England. There he would meet up with his wife, Lucretia, who was recuperating from a bout of malaria. Blaine and Garfield slowly finished their meal and enjoyed their carriage ride to the Baltimore and Potomac Railroad station in the heart of the city. They were joined by Garfield's two sons, Harry and Jim, who, after visiting their mother, were going to enroll at Williams College. They were also joined by Robert Todd Lincoln, who had watched his father die from an assassin's bullet years earlier. The president was eagerly anticipating the trip and looked forward to spending time with his wife at the beach they both loved so much.

Upon arriving at the railroad station, the president and Blaine stepped out of the carriage and greeted a small group of supporters who had gathered there. After walking about halfway into a deserted waiting room, a nervous-looking stranger slowly approached them. Blaine immediately recognized the stranger as Charles Guiteau, a disappointed, mentally unstable man who had repeatedly asked for, and been denied, a position in the Garfield administration.[1] Owing to Guiteau's delusions about himself and his "role" in Republican Party politics, Garfield would become the second president to die in office as the result of an assassin's bullet,[2] only sixteen years after Lincoln.[3]

JAMES ABRAM GARFIELD

The twentieth president of the United States, James Garfield, was born November 19, 1831, in northeast Ohio.[4] His family belonged to a church called the Disciples of Christ[5] in which Garfield became an ordained minister.[6] In 1851, Garfield decided to attend a school sponsored by the church in Hiram, Ohio, called the Western Reserve Eclectic School, later named Hiram College.[7] While there, Garfield discovered he was a "natural speaker" and could sway audiences.[8] He also met his future wife, Lucretia "Crete" Rudolph, the daughter of one of the school's trustees.

In 1854, after three years at Hiram, Garfield decided to attend Williams College in Williamstown, Massachusetts. He continued to perfect his speaking skills as a member of the debate team. He graduated in 1856 and became a professor of Latin and Greek at Hiram College.[9] At first, he was not happy there because he believed the college president to be incompetent.[10] When the president resigned in 1857, some members asked Garfield to step in as president, even though others thought he was too young and inexperienced. As a compromise, they named him "chairman of the College," but a few months later, he formally became the college's president. Garfield instituted many reforms, including science courses and antislavery ideals.

In November 1858, Garfield married Lucretia.[11] In all, they had seven children, two of whom died at an early age. The next year, Garfield began to study law, but was also given the opportunity to run for office as an Ohio state senator. He had become well known for preaching, lecturing, and debating the issues of the day. In his campaign, he spoke against slavery and supported free labor.[12] He won the election and served in the Ohio State Senate for the 1859–1861 term. From that point on, politics was his chosen career, though he maintained his interest in law and was admitted to the Ohio bar in 1861.[13]

Garfield also established a strong military career. He enlisted in the Union Army in 1861 during the Civil War.[14] At first, he was appointed to the rank of lieutenant colonel of the 42nd Ohio Volunteer Infantry.[15] During the war, the 42nd Ohio Volunteer Infantry joined three other regiments and a cavalry unit to form the 18th Brigade. Garfield was promoted to colonel and put in command of the brigade.[16]

During the war, Confederate soldiers had marched into Kentucky from Virginia. Garfield was ordered to drive the Confederate forces out of eastern Kentucky. The Confederates, who outnumbered Garfield's troops, met Garfield's men in Kentucky's Big Sandy Valley on January 10, 1862, in a battle later called the Battle of Middle Creek. In the end, Garfield successfully drove the Confederates out of Kentucky with few casualties. Garfield was considered a hero.[17] Because he was such an effective leader, Garfield was made a brigadier general. He worked alongside General Ulysses S. Grant to drive the Confederate Army from Union territory.

Garfield's military career continued to advance. In 1863 he became chief of staff to Major General William Rosecrans,[18] and distinguished himself at the Battle of Chickamauga in September. When his horse was shot out from under him, he safely delivered a message that saved the Army of the Cumberland from disaster. Even though the Union lost the battle, Garfield helped the Army of the Cumberland survive. For his bravery, he was promoted to major general.

After the war, President Lincoln urged Garfield to return to political life.[19] While serving in the Army in 1862, Garfield was elected to the U.S. House of Representatives. Garfield served in the House for seventeen years, from 1863 to 1880.[20] He was respected for his military expertise, and served as chairman of the Military Affairs Committee, chairman of the Banking and Currency Committee, and chairman of the Appropriations Committee. He was also a member of the Ways and Means Committee, for which he inspected hospitals, offices, and schools to find wasteful spending.[21]

One issue the House had to address after the war was Reconstruction of the South. There was much disagreement as to what role the federal government should take. Garfield believed that Lincoln was weak and was being too generous with the South. He called for much harsher measures than Lincoln proposed. Garfield was opposed to readmitting the southern states into the Union with full states' rights, and he wanted the South to be occupied by Union troops until Southerners agreed to give full rights to their former slaves.[22]

Garfield was also outspoken about slavery.[23] He opposed slavery and believed that the freed slaves should be allowed to vote. There was great debate about this issue. Some argued that the slaves were unable to read or write and had no education, and were thus not capable of voting. Garfield promptly pointed out that the slaves were no different from the European immigrants coming into the country at the time, many of whom were also unable to read or write.

After Lincoln's assassination, President Andrew Johnson continued the policies of the Lincoln administration; this led to numerous conflicts with Congress. Garfield found himself acting as a mediator between the president and Congress, and most times supporting Congress. In 1866, when Johnson vetoed civil rights legislation that gave citizenship to blacks, Garfield voted in favor of the act over Johnson's veto.

Ulysses S. Grant, whom Garfield initially supported, succeeded Johnson to the presidency. However, Garfield believed that Grant was giving offices to unqualified supporters simply to reward them for their support. Garfield favored the practice of appointing people to office based on their qualifications, and sought to reform the patronage system and create a civil service system whereby people would be hired on their merit by an independent agency.

Garfield became a highly respected member of Congress and a leader of the Republican Party. He developed a greater knowledge of the inner workings of the government than any other president. Unfortunately, in 1872 he was accused of taking bribes from a fellow congressman for stock in a railroad construction company called Credit Mobilier. At the time, Credit Mobilier was receiving government appropriations to build the Union Pacific Railroad. The owners of the company offered to sell stock in the company to members of Congress at low prices. Some argued this was bribery, since congressmen could vote for higher appropriations for the company, making sure that their stock would rise in price. In the end, there was no proof that Garfield bought any stock, and he was cleared of the charges. Nonetheless, his name remained connected with political corruption for many years.

In 1876, Garfield was appointed to serve as a member of the electoral commission that would decide between Rutherford B. Hayes and Samuel J. Tilden for president. This resulted in the Compromise of 1877. In the bargain, Republicans promised to remove federal troops from the South, to be fair to southerners in giving out federal jobs, and to vote for federal funds for improvements in the South. In return, the southern Democrats agreed to give the election to Hayes and to deal fairly with blacks.

In January 1880, the Ohio legislature elected Garfield to the U.S. Senate. That same year, at the Republican convention, the members of the Republican Party were split between a more moderate group, referred to as the Half-Breeds, and the more conservative faction, known as the Stalwarts.[24] Garfield, as head of the Ohio delegation, refused to take a side.

Former President Grant had been retired for four years, but decided to run for the nomination for president. He was supported by the Stalwarts. The Half-Breeds supported James G. Blaine. The compromise candidate was John Sherman. Although Garfield differed with Sherman's policies, he supported Sherman because of past support Garfield received from him. Meanwhile, a group of Republicans was working behind the scenes for a Garfield nomination. In the end, the Half-Breeds gave their support to Garfield, and on the thirty-sixth ballot, Garfield was nominated as the Republican candidate for president.[25] His opponent was Democrat and Civil War hero Winfield S. Hancock.[26]

In the campaign, Garfield decided to stay home and let people come to his house to visit him and hear his speeches. Thousands of people came to his home, Lawnfield, in Medina, Ohio, during the summer and fall of 1880. The railroads established special rates for people interested in making the trip. When the election was over, Garfield beat Hancock by a margin of just under 10,000 votes.[27] The Electoral College chose Chester A. Arthur, a Stalwart, as the vice presidential candidate.[28] Garfield was inaugurated and became president in 1881. Soon after, he, like Lincoln, began to have strange nightmares about his own death.

One of the first issues for Garfield was dealing with the hundreds of people who came to him requesting a job or a favor. One of those job seekers was Charles J. Guiteau. Garfield's advisors found Guiteau unsuitable for any position in the administration, but Guiteau believed otherwise.

CHARLES GUITEAU

Charles Jules Guiteau, the man who shot President Garfield, was born on September 8, 1841, in Freeport, Illinois. He was the fourth of six children, only three of whom survived to adulthood. Guiteau's mother, who reportedly had postpartum psychosis after Guiteau's birth, passed away when he was only seven, leaving his father, Luther, to raise him. Luther, once a cashier at the Second National Bank of Freeport, was profoundly religious and raised Guiteau with strict tenets of good and evil. He sometimes used physical discipline to teach Guiteau proper behavior. Luther was a pillar of the community, even serving as superintendent of the schools in Freeport for a short time. However, one of Charles Guiteau's brothers died insane, as did a niece and nephew.

Charles went to school in Illinois until he was twelve. About that time (in 1853), his father remarried, but Charles resented his new stepmother and chose to live with his sister and her husband in Chicago.

In the meantime, Guiteau's father joined a religious group led by John H. Noyes. Noyes preached a doctrine called *perfectionism*, through which man could strive for holiness sufficient for eternal salvation. Noyes believed in "free love," shared labor, and mutual criticism. He also believed in communal living in which the good things in life were shared with other members. Noyes and the community members believed in "open relationships" and shared marriage among its members. The Guiteau family eventually moved to Oneida, New York, to be part of Noyes's community. After a brief stay there, Charles left in 1865 and moved to New Jersey, but returned later that same year.[29]

Guiteau again left the community in 1866 and moved to New York City. By then he was a religious fanatic who tried to make a living lecturing on the Second Coming of Christ. He also tried to publish a newspaper called the *New York Theocrat*, but it failed because he could not find sufficient financial backing.[30] When the publishing attempt failed, Guiteau moved back to Oneida to live in Noyes's community. He became moody and complained about doing manual work in the kitchen or the factory. He was unpopular, and many of the females in the group shunned him.

Noyes and Guiteau had a falling out over several thousand dollars which Guiteau claimed Noyes owed him in back pay. Guiteau again left the community, this time attempting to sell an exposé of his life at the Oneida community, but this attempt to publish also failed. At one point, he had an idea to purchase the *Chicago Tribune*, even though it was not for sale. He approached the president of his father's bank and asked for $25,000, promising him that he would make him governor of Illinois if the loan was made. It was not.

When his publishing career failed, Guiteau began a career in law. For a short time, he worked as a clerk in a law firm and was admitted to the Illinois bar.[31] By the end of 1868, he was in practice for himself. To most people, Guiteau seemed to be a respectable member of the community and someone with moral character. He did not drink, smoke, or gamble. When he was twenty-seven, he married a sixteen-year-old girl named Annie Bunn, who worked in the library of the Chicago YMCA.

Guiteau had expensive tastes, but often could not pay his bills, forcing him to run away when the bills came due. He and his new wife were frequently forced to sneak out of their lodgings at night. Guiteau learned how to stay one step ahead of bill collectors and became a great con man.[32] Sometimes, he would ride trains without purchasing a ticket by claiming he was a minister. When Annie complained to Charles about their lifestyle, he locked her in a closet, beat her, punched her, and kicked her. After about five years, she grew tired of his temper, the constant lack of money, hiding from bill collectors, and fleeing apartments for lack of rent money.[33] Charles found he enjoyed the company of prostitutes, even contracting syphilis from one. One prostitute testified in court that she slept with him to allow him to get a divorce. His wife left him in 1874 on the grounds of adultery.

Not long after, the *New York Herald* ran a story about Guiteau, printing an article that described how he destroyed his own practice. In response, Guiteau brought a suit against the paper for $100,000. He eventually dropped the lawsuit because he did not want to have the *Herald* as an enemy if he ever ran for president of the United States.[34]

Guiteau was caught one night while trying to escape without paying for a room, and was taken to the police station, where he was charged with fraud. He ended up spending five weeks in jail. His sister Frances came to get him, and he lived with her until he attacked her with an axe. Frances tried to have him committed to an asylum, but Guiteau fled to Chicago and disappeared.

In the 1872 presidential campaign, Guiteau became interested in politics and supported Horace Greeley's campaign. He often hung around the Democratic headquarters in New York, but most people there avoided him. He was convinced if Greeley won, he would be appointed minister to Chile. Greeley lost the campaign, and Guiteau received no appointment.

In 1880, Guiteau again took an interest in the presidential campaign, this time as a Republican. Early in the campaign he supported Grant, but then switched his support to Garfield. Guiteau considered himself to be a Stalwart. At that point, he was almost thirty-nine years old and living in Boston, where he sold insurance. He was not successful in that job. He also occasionally gave religious speeches and wrote and self-published a book called *The Truth*. Because he had little income, Guiteau was forced to wear old clothes and had a shabby appearance.[35]

During the campaign, Guiteau wanted to take an active part and offered his services to the National Republican Committee. In order to be more available, he decided to leave Boston and travel to New York on a steamer called the *Stonington*. During the trip, it became very foggy and the ship ran into another ship, the *Narragansett*. The *Narragansett* sank within minutes. Some of the passengers were burned alive, and others died of hypothermia. In all, eighty people were feared dead, but Guiteau survived.[36]

Guiteau wrote a speech for Grant that he wanted to give at the 1880 Republican National Convention, but Guiteau was never asked to deliver the speech. Even though it was written for Grant, Guiteau discovered that it could easily be edited for Garfield.[37] When Garfield's name was mentioned as a possible contender, Guiteau sent the speech to Garfield. Guiteau seriously believed that his speech would tip the election for Garfield.

Guiteau left New York City and traveled upstate to places like Poughkeepsie and Saratoga and tried to deliver the speech there, but was unable to find an audience. He returned to the city to find work, but was not able to do so. He even called at the home of Chester Arthur, the vice presidential candidate, but was turned away. One day, Guiteau was able to get through and enjoyed several minutes talking face-to-face with Garfield. Guiteau told Garfield about his speech,[38] and for the next few months, Guiteau barraged Garfield, Blaine, and others with letters and copies of it. When no one responded to him, he started to have thoughts of killing the president. Guiteau believed that the act of assassinating a president (not necessarily Garfield) would bring attention to himself and his cause.

Guiteau continued to attend Republican events even though many Republicans considered him to be a nuisance. He went to the Fifth Avenue Summit of August 1880 (at the Fifth Avenue Hotel), where Republicans were meeting to choose the party's leaders. Guiteau attended every meeting he could, often just waiting in the hotel lobby to hobnob with the political elite. He was friendly, but his awkward style and dirty appearance kept him from being accepted. He was able to introduce himself to many of them and gave each a copy of his speech. He even gave another copy of his speech to Garfield. Guiteau knew that if the Republicans won the election, there would be plenty of political jobs that needed to be filled, and those who gave speeches or worked in the campaign would get the best appointments.

All through the month of August (and throughout the campaign), Guiteau frequented the Republican offices, often staying for hours at a time, claiming to have seen Chester Arthur about twenty times. Finally, Arthur arranged to have Guiteau give his speech to a rally of black New York voters on Twenty-Fifth Street. The *New York Times* listed Guiteau as the lead-off speaker for the event. When he began his speech, Guiteau became uncomfortable and stopped after only a few paragraphs. He later claimed he did not like the crowd.

After the election, Guiteau was convinced that he played a vital role in the Republican victory of 1880. On March 5, 1881, he went to Washington, where he told people that he had worked at Republican headquarters and on the campaign alongside Chester Arthur, and that he had given a speech in support of Garfield. Because of his support for the party, he expected the reward of a diplomatic appointment. At first he sought to be the minister to Austria, and later the consul to Paris.

He wrote to Garfield and said he had plans to marry a wealthy woman in New York, which would give him adequate resources and prestige to represent the U.S. government at the court of Vienna with dignity and grace.[39] In reality, the "wealthy lady" to whom Guiteau referred was a lady who he had seen at church one Sunday morning, and even though they had never been introduced, he was sure she would marry him if he asked her. He sent her letters, but she complained to police detectives, who arrested him and ordered him to stay away.

Even though Guiteau got no reply from Garfield about the position, he still traveled to Washington the day after the inauguration to meet with the new president. At that time, it was tradition that the White House was open to everyone.

On March 8, Guiteau went to the White House to meet with Garfield. He walked to the front door of the building and went right in. Garfield normally talked to visitors between noon and one o'clock every day. When Guiteau arrived, he found over a hundred others there as well, almost all of them interested in a job.

Over the next few weeks, Guiteau continued to visit the White House in hopes of meeting Garfield and getting a job. Most of the time, he was ignored. One day, Guiteau was called into Garfield's inner office, where he was able to meet personally with the president. He returned to the White House a few days later but was not able to meet again with the president. Finally, Guiteau was politely but firmly rebuffed. Nonetheless, he was convinced he was going to get a job as a diplomat. He spent many days in Lafayette Park across the street from the White House, feeding the squirrels and waiting for Garfield to have time to see him.

While in D.C., Guiteau rented a room at Mrs. Lockwood's Boarding House. At one point, he entered the room of Illinois Senator John Logan, who was also residing at the boarding house. The senator greeted him and spoke with him briefly, and Guiteau gave him the speech he had written. He told the senator that he had delivered the speech in New York and as a result was promised an appointment of consul-general to France. He asked Logan for a recommendation, but Logan politely refused. Afterward, Mrs. Lockwood asked Guiteau to leave the boardinghouse and gave him a bill for his first two weeks' rent. The next day, his room was empty.[40]

Guiteau made it a point to attend White House receptions frequently in order to keep his name in front of the officials there. He was able to introduce himself to Mrs. Garfield, and they spoke briefly. He gave her his calling card and told her that he was one of the men who had made her husband president. She chatted politely with him for a short moment, and then moved on to greet the next person.[41]

Garfield continued to appoint people to positions in his administration, but some Stalwarts were upset about his choices. Guiteau wrote a series of letters to Garfield condemning some of the appointments and requesting that Garfield appoint a Stalwart, like himself, instead. He also reported that Blaine approved him for the Paris job.[42]

Guiteau was a voracious reader of newspapers, especially the anti-Garfield *New York Herald* and the Washington-based *New Republican*.[43] From these sources, Guiteau developed fears about Garfield and Blaine and how their policies were dividing the country and destroying the harmony within the Republican Party.

In March, a clerk at the White House told Guiteau that his appointment had been referred to the State Department.[44] He immediately went to the State Department to apply for the Paris consulship with Secretary of State Blaine. He continued to go there almost every day through March and April. He still was confident that the job was his. While he was waiting, he wrote letters to Garfield that gave him pointers, tips, and advice on his reelection.

On May 14, Guiteau visited the State Department, where Blaine told him, "Never speak to me again on the subject of the Paris consulship," and to stop bothering the State Department secretaries.[45] Despite that, Guiteau continued to write the president letters about the appointment, assuming it was his. The clerks at the State Department considered him more of a nuisance than a bona fide office seeker. But he grew so demanding that by June 6 he was barred from entering the White House at all.[46]

Guiteau began to believe that Garfield disliked him because he supported Grant in the campaign.[47] He also believed that Garfield was the cause of all the trouble within the Republican Party and needed to be removed. He decided that Garfield must die.[48] By shooting Garfield, he would heal the dispute within the party and save it. Further, removing Garfield would prevent another civil war. He convinced himself that God commanded him to kill Garfield and that he could be God's executioner because he had the brains and nerves to do the job.[49]

His plan to shoot the president was not personal, but rather a political necessity. He had met the president and Mrs. Garfield and liked both of them. But in his eyes, Garfield was a dictator and a traitor, and Guiteau believed that the country would rally around him when he freed them from the president's tyranny. Once the shock wore off, people would applaud him and Chester Arthur would treat him politely and respectfully. He also believed that after the assassination, Americans would consider him a hero, Arthur would give him a presidential pardon, and the gun he used to save the country would be on permanent display in Washington.[50]

On June 6, Guiteau went to O'Meara's Gun Shop and bought a relatively expensive .44-caliber snub-nose British Bulldog revolver with a white bone handle.[51] The gun was named a British Bulldog because of its destructive power. The same model with a wooden handle was a dollar cheaper, but Guiteau wanted the white one because it would show better on display in a museum once he killed Garfield. He also bought a box of cartridges and a penknife. In order to pay for the gun, he had to borrow ten dollars from a cousin. Guiteau had never handled a gun before, and was even afraid of them.[52] For the next four weeks, he practiced firing the weapon along the Potomac River. He also practiced stalking the president.

He stalked the president for weeks before the actual assassination. He had decided against shooting him at the White House, because it was too crowded, and he was no longer allowed inside.[53] Three times before the assassination, he was within firing range of the president, but each time he backed down. One time, he watched Garfield walk through Lafayette Square Park. Another time, he followed Garfield to the Disciples of Christ Church, where he stood in the back of the congregation and noted where Garfield sat during the service.[54] Afterward, he walked outside the church to locate the window nearest to Garfield's pew to determine whether it would be possible to shoot through it. He thought the church would be an ideal place to kill Garfield, and decided to do it the next Sunday, June 19. But Guiteau read in the newspaper that Garfield would not be attending church that day because he and his wife were going on vacation. Lucretia had been recuperating from malaria, and they were going to the seashore for some fresh air.

Guiteau decided to shoot Garfield as the couple left for vacation. When the Garfields left, Guiteau was at the train depot. He watched the couple walk toward the train, but decided at the last minute not to shoot the president. He felt that Lucretia seemed too frail, and he did not want to shoot the president in front of her.[55]

While waiting for the president to return from his vacation at the seashore, Guiteau walked past the Washington, D.C., jail, the Bastille, and asked a warden if he could go inside. He wanted to see where he would be staying after the assassination and if the conditions met with his approval. He also wanted to make sure it was safe enough, just in case there was an angry mob that might try to lynch him after the assassination.

Garfield returned to Washington, D.C. from his vacation on June 27, leaving Lucretia at the seashore to recuperate. Once again, Guiteau carefully tracked Garfield. On Friday night, July 1, Garfield walked to Blaine's house. Guiteau followed him, but decided not to shoot him there because it was a hot night and he was tired from the heat.[56] But he knew he had to do it soon. Guiteau asked the doorkeeper at the White House when Garfield would be departing in the morning. He then returned to the boardinghouse and wrote one last explanation of his reasons for assassinating the president. Later, he would give the letters to reporters so they would be published after the shooting.[57]

THE ASSASSINATION

Despite the assassination of Abraham Lincoln sixteen years earlier, the president still had no bodyguards. Newspapers published his daily schedule. On this day, Garfield was returning to New England to visit his wife, who was already there. He was going to give his boys a personal introduction to the faculty at Williams College. He was in a good mood and was looking forward to this two-week vacation through New England.

On the morning of July 2, 1881, after a breakfast with his friend James Blaine, the men went to the Baltimore and Potomac Railroad station, where Garfield was to catch the train to New Jersey. At 9:30 A.M., Garfield climbed out of the carriage and stopped to greet a few well-wishers. Blaine went inside the station to say goodbye to Garfield and other cabinet officers and their wives who were going with the president. Also joining them were Garfield's two sons, Hal and Jim, and Robert Lincoln.[58]

Meanwhile, Guiteau, who was thirty-nine at the time of the shooting, woke early, at around 4:00 A.M., and ate a big breakfast. He then walked to Lafayette Park and sat on a bench where he could watch the White House. At about 9:00 A.M., he left the bench and checked his pocket to make sure the pistol was there. He had wrapped the weapon in paper to make sure that no sweat or dirt would get into the firing mechanism. He took a tram to the railroad station, arriving about ten minutes past nine. He had his shoes shined at a shoeshine stand.

Garfield and Blaine walked arm in arm to the entrance of the ladies' waiting room, which was empty because it was early. Since men were allowed into the area, there were a few other men there. The two men separated as the president asked a policeman how much time he had before the train left. He was told he had about ten minutes. Blaine stepped ahead of the president to allow him more room through the doorway. The president remarked that he wished Blaine was going on the trip with them.

A female attendant was on duty, and there were several passersby, and a down-and-out looking man who moved nervously about in the shadows of the entrance, pacing nervously back and forth. He was a thin man, about 130 pounds, and of medium height.[59] Garfield and Blaine were halfway into the room when the stranger moved toward them. When he was six feet behind and to the extreme right, the man drew a revolver from his coat and fired. Two shots rang out. The assassin said nothing and gave no warning, but aimed at the president's heart. Some thought a firecracker had been lit to honor the president.

The first bullet passed through Garfield's right sleeve and gave the president a slight flesh wound. The second bullet, fired at point-blank range, entered the middle of the right side of Garfield's back, fracturing two ribs and narrowly missing the president's spinal cord. The bullet lodged in his back near the pancreas.[60]

Garfield turned, flinched, then straightened up and threw his head back, confused, as he cried out, "My God! What is this?"[61] At that point, a third shot hit him square in the back on the right side and flattened his lungs. Garfield reeled sharply to the right and fell over, hitting the floor hard. He lay on the floor, bleeding profusely. He vomited but did not lose consciousness.[62]

Blaine turned to help the president and exclaimed, "My God, he has been murdered! What is the meaning of this?"[63] Garfield's sons, Harry and Jim, raced to their father's side and found that he had been severely wounded. James was in tears. Robert Todd Lincoln, who had come to see the president off, stood off to the side, thinking back to the night his own father was assassinated.

No one on the outside knew about the shooting. They were joking and laughing as they waited for their vacation to begin. Inside the train station, there was confusion in the waiting area. Garfield lay on the ground, semiconscious. Nobody seemed to know what to do. Some bystanders held his hand, while others his head. His teenage sons remained by his side. The crowd yelled, "Lynch him" or "Hang him."[64]

The first doctor to reach Garfield was Dr. Smith Townsend, the public health officer. He arrived just a few minutes after the shooting.[65] The doctor found that Garfield had almost no pulse and had cold, clammy skin and shallow

Figure 3.1.   Lithograph of President James A. Garfield's assassination by Charles Guiteau on July 2, 1881, at the Baltimore and Potomac Railroad Station in Washington, D.C. (Courtesy of the Library of Congress.)

breathing. He immediately concluded the president was dying. The doctor asked someone to bring brandy and ammonia aromatic smelling salts, and after that Garfield became more alert. He told the doctor that his right leg and foot had a severe "prickling sensation."[66]

The next doctor to show up was Dr. Charles Purvis, an African American physician. He ordered bottles of hot water be placed around Garfield's leg and feet and a blanket wrapped around his torso. Garfield was given more brandy. Soon after, two more doctors appeared and moved Garfield to a room on the second floor of the train station, where members of his cabinet gathered.

To investigate the extent of the bullet wound, the doctors stuck their unwashed fingers and unclean instruments far up into the bullet hole in Garfield's back. While many of the doctors probed his wounds, they created a much larger wound. Doctors did not find the bullet, but did not think the wound was too serious and believed Garfield would recover. Garfield asked about the injury. The doctors lied to him and said it was not serious, even though most of them thought the wound was fatal. Garfield disagreed with them, and said to one doctor, "I thank you doctor, but I am a dead man."[67]

Robert Todd Lincoln asked for Dr. Willard Bliss, a Civil War surgeon who was considered to be an expert in gunshot wounds. Bliss arrived within fifteen minutes. He also put his little finger in the wound, and used two metal probes. Based on his exam, he concluded that the bullet entered Garfield's liver. Temporary and unclean dressings were applied.[68] Garfield asked that someone send a telegraph to his wife and tell her what happened, and asked to be taken back to the White House.[69]

A horse-drawn ambulance carried Garfield back to the White House. Throughout the ride, he was jostled to and fro on the cobblestone streets. He was taken to the second floor of the White House, where he continued to complain of leg pain and was given shots of morphine. Garfield received around-the-clock care from Dr. Bliss, who was the attending doctor from that point on. He was assisted by a team of surgeons who ordered that Garfield remain fully clothed so there was no unnecessary movement. But it was hot outside, so after eight hours, his shirt and trousers were removed. This allowed for the first thorough physical exam. Afterward, his condition stabilized and he was upbeat and talkative.

Later, it seemed unlikely that the president would live through the night. Garfield vomited, his fever spiked, and he could not eat. Although there were never less than three doctors in the room at a time, they fought among themselves as to the appropriate procedures. Trained nurses were scarce at the time, so Bliss was forced to turn to the wives of various cabinet members to tend to his needs. They had no knowledge of basic nursing responsibilities.

Two surgeons came to the White House on Saturday, July 23, but Bliss said it was best not to disturb him. Instead, he could be examined the next day. On Sunday, a surgical incision was made to drain pus. The incision was not long enough, and two days later they had to open it again. There was no anesthesia. Fragments of rib were removed and drainage tubes fastened. In all, three separate operations were performed to drain abscesses and to remove bone fragments, but the president's condition did not improve.

Bliss invited Alexander Graham Bell to demonstrate a new electromagnetic bullet-finding device he had recently invented. Bell came to the White House, but his attempt to locate the bullet proved unsuccessful, partly because the doctor (Bliss) had told him the wrong area, and the steel springs in the bed may have interfered with the device.[70] One New York surgeon fired shots into cadavers hoping to replicate Garfield's injury and find the location of the bullet. This did not work, either.

By late July, Garfield suffered chills, signs of infection, and blood poisoning. His fever rose and he continued to vomit. He had a rapid pulse. Nonetheless, on Friday, July 29, Garfield presided over a brief cabinet meeting. It was mostly for appearances, to show the public he was improving and still capable of being president.

By the middle of August, it was clear that Garfield was not improving and that the wound was not healing properly. Secondary areas of infection had developed. On Sunday, August 14, Garfield vomited what little he ate. He was taken off all food, instead getting nutritive enemas made of beef bouillon, egg yolks, milk, whiskey, and opium. In reality, he was starving to death.

Garfield lay between life and death in the White House for weeks. Some days he could eat and did not feel pain, but other days were different. During the course of several weeks, he lost nearly a hundred pounds.[71] A bullet remained in his spine, but it could not be located. There were no antibiotics, so he faced an extremely high risk of blood poisoning. Because the doctors poked him so much looking for the bullet, the wound repeatedly became infected. Garfield had been lying in a room in the White House that overlooked the Potomac, but there were a lot of mosquitoes, too, and there was concern about the president contracting malaria.

Many people sent telegrams to the president to wish him well, including Queen Victoria; Prime Minister William Gladstone; the emperors of Russia, Austria, and Germany; and the kings of Denmark, Norway, Sweden, Belgium, Portugal, Italy, and Spain.[72]

It was very hot in Washington, and Garfield longed for cool sea breezes. He asked to be moved to the family's seaside cottage in Elberon, New Jersey, for fresh air. The doctors thought the fresh air would be beneficial for the president, so they agreed to allow him to travel. In September, more than 2,000 volunteers worked to construct a railroad track to the front door of his vacation home.[73] They laid 3,200 feet of temporary track to the door of the Garfields' cottage. They also built a special train car that minimized movement, with an extra-thick mattress on springs.

In the first few days at Elberon, Garfield seemed to improve, but he soon developed bronchopneumonia and drifted in and out of consciousness. He was still nauseous and had chills and a fever. On Saturday, September 17, Garfield complained of a throbbing pain in his chest. Shortly after 10:00 P.M. on Monday, September 19, Garfield awoke, cried out, "Oh Swaim [chief of staff, David G. Swaim], this terrible pain," and placed his hand over his heart.[74] He fell on his pillow and became unconscious. He died at 10:35 P.M. on September, 19, 1881, only two months before his fiftieth birthday.

Garfield's body lay in state in the Rotunda of the Capitol building rather than in the White House for two days. More than 150,000 people came to see the open coffin, including Garfield's mother. After everyone left, Mrs. Garfield was given one hour with her husband. There was a service in the Rotunda on September 23, and then a funeral train with Garfield's body left Washington, D.C. for Ohio. Thousands of people lined the train route. He was buried in Lakeview Cemetery in Cleveland. In all, Garfield had spent 200 days as president, and for eighty of those days he lay in pain. He was shot in broad daylight in a time of peace.

Chester A. Arthur took the oath of office at 2:15 A.M. on September 20. Judge John R. Brady was the first judge to arrive and administered the oath of office. Arthur was fifty-one years old. He then took the oath again in front of dignitaries from Chief Justice Morrison R. Waite. One of the first things he did as president was to proclaim Monday, September 26, as a national day of mourning.[75]

THE AFTERMATH

Immediately after the shooting, Guiteau walked through the waiting room toward the exit and the carriage he had waiting for him to take him to jail.

People were yelling, "Stop him! He shot the president!"[76] There were calls to lynch him. Guiteau stepped out onto the sidewalk, and a policeman and a ticket agent blocked his path. He was still holding the pistol he had used to shoot Garfield. He was arrested by Washington, D.C. policeman Patrick Kearney, who had rushed into the station at the first sound of gunfire. The policeman grabbed his arm and started to pull him back into the station. Guiteau fully expected to be caught and told the police, "I did it. I will go to jail for it. I am a Stalwart and Arthur will be president."[77]

Guiteau kept quiet as officers quickly dragged him to police headquarters. They searched him and took his gun. They found letters he had written and put him in a cell. At the jail, he answered all their questions. He told the detective in charge that Arthur was his friend, and that he would have him made chief of police. In one of the letters, written on the morning of the assassination, he wrote, "The President's tragic death was a sad necessity, but it will unite the Republican Party and save the Republic . . . [I] had no ill-will toward the president. His death was a political necessity."[78]

Before his trial, Guiteau seemed to enjoy being in jail, where he received free food and a free place to stay. He also received many letters congratulating him for shooting the president.[79] He courted the press and prepared statements for newsmen, and seemed to be enjoying his new celebrity status. He dictated a lengthy biography from his jail cell to the *New York Herald* and wrote a letter to incoming President Arthur, taking credit for his elevation to the presidency. "My inspiration is a God send to you and I presume that you appreciate it. . . . It raises you from a political cipher to the president of the U.S. . . . Never think of Garfield's removal as murder. It was an act of Garfield resulting from a political necessity for which he was responsible."[80] He then proceeded to advise Arthur on the selection of a new cabinet.

Guiteau was charged with murder. The trial started on November 14, 1881, nearly two months after Garfield's death. It lasted fifty-four days and attracted great public interest. Guiteau was the target of two assassination attempts during the hearings. One was by a disgusted guard, and a second attempt occurred on the sixth day of the trial. As Guiteau was brought to the trial in a prison van, a man with a pistol chased the van on horseback, rode up to the rear, fired a shot through the back of the van, and rode away. The man was pursued, captured, and jailed. Guiteau was not hurt, although the bullet grazed his arm.[81]

Guiteau tried to plead insanity. During the trial, he laughed, told stories, acted as his own lawyer, and insulted the judges, lawyers, and witnesses.[82] He regularly threw the court into an uproar with impromptu speeches. He once interrupted the proceedings to suggest that members of the jury be taken out for walks to improve their digestion. At times he was foul-mouthed and abusive, and sometimes he mocked his lawyers. He told the court that God had ordered him to kill the president. His father wrote a letter that said he was a "fit subject for a lunatic asylum."[83] The judge did not restrain Guiteau's outbursts because he wanted the jury to view his behavior firsthand. He called witnesses "dirty liars," and called the prosecutor a "low-livered whelp" and an "old hog."[84] He claimed that by murdering Garfield, he could deliver the Republican Party into the hands of its conservative Stalwart wing. Now the Stalwarts owed him a federal appointment for his service to them.

At the same time, he objected to being characterized as insane and denounced his chief counsel, brother-in-law George Scoville, for attempting the defense. Guiteau pointed back to his survival of the shipwreck, saying that he survived because God had important plans for him and had saved his life for a purpose. He argued that Garfield died of medical malpractice and that the doctors should be indicted for murdering Garfield. "The doctors did that. I simply shot at him."[85] He said the doctors said Garfield would recover. He also told a government psychiatrist that he knew if he could convince a jury of his belief the shooting had been divinely inspired, he would not be convicted.

If he was found insane, then he would not be hanged, which most Americans felt he deserved. Most people felt that Guiteau knew what he was doing. Some pointed to the spoils system as the real cause for the assassination. They argued that a reformed civil service based on merit would avoid the patronage squabbling that had spun out of control. The judge chose to believe Guiteau, who said he was not insane, rather than believe the attorney, who said Guiteau was insane.[86]

At the time, the standard for insanity was the M'Naghten rule, which held that the defendant was to be considered responsible if he was aware of the nature of his act and knew it to be forbidden by law. At the same time, it was alleged that the state's lawyers coached witnesses and bribed experts to testify that Guiteau was sane. They suppressed or destroyed letters and documents that might show he was crazy.[87]

At the end of the trial, Guiteau asked to talk to the jury. He took the stand for four days and told the jury that the Lord had chosen him to remove the president, and nothing that one does in response to divine command can violate any law. He said that in any case, everyone was happy over the change in administrations. He said that there would be a terrible day of reckoning if he was executed, and sang a portion of "John Brown's Body."[88]

The jury deliberated one hour before returning a verdict, and on January 25, 1882, Guiteau was found guilty. Guiteau shook his finger at the jurors and said, "You are all low, consummate jackasses."[89] Judge Walter Cox sentenced him to be hanged. The Supreme Court denied a writ of habeas corpus, and President Arthur declined to grant a reprieve.

He was hanged at noon on June 30, 1882. Before being hanged, he read aloud from the Bible and sang a hymn he had composed for the occasion that began, "I am going to the Lordy; I am so glad."[90] Two hundred and fifty people watched the execution, some of whom had paid $300 for admission.

An autopsy on Guiteau's body showed nothing more abnormal than an enlarged spleen. Medical professionals preserved his skeleton, spleen, and brain and put them in storage at the National Museum of Health and Medicine in Washington, D.C., where they remain to this day.[91]

Garfield's untimely death brought pressure for civil service reform. In 1883, Congress passed the Pendleton Act, which established a bipartisan Civil Service Commission. Because of that, many federal government jobs could be obtained only through a process of competitive examinations. The commission would also protect federal government workers from dismissal for political reasons. At first, members of both political parties resisted the plan because it would reduce their power to use government jobs as rewards for party loyalty. But Garfield's death cast a harsh light on the old patronage system.

Some citizens called for stricter control of guns after the assassination, although Guiteau was not a "gun nut" and had bought his revolver legally. There were no changes in the law after Garfield's death, but the topic was brought up and added to the public's agenda, even if only for a short time.

The question of presidential succession was also raised as a consequence of Garfield's assassination. As Garfield laid disabled, there were questions about who would succeed him in office. Vice President Arthur did not want to have anything to do with the conversation, and he spent much of the time in New York trying to distance himself from the discussion. But Grant knew that Garfield was disabled and more than likely unable to continue as president, and conceded that the Constitution did not specify how a successor should be chosen. Grant felt that the president's physicians should inform the cabinet as to Garfield's incapacity, and that the cabinet should then invite Arthur to act as president. In the end, nothing was done, probably because there were no critical issues facing the country that summer which could not be either deferred or handled within the departments themselves.

The months when the president was ailing showed how America, in a time of emergency, could survive without a president. During that time, Garfield signed only one document, which was largely unimportant, and he had few discussions with members of his cabinet. There were discussions in newspapers about the meaning of the word *disability* in the Constitution and the circumstances in which the vice president might assume the duties of the presidency. Since most thought Garfield would live, there was no demand that the question be settled in any hurry.

Garfield may have lived after the shooting had his doctors practiced correct sterilization procedures.[92] The autopsy showed that a cyst had formed around the bullet, rendering it harmless.[93] With the proper medical care, Garfield's wound would not have been fatal, and the president could have been back to work in a few weeks. The lack of proper procedures led to blood poisoning, the immediate cause of the president's death. Garfield's death brought about medical changes, such as the need for antiseptic surgery. The absence of trained nurses was also criticized, and as a result of Garfield's death, new nursing schools were established.[94] The procedures for X-rays were also further developed.

CONCLUSION

President Garfield had been president for only six months when he was assassinated. He did not have much time to distinguish himself as a leader. He was trying to put together a balanced cabinet and return balance to the Republican Party. His assassination brought calls for civil service reform. The passage of the Pendleton Civil Service Reform Act of 1881 was a direct response to Garfield's death.

Lucretia outlived her husband by thirty-six years. She lived quietly in Mentor, Ohio, in the family home of Lawnfield and eventually built a house in Pasadena, California. She died on March 14, 1918.

Charles Guiteau, a mentally unstable middle-aged man who became the second individual in American history to assassinate a sitting president, was, as mentioned, executed by hanging on June 30, 1882.

—— 4 ——

William McKinley

INTRODUCTION

At about 3:30 on the very hot afternoon of September 6, 1901, President William McKinley and his wife, Ida, arrived at the train depot at the World Exposition in Buffalo, New York. They had spent the morning enjoying the sights in Niagara Falls. Mrs. McKinley returned to their lodgings for a short rest while President McKinley made a brief appearance at the exposition to greet the public.

McKinley was eager to greet the public and shake their hands. The crowd quickly moved forward toward the president. Many in the crowd wiped perspiration from their hands with handkerchiefs as they waited. No one noticed a short, clean-shaven young man in a suit near the door. He was an unemployed loner, an anarchist who was looking for a way to make a mark on history. He seemed to have an injured right hand, because it was wrapped in a handkerchief, so the president extended his left hand instead of his right.

What nobody knew was that concealed beneath the handkerchief was the weapon that would render William McKinley the third American president to be killed by an assassin's bullet.[1]

WILLIAM MCKINLEY

William McKinley, the twenty-fifth president of the United States, was born on January 29, 1843, in Niles, Ohio, the seventh of nine children. His family lived in a two-story farmhouse that had a country store downstairs.[2] McKinley's mother was deeply religious and allowed no drinking or dancing. As a child, McKinley liked school and learning, and especially enjoyed debating.[3] He attended the Poland Union Seminary in Ohio,[4] a Methodist high school. He joined the Methodist church in 1859, and remained very religious throughout his life.[5] When he was seventeen, he went to Pennsylvania and entered Allegheny College, a Methodist college, but withdrew after one term because of illness and a lack of funds.[6]

When the Civil War broke out, McKinley enlisted in the Poland Guards and was inducted into the U.S. Army. It was 1861, and McKinley was only eighteen. The Poland Guards joined the 23rd Ohio Volunteer Infantry Regiment,[7] where McKinley learned how to march in formation and shoot muskets. The unit marched into West Virginia and guarded the region against Confederate soldiers.

On September 10, 1861, the unit met Confederates at the Battle of Carnifex Ferry in West Virginia.[8] The Confederates were forced to retreat. The group then joined the Army of the Potomac. There, McKinley became the commissary sergeant and was responsible for distributing food rations to troops and making sure the horses got fed.[9] He also supervised the transportation and unloading of supplies.

On September 17, 1862, the Army of the Potomac fought General Robert E. Lee's Confederate Army at Sharpsburg, Maryland. The unit had gone into battle long before breakfast could be served. During a break in the fighting, McKinley supplied food and drink to the soldiers. He was ordered back several times by officers who thought he could not make it, but he ignored the orders. Because of his bravery, McKinley was promoted to second lieutenant. He was promoted to first lieutenant in March 1863, then to captain in July 1864, and finally given the rank of brevet major in 1865.[10]

When the war was over, McKinley became a clerk in a law firm in Youngstown, Ohio.[11] He attended Albany Law School in New York and passed the bar exam in 1867, even before finishing all of his courses. He returned to Canton, Ohio, to practice law, where his caseload consisted mostly of illegal liquor sales, burglaries, and assault cases.

McKinley, who was handsome and good-natured, had high ideals and made friends easily. He became the head of the Sunday school in the First Methodist Church and president of the Canton YMCA in 1868.[12] He also became active in local politics in Canton, campaigning for Rutherford B. Hayes when he ran for governor of Ohio, and for Ulysses Grant for president. Many people were impressed with him, so they asked him to run for the position of county prosecuting attorney. He did, and won the 1869 election.[13]

In 1871, McKinley lost his bid for a second term by just 143 votes.[14] Some said that his aggressive prosecution of liquor interests caused his defeat. Saloons, distilleries, and bar patrons mounted a strong campaign against him. McKinley returned to practicing law.

One day at a picnic, he met Ida Saxton, a frail socialite from a prominent family in Canton, Ohio. They were married in January 1871. The couple had two daughters, both of whom died in childhood. At about the same time, McKinley accepted a part-time job in his father-in-law's bank to supplement his law income.[15]

Despite Ida's health concerns, McKinley remained politically active. He was elected to the U.S. House of Representatives in 1876.[16] He served there for seven terms, from 1877 to 1884, and then from 1885 to 1891. There was a break in his service in the mid-1880s while a special election committee in the district unseated him, upholding the claim of Johnathan Wallace, a lawyer, that he had defeated McKinley in the election of 1882. McKinley reclaimed his congressional seat in the 1884 election, then won again in 1886 and 1888.

While in the House of Representatives, McKinley voted in favor of civil service reform and full rights for the nation's freed blacks. Tariffs were a major issue of the time. McKinley supported tariffs because they made imported products more expensive for the consumer and protected American industries by encouraging the purchase of items made in the United States. McKinley remembered that cheap, imported iron had ruined domestic production of iron, along with his father's income. Over time, McKinley became the nation's leading expert on tariff laws.[17]

Because he felt so strongly about the issue, he proposed the McKinley Tariff Act of 1890, which was designed to put higher taxes on certain goods from other countries, thereby pushing the tariffs higher. The bill also gave the president the power to raise or lower tariffs as he thought necessary. It was signed into law by President Benjamin Harrison.

Some people were angry about the higher prices on foreign goods that resulted from the new tariffs. Many believed that the tariffs only helped the large American companies producing goods that competed with foreign products. As a result, McKinley was accused of being a "friend of big business."

McKinley became chairman of the House Ways and Means Committee in 1889, but did not hold the position for long. He lost a reelection bid in 1890, and it appeared as if his political career was over. But it was not. McKinley ran for governor of Ohio and won, serving from 1892 to 1896. As governor, he worked for laws to ensure greater safety in Ohio's factories and on railroads. He allowed workers to form trade unions and peacefully strike for better working conditions. He also worked to find ways to stop child labor. At that time, it was not uncommon for children to work long hours at difficult jobs. He proposed laws to protect railroad workers, provide relief to destitute miners, and abolish waste in the bureaucracy. In addition, he spoke out on the evils of alcohol abuse, supporting temperance groups with many speeches and appearances.[18]

In 1892, McKinley attended the Republican National Convention as a delegate-at-large and was made permanent chairman. At that convention, President Harrison won renomination, but McKinley received a few votes and some Republicans spoke openly of making McKinley their presidential candidate in 1896. In the meantime, McKinley ran for governor again in 1893. He often wore a red carnation in his buttonhole for good luck. This later became Ohio's official flower.

In June 1896, McKinley received the Republican nomination for president. During the campaign, he reached out to business leaders and had significant support from labor. His speeches were carefully prepared and delivered in a formal style. He was the first candidate to hand out campaign buttons and other items to promote himself as a candidate. Like other candidates of the time, McKinley stayed home and paid the train fare for people to come to Canton to hear him speak from his front porch. In the end, McKinley won the election and became president.[19]

As president, McKinley continued his support for tariffs.[20] He had a good relationship with Congress, which allowed him to push for an even higher protective tariff, called the Dingley Tariff Act. This new law provided for the highest tariffs yet to be placed on foreign goods. It also helped McKinley make new trade agreements with other countries.

Reporters noted that the McKinley White House had a more relaxed atmosphere than previous administrations.[21] The president frequently shrugged off the Secret Service to walk freely through the streets of Washington like an ordinary citizen. During his administration, the public could once again stroll through the White House gardens.

But the events surrounding the Spanish-American War changed that.[22] Spain had occupied Cuba since the days of Christopher Columbus, and the Spanish were often brutal to the Cubans. There were many reports of Spanish atrocities against Cubans. The Cubans revolted in 1895, seeking independence. McKinley worked for a diplomatic solution for over a year, believing that the Cuban conflict could be resolved without U.S. military involvement. He urged Spain to adopt a more humane policy toward Cuba and to stop the fighting.

Many Americans called for the United States to get involved in the war. Americans owned land and grew sugar on the island and were losing money because of the uprising. Others urged America to get involved so the United States could obtain new territory. When a letter from Enrique Dupuy de Lome, the Spanish minister to the United States, was published in the *New York Journal* in which de Lome characterized McKinley as weak, many Americans were angered.[23]

McKinley eventually sent the battleship *Maine* to Cuba. While it was there, an explosion ripped open the hull of the ship, sinking it in the Havana Harbor and killing 266 men. The cause of the explosion was never determined, but many believed that Spanish mines were the cause.[24] McKinley told Spain that the United States wanted peace in Cuba immediately, and although Spain realized that Cuba was lost to them at that point, they regarded defeat in war as more honorable than surrender without a fight. Thinking that Congress might declare war before he had time to negotiate with Spain, McKinley sent a letter to Congress asking it to declare war, and Congress did so on April 25, 1898.

The Spanish-American War was short, lasting just over three months. The United States fought the Spanish on two fronts: Cuba and the Philippines. On May 1, 1898, Commodore George Dewey, with a fleet of six ships, destroyed Spain's ten-ship Pacific fleet under Admiral Patricio Montojo in Manila Bay, Philippines, without losing a single man. The Spanish casualties totaled 381. In

August, U.S. troops captured Manila and took possession of the Philippines. In July, American troops captured Santiago, Chile. That same month, the United States destroyed Spain's Atlantic fleet, and American forces captured Puerto Rico. Spain sued for peace, and a ceasefire was declared on August 12. The Paris Peace Treaty was signed on December 10, 1898, and ratified on February 6, 1899. In the treaty, Spain relinquished its claim to Cuba and ceded Puerto Rico, Guam, and, for $20 million, the Philippine Islands to the United States. With the acquisition of the Philippines, the United States joined the ranks of the world's colonial powers.[25]

After the war, McKinley became interested in developing a relationship with China, which had the potential for rich trade opportunities. McKinley proposed an "open-door" policy, and the United States joined Britain, France, Germany, Russia, and Japan on an equal footing in the China trade. This allowed the United States the opportunity to buy Chinese goods as well as sell American goods in China. There were no tariffs that would help one nation over another.

McKinley ran for reelection to the presidency in 1900, with Theodore Roosevelt as his running mate.[26] They easily won the election. One thing McKinley had to deal with as president was the spoils system. He supported civil service reform and issued orders to extend the merit system. However, he also tried to exempt a number of positions from competitive testing.

McKinley also had to deal with civil rights violations in the South. At the time, violence against blacks in the southern states was commonplace. The number of men lynched by the white supremacist Ku Klux Klan (KKK) disturbed the president, and he spent a lot of time trying to reconcile differences that still remained years after the end of the Civil War.[27] Many black Americans were not much better off than they were before 1865. McKinley believed that black Americans should be entitled to vote because so many had fought for the country in the Civil War. McKinley maintained his political ties with the South, but because he sometimes held back in pressing for civil rights, some black leaders turned toward the Democrats to seek justice.

McKinley dealt with other issues as president, including troubles with Canada over the Alaskan boundary. Canadians complained about American infringement on hunting, fishing, and mineral rights. In 1898 McKinley signed a joint congressional resolution that annexed the Hawaiian Islands. McKinley also played a key role in establishing an international court of arbitration, a forerunner of the World Court.[28]

McKinley was a likable, honest leader. He set aside an hour each day to meet with the public. During these visits, he gave away scarlet carnations, his favorite flower. He often traveled around the country to talk with supporters and listen to public opinion. He maintained a good relationship with the press. The United States was enjoying a healthy economy, and most people were happy—except for one man, who felt that the nation would be better off without President McKinley.

LEON CZOLGOSZ

Leon Czolgosz was twenty-eight when he shot President McKinley. He was an anarchist and a devoted follower of Emma Goldman, the leading anarchist at the time, who had emigrated from Russia in 1885. Goldman opposed all forms of government and led crusades against them. She served time in prison for advocating anarchy, birth control, and women's rights. Goldman lectured throughout the East and Midwest, appealing to oppressed people to protest or use violence to achieve their goals. After shooting the president, Czolgosz openly admitted his actions and seemed proud of what he had done. He said he did his duty: "I don't believe one man should have so much service and other men should have none."[29]

Czolgosz was born in Detroit, Michigan, in 1873, the fourth child of Polish immigrants.[30] The family moved frequently, following the available work. For a while, his father worked for the city sewer system in Detroit, and his mother washed others' laundry. When Czolgosz was twelve, his mother died after giving birth to her eighth child. Four years later, when he was sixteen, his father remarried, and they settled near Pittsburgh, Pennsylvania, where Leon worked in a bottle factory. Later the family moved to Cleveland, Ohio, where Czolgosz got a job in a mill.

The family was poor, but Czolgosz and his five brothers worked and the family saved enough money to buy a small farm and a store near Cleveland. He continued to work in the mill and was considered a good worker. Coworkers said he was neither friendly nor quarrelsome. He was a loner who read radical papers and magazines and attended some socialist meetings. When the workers at the mill went on strike in 1893, it gave Czolgosz more free time to read and think about anarchism and capitalism, and he even joined a socialist discussion group. After the strike, he went to work as Fred C. Nieman, German for "nobody," using the alias because he feared retaliation from the company for striking and for his involvement with a socialist group.

In 1898, when he was twenty-five, Czolgosz had a nervous breakdown. He quit his job at the mill and went back to live with his family in Cleveland. He fought with his stepmother constantly and became more irritable and reclusive. He refused to eat dinner with the family, instead eating in his room. He demanded his family pay him for his portion of the farm, then left home.

Czolgosz did not have many friends and spent much of his free time reading newspapers and books. He was growing tired of the widening gap between America's rich and poor and between the races. He saw that power was centralized in the hands of a few, particularly those who owned railroads and steel mills. He attended a socialist meeting and was captivated by a speech by Goldman. Czolgosz agreed with Goldman's denunciation of American expansionist policy, which had cost the lives of Americans, Cubans, and Filipinos in the Spanish-American War. He started to hate the American system of government and believed that all government officials were against working people.

He believed that the president was "an enemy of the people" and that it was acceptable to kill him.

The philosophy of anarchism interested him. He knew that four world leaders had been assassinated in the name of anarchism, including King Humberto of Italy, who was killed in 1890. Czolgosz was fascinated with Humberto's assassination.[31]

Czolgosz tried to get more involved in the anarchist movement and requested to join different anarchist groups, but they denied his requests.[32] He wanted to meet Emma Goldman. But many anarchists thought he was crazy and that he must be a police plant. They warned each other against him, and decided that all should steer clear of him.

Czolgosz believed that if he shot McKinley, it would prove something to the anarchists and they would finally accept him. He would prove to them that he hated the politics of state-supported capitalism that the president and his party represented. He wanted to strike at the American leader to prove the nation vulnerable and to shatter its illusions of safety. He also knew what he was doing and that he would die if he succeeded.[33]

Czolgosz purchased a five-shot .32-caliber Iver Johnson revolver for $3.10 from the Sears and Roebuck catalog.[34] He chose that weapon because it was the same one used by Humberto's assassin. He moved to West Seneca, New York, then to Buffalo, where he rented a room for $2 a week under an assumed name over John Nowak's saloon in the very center of the city.[35]

It is not known exactly when Leon Czolgosz decided to shoot McKinley. More than likely, he stalked the president for several weeks prior to the assassination at the Buffalo Exposition.[36] There is some evidence that Czolgosz may have tried to kill McKinley in a park in Canton, Ohio. According to an employee at Meyers Lake Park, Czolgosz was there in the early summer of 1901. Whenever the decision was made, Czolgosz was able to get close enough to McKinley on a fateful day in September to carry out his plan to impress the anarchists who did not accept him.

THE ASSASSINATION

In mid-1901, McKinley decided to tour the country. The trip would serve many purposes, but a major issue at the time was the expansion of trade, which Congress opposed. Congress was dragging its feet on seven trade agreements, which made the president angry. He wanted to rally public support for the agreements, and at every stop during his nationwide tour he gave patriotic and uplifting speeches designed to convince the public of the need to expand trade opportunities. The trip was to end in June in Buffalo, New York.[37]

During the trip, Ida became seriously ill with an infected finger. It was so serious that word was sent to the White House suggesting funeral arrangements be made.[38] But she regained her strength, and the couple decided to interrupt the trip and go home to Canton for rest and relaxation. They postponed their appearance at the Buffalo Exposition until September.

The couple finally arrived in Buffalo on September 4. Ida did not want her husband to go because she had forebodings of bad things that were to happen. But McKinley was eager to visit the expo. It was the first World's Fair of the twentieth century, a celebration of technological progress. Thousands of visitors witnessed American technical advances in electrical machinery, the automobile, and the telephone. The ornate buildings were called *temples*.

Many came to the fair in September simply to get a glimpse of the president. Czolgosz was part of the crowd that met the president's train. He did not kill the president at that time because of some police who pushed him back and away from McKinley. Czolgosz knew he could not get close enough to kill McKinley and decided to wait.

McKinley had been invited to speak at the expo on September 5, 1901, on any subject he wished. He chose to mark the end of American isolationism. The United States had become a world power, and he wanted to promote world trade. This marked a switch in his policy. He even broke with his commitment to a high protective tariff, arguing for greater reliance on reciprocal trade agreements.[39]

He spoke about America's role in the world and the new trade agreements he was negotiating. He spoke about inventions that had changed American life and explained that, because of greater ease of communication, "isolation is no longer possible or desirable."[40] McKinley spoke of the unity of the modern world and the "almost appalling" prosperity of the United States. He reminded listeners that distance had been effaced by the telegraph and cable, by swift ships and fast trains. He finished by speaking about his policy goals for his second term. He praised America's progress and America's bright future.

About 50,000 people heard his speech, including regular citizens, high U.S. officials, and representatives of foreign countries, including the duke of Arcos, who represented Spain, the Turkish minister, and a contingent from China.[41] The speech was well received by both Americans and others. Czolgosz was there, in the front row, but apparently lost his nerve to shoot. After the speech, he followed the president to his carriage, but was shoved back by a guard. He then followed the president to the stadium, but guards would not allow him through the main entrance.

The next day, September 6, McKinley and his wife began the day by visiting Niagara Falls.[42] Once again, Czolgosz followed him but was not able to get close enough to shoot the president. He decided to return to the expo, where he would have another chance later that day at the Temple of Music.

McKinley was expected to hold a ten-minute public reception at the Temple of Music on the exhibition grounds. It was one of the most spacious buildings built for the expo. Ornate and easily accessible to the crowds, it was a good setting for a reception. McKinley was looking forward to meeting the public and shaking hands.

There were many people with McKinley that day, including the president of the exposition, John G. Milburn. George Cortelyou, the president's personal secretary, worried about McKinley's safety. Cortelyou urged McKinley to cancel the reception, but the president did not think there was anyone who would want to hurt him. Cortelyou actually removed the visit from the president's agenda twice, but it was put back at the president's insistence. Three Secret Service agents were assigned to protect McKinley. Cortelyou had extra Secret Service men and city police detectives watch for danger during the reception.[43]

Inside the building, a space in the center of the floor was cleared for the president to stand and greet people. It was a very hot day in Buffalo, and many people had stood in line in the blazing sun for a long time to see the president. Many visitors wiped perspiration from their faces with handkerchiefs. It would be impolite to meet the president while heavily perspiring.

McKinley entered the Temple of Music through a side door. At 4:00 P.M., he indicated that he was ready to meet the people who were waiting outside.[44] Czolgosz had been standing at the doors of the Temple and was one of the first to enter. The crowd moved forward to the area where McKinley was ready to shake hands. The president bowed to the right and to the left, and the crowd let out a great shout of welcome to the president. He greeted each person as they approached, and attendants kept the line moving. They were eager to meet him, especially the children. A twelve-year-old girl, Myrtle Ledger of Springbrook, New York, asked if she could have the red carnation in the president's lapel. The president did not typically remove the flower because he thought it was a good omen. But this time, he unpinned the good-luck flower and gave it to her.

An orchestra played a Bach sonata, and people continued to meet the president. He was an expert at moving people along quickly. He would grasp an outstretched hand, gently shake it, and then guide it past him as he turned to the next person in line. This technique allowed him to meet thousands of people at a function.

Many police officers and guards surrounded McKinley, but because of the heat they did not enforce the rule that any person who walked toward the president must have both hands clearly visible and empty. The Secret Service agents and guards became concerned when they spotted a suspicious-looking man in the line. He was a short, dark-complexioned young man dressed in a dark suit, and he appeared restless. The agents were relieved when the man shook McKinley's hand and moved on without incident. Unfortunately, they focused on this man and not the man next in line.

At 4:07 P.M., George Cortelyou signaled for the doors to close. At that time, a young, short, clean-shaven, well-dressed man in a black suit and a workman's cap stepped up to shake the president's hand.[45] He seemed to have an injured right hand because it was wrapped in a handkerchief, so McKinley reached out with his left hand to greet the man. Leon Czolgosz turned his eyes squarely on the president's face and extended his left hand, leaning forward to grasp the president's hand, drawing McKinley toward him. His right hand flashed from beneath the coat lapel and exposed the weapon that had been hidden by the handkerchief. Czolgosz thrust the weapon against the president's breast and pulled the trigger.[46] Two quick shots rang out. McKinley dropped the man's hand and rose to his toes in astonishment.

Before Czolgosz could fire a third shot, two men, a marine and John Parker, a six-foot-one-inch black man from Georgia, both grabbed the revolver. Others in the crowd jumped on Czolgosz and wrestled him to the floor. Some in the crowd started to hit him, yelling, "Lynch him!"[47] The band stopped playing. Secret Service agents and police swarmed on him, but Czolgosz twisted back around in an attempt to see the consequences of his action. He craned his neck to watch the president bleed. This action so enraged the Secret Service that an agent hit him in the jaw.

The first bullet had bounced off a button on McKinley's jacket. McKinley then turned his body slightly to the right and the second bullet entered his abdomen between the navel and the left nipple.[48] The bullet passed through the stomach, nipped the top of the left kidney, and lodged in the pancreas. He shivered and staggered backward into the arms of a Secret Service agent. He was obviously badly wounded.

McKinley asked a Secret Service agent if he had been shot. Cortelyou tore open the president's vest, and blood covered his shirt front. McKinley said, "Do not be

Figure 4.1.   The assassination of President William McKinley by anarchist Leon Czolgosz on September 6, 1901, at the Buffalo, New York, Pan-American Exposition. (Courtesy of the Library of Congress.)

alarmed, it is nothing."[49] He also said, "Don't let them hurt him,"[50] and, "May God forgive him."[51] While it was reported in the newspaper that he said, "Let no one harm him," he actually said, "Be easy with him, boys."[52] McKinley said that he must be a "misguided fellow."[53] He was also very concerned that they be careful when they told his wife about the shooting.

Meanwhile, guards threw Czolgosz to the floor. They seized his pistol. Some continued to punch him. They led him to a chair in the middle of the room. His face was bleeding. The police were determined there should be no lynching, so he was removed from the room and taken to a small area off the west stage of the temple to protect him from the crowd. They then took him by carriage to the Buffalo police station. On the trip, Czolgosz cowered in the corner of the carriage, occasionally lifting his head to look out the window. When he heard the noise from the mob as they struggled to get close to him, shivers ran through his body and his eyes rolled wide with terror.

While Czolgosz was at the police department, thousands of people gathered in the streets, many still calling for his lynching. He was saved from the angry mob by the detectives, who placed Czolgosz in the dungeon at police headquarters. He told police that his name was Fred Nieman, that he was from Detroit, and that he had been in Buffalo about a week, staying at John Nowak's saloon. The owner of the hotel, Nowak, said he knew little about the man, saying he had been alone at all times and had no visitors.

Czolgosz told police, "I am an anarchist, and I did my duty."[54] He said he had shot the president for the working-class people of America. Later, when he told police his real name, he also said he was a follower of Emma Goldman. He signed a confession stating that he had no partners, that he had decided three days before to commit the crime, and that he had bought the revolver in Buffalo. He did not appear to be uneasy or remorseful for his actions, nor did he show any signs of insanity.[55]

McKinley was carried to the exposition's electric-powered ambulance, which arrived four minutes after the shots were fired. As the crowds stared, McKinley was taken to the fairground's small emergency hospital. A preliminary exam was underway within five minutes of the shots being fired. McKinley agreed to an immediate operation. He was given an injection of morphine to ease his pain. Before ether was given, he recited the Lord's Prayer. When the doctors placed him on the operating table, one bullet dropped out of his clothes. It was the bullet that had been deflected by a button and had only grazed his ribs.

The operation was performed by Dr. Matthew D. Mann, a gynecologist who had never operated on a male patient or treated a gunshot wound.[56] Nonetheless, the doctor spent an hour and twenty minutes in surgery. McKinley was heavy, and at first the doctor had trouble getting in. The doctor closed some holes in the president's stomach. The bullet had gone deeper into his back, but the doctor was unable to find it because the light was poor. Since they were using ether, they could not use candles as a source of additional light. Even though electric lights were located throughout the exposition, there were none in the medical rooms.

For a short time, a metal pan was used to reflect sunlight. Needless to say, the operating conditions were not up to par.

When the president's pulse rate began to increase, they sutured the stomach wounds. Dr. Roswell Park, a leading expert in abdominal surgery at the time, arrived just as the operation was ending. He was hesitant to interfere.[57]

Even though there was a new X-ray machine at the exposition, it was never used to locate the bullet.[58] Thomas Edison was one of the few people who knew how to use the machine, and he was not there.

Mrs. McKinley was not told of the shooting for over two hours. When the incident occurred, she was at the Buffalo home of the exposition director, John Milburn, resting from fatigue after their morning excursion to Niagara Falls. It had been ordered that she should not be told until the last possible moment. She woke from a nap, and got worried when it got dark and the president had not arrived at the house. At 7:30 P.M., the family physician arrived and told her what had happened.[59]

It was announced to the public that the president was in no immediate danger and that a full recovery was expected. They took McKinley to Milburn's home to recuperate. He requested a cigar, but was denied. His condition fluctuated over the next several days. He sometimes asked to see the morning paper, but this request was also not granted.[60]

The upstairs of the Milburn home was kept absolutely quiet. The downstairs was transformed into an office, with many people answering telegrams and letters.

McKinley rallied briefly and on September 7, a medical bulletin told the public that no serious symptoms had developed and it appeared as if the president would fully recover. He was conscious and talking cheerfully with visitors. The public was told that if no further complications arose, McKinley's recovery would be rapid. At first the bulletins reported that the president was "more and more satisfactory"; then, that he had had "the most comfortable night since the attempt on his life"; then, that he "continues to gain."[61] For almost six days, the public was told that the president was getting better; the doctors did not detect any significant infection. On September 11, physicians publicly pronounced him out of danger. Vice President Roosevelt left Buffalo for a trip through the Adirondacks, and the members of the cabinet returned to Washington.

Four days after the shooting, minor surgery was performed to remove a small fragment of clothing the bullet had carried into the abdomen. The wound was treated with antiseptic, and the dressing was changed three times a day. McKinley's food consisted mostly of beef broth. Solid food was withheld since he could not digest it easily.[62]

No one could tell that McKinley was getting worse. By September 13, his health declined rapidly. A gangrenous infection set in and he became feverish. He was unable to eat and his heart began to fail. The doctors admitted that the president was in critical condition.[63] It soon became obvious he was going to die. Physicians worked all night to keep the president alive. Ida came to his bedside and said she wanted to die with him.

On September 14, at 2:15 A.M., McKinley died. It was eight days after the shooting. His last words were the words of his favorite hymn: "Nearer, my God to thee, nearer to thee."[64]

THE AFTERMATH

After McKinley's death, the exposition closed briefly as a sign of respect for the president. Dr. Mann, along with thirteen other physicians, performed an autopsy. The adrenal gland and pancreas were damaged, and they also found degeneration of the heart muscle. The bullet was never found. The proximate cause of death was gangrene, which had developed around the holes created by the bullet. A plaster death mask was made of the dead president.

Private ceremonies were held in the Milburn home. The body was then moved to Buffalo's city hall, where a funeral service was held. About 90,000 people came to pay their respects.[65] A funeral train took the body to Washington, D.C. The cedar casket that held the president's body was attached to the rear of the train, elevated so that it could be easily seen by the public. It was guarded by men from the Army and the Navy. The locomotive was heavily draped in black, and the windows of the train were shaded. Along the way, church bells tolled, flags were hung at half-mast, and people threw flowers on the train track.[66]

In Washington, McKinley's body lay in state first in the White House and then in the Capitol Rotunda. There, thousands more people waited for hours in the rain to pass by the casket. The train then took the body back to Canton, Ohio. Ida rode the funeral train back to Canton and then withdrew as the nation mourned.[67]

McKinley's body arrived in Canton on September 18 at 11:00 A.M. It lay in state at the Stark county courthouse. Once again, for more than seven hours, a constant stream of people passed the bier. At Mrs. McKinley's request, the casket was moved to their house on North Market Street so family members and relatives could pay their final respects. The following day, a memorial service was held in the First Methodist Church. Statesmen, diplomats, and representatives of other nations gathered with the family. Ministers of five religious denominations delivered the simple service. McKinley was laid to rest in a temporary receiving vault at Westlawn Cemetery, then later moved to the McKinley National Memorial Tomb in Canton.[68]

For many days after McKinley's death, the nation mourned. Leaders from nearly every nation sent condolences. As McKinley's body was laid to rest, economic activity in America came to a halt. Telegraph lines remained silent, and streetcars and trains stopped running. Homes and businesses were draped in black.[69]

There were memorial services for McKinley in London, Germany, Canada, Paris, St. Petersburg, Brussels, Vienna, Colombia, Copenhagen, Bombay, Constantinople, Gibraltar, Rome, Peking, the Philippines, and Venezuela. In the United States, there were services in Cleveland, St. Paul, and Chicago.[70]

When McKinley died, messengers had to go looking for Theodore Roosevelt, who had gone to Mount Marcy, the highest peak in the Adirondack Mountains in New York, after being reassured that McKinley would recover. They found him late in the afternoon. At that point, the nation had been without a president for twelve hours. He returned from his camping trip to become the next president, taking the oath of office in the library of the Milburn House by John R. Hazel, U.S. District Judge for the District of New York.[71] He promised to continue the policies of President McKinley, but he was very different. McKinley was reserved, and from a lower-class upbringing; Teddy Roosevelt was outgoing and from an upper-class family. Roosevelt was young and was described as creative, smart, and a wild cowboy.

Czolgosz admitted to killing McKinley. He said, "I killed President McKinley because I done my duty. I don't believe one man should have so much service and another man should have none."[72] Although Czolgosz said he was guilty, a technical plea of not guilty was entered.[73] In New York, defendants accused of capital crimes were required to enter a plea of not guilty.

On September 16, a grand jury found an indictment against Czolgosz, charging him with murder in the first degree. When he was asked if he wanted an attorney, he did not reply. Czolgosz declined legal counsel because, as an anarchist, he did not acknowledge the right of a court to try him.[74] Since Czolgosz declined legal counsel, the court appointed two prominent former New York State Supreme Court justices to represent him. But Czolgosz refused to answer a single question for them.

He was given a speedy, fair, and dignified trial. It began September 23, 1901, in city hall, and was presided over by Judge Truman C. White.[75] Throughout the process, Czolgosz maintained a solid demeanor, declaring that he had no accomplices. His mental condition was questioned, and many experts were called to examine him. However, he did not seem to be interested in establishing his insanity. On September 9, he was declared to be sane. If he had been found insane, it would be required to let him go free and he could not be executed. But if he was found guilty of killing the president, then he would have to be executed.

The defense argued that Czolgosz could not possibly bear responsibility for his actions because the powerlessness and hopelessness of industrial life had driven him mad. He had been paid poorly and put out of work by the tycoons with whom McKinley had close ties. This had caused him to go insane and have delusions.[76] He shot the president in broad daylight in front of thousands of people. His lawyer questioned, "How can a man with a sane mind perform such an act?"[77]

The trial was quick. The defense did not present evidence on Czolgosz's behalf. After nine hours, the case went to the jury, and in only thirty-four minutes, the jury found him guilty.[78] Czolgosz was executed on October 29, 1901, at New York's Auburn State Prison in the electric chair, after telling onlookers, "I am not sorry for my crime."[79] Witnesses said Czolgosz was calm and kept his head erect. He said he killed the president because he "was the enemy of the good people—the good working people."[80] When Czolgosz's body was placed in its coffin, officials poured sulfuric acid on it so that his remains would decompose as quickly as possible. The coffin was then buried in the prison graveyard.

McKinley's murder terrified the leaders of the country; they began to treat immigrant working classes differently. His murder pressed Americans to give voice and clarity to their opinions of a working class that was largely immigrant in its composition.[81]

The working people were not helped by Czolgosz's act. Hundreds of communists and anarchists were arrested after McKinley's death. Many were put out of work or fired. Within days of the shooting, Emma Goldman was arrested in Chicago after Czolgosz admitted he was inspired by her to kill the president. Those affiliated with the Communist Party had to prove they were innocent. New laws banned the immigration of known anarchists. The trial also raised the question of what constitutes sanity in a murder. There were calls for a more precise definition of "madness" in those accused of crimes. Finally, after this assassination of a third U.S. president, the U.S. Secret Service began to provide full-time protection for the president.[82]

CONCLUSION

William McKinley, who had aided the growth of big business and industry, and helped to put America onto the world political scene, became the third president to die by an assassin's bullet.[83] The ascent of Vice President Theodore Roosevelt would dramatically change the dynamics of politics and would help America launch into the Progressive era.

Ida McKinley's health steadily declined after her husband's death, although her epileptic seizures appeared to stop. She withdrew to the privacy of her home. Relatives looked after her, and every day she dressed in black. She made a concerted effort to visit her husband's grave on a regular basis. She died on May 26, 1907. Ida and President McKinley and their two daughters were permanently laid to rest four months later in the McKinley National Memorial Tomb in Canton.[84]

Leon Czolgosz, a twenty-eight-year-old self-professed anarchist, shot and killed President McKinley at the Buffalo Exposition in New York. He claimed that McKinley had too much power and was unfair to the working man. Czolgosz was arrested, tried, and convicted of assassinating the president and was executed later that same year.

Although President McKinley had Secret Service protection while at the Buffalo Exposition, the protection duties were still not a permanent assignment for the special agents. The next president, Theodore Roosevelt, would have Secret Service protection on a full-time basis.

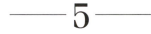

5

Theodore Roosevelt

INTRODUCTION

The presidential campaign of 1912 was beginning to wear on Progressive Party candidate and former Republican President Theodore Roosevelt. He was losing his voice. Yet, when asked to speak in Milwaukee, Wisconsin, to a crowd of 9,000, he could not resist the challenge. He checked into the Hotel Gilpatrick, and a little before 8:00 P.M. prepared to travel to the convention center via his awaiting car. It was October 14, 1912.

Roosevelt exited the hotel, then stepped across the sidewalk and into the waiting car. He immediately sat down, but a crowd had gathered and he decided to engage them. He stood back up and began waving at the crowd. At the same time, a short and somewhat stocky man appeared between two people not more than thirty feet from the former president. Roosevelt was about to experience an attempt on his life as he sought to reclaim the office he had first held because an assassin in 1901 had been successful.

THEODORE ROOSEVELT

Theodore Roosevelt, the twenty-sixth president of the United States, was born on October 27, 1858, in New York City to Theodore Roosevelt Sr. and Mittie Bulloch.[1] Theodore Sr.—or Thee, as he was called—was a New York City merchant and philanthropist; his wife was a southern belle from a slave-owning family in Georgia who retained Confederate sympathies.

Theodore Roosevelt Jr. (called Teedie) was a sickly and asthmatic child who was often sick for months on end but would then have fitful bouts of hyperactivity. He was also a very curious boy, always interested in the outdoors, zoology, natural history, and, after discovering he needed glasses, ornithology. As he seemed to be sick more often than healthy, his father started him on boxing lessons and two hours of calisthenics daily, telling Theodore that he would have to overcome his illnesses.

The family took two trips around the world, the first to Europe from 1869 to 1870, and the second to the Middle East from 1872 to 1873. He managed to stay healthy more often than not during these trips, and he continued to perform his daily calisthenics. In between trips, while the family was at home in New York City, Teedie was home schooled.

Theodore entered Harvard College in 1876. He did well there, but was taken aback by his father's death in 1878. He redoubled his efforts and excelled at his studies. He also took up rowing and boxing and joined the Delta Kappa Epsilon fraternity. After graduating Phi Beta Kappa from Harvard in 1880, he went on to Columbia Law School.

Theodore's career began to take off in multiple directions. While at Harvard, he wrote a history of the Naval War of 1812. The book was well received and became the standard study of the naval aspects of this war for decades. He met Alice Hathaway Lee, courted her, and eventually won her hand in marriage. In 1881, he dropped out of Columbia to run for New York assemblyman. He won the election and became one of the most active, if not annoying, assemblymen to that point in time. To top it all off, he found out he was going to be a father. Then tragedy struck.

His wife had difficulties with the pregnancy and was tended to by Theodore's mother. On February 12, 1884, daughter Alice Lee was born. Her mother, Alice, was not doing well after the birth, so rather than a time of celebration, it was a time of concern. In addition, Theodore's mother had become sick, and on February 14, 1884, at 3:00 A.M., she succumbed to typhoid fever. Eleven hours later, Theodore's wife succumbed to kidney failure, the result of Bright's disease. Theodore was struck hard. His diary entry for that day was simply a large X. Distraught, he began making plans. He wrote a short tribute to his wife, then never spoke of her again, not even in his old age, nor among friends, nor in his autobiography. She was expunged from his life.

He turned over the care of his daughter to his sister Anna (Bamie), and fled west. He spent the next two years in the Badlands of North Dakota, improving on his riding and hunting skills. He bought some land, had a ranch house built for him, and developed a large herd of cattle. In the severe winter of 1886–1887, although Theodore would survive, his cattle did not, and his entire investment was wiped out. He moved back east.

Theodore began to rebuild his life. He ran for mayor of New York City and lost. He built his home, Sagamore Hill, in Oyster Bay, New York. And in 1886, he married his childhood sweetheart, Edith Kermit Carow. He began writing some additional books, two biographies and a four-volume frontier history called *The Winning of the West*. In 1888, he returned to politics, campaigning for Benjamin Harrison for president who, upon winning the White House, appointed Theodore to the U.S. Civil Service Commission in Washington, D.C. There he fought against corruption and attempted to honestly enforce the civil service laws. He was reappointed to the post in 1892 by President Grover Cleveland.

In 1895, Roosevelt accepted a posting to the wholly corrupt New York City Police Department's board of commissioners. Roosevelt was immediately elected president of the board, thus becoming the police commissioner. He remained in the post for several years, initiating a number of reforms, until he was appointed assistant secretary of the U.S. Navy by President William McKinley. He was instrumental in preparing the country for the oncoming Spanish-American War. When war was declared, he resigned as the assistant secretary in order to lead troops into battle. He achieved national renown for the taking of San Juan Hill in Cuba.

Colonel Theodore Roosevelt, as he would liked to be called for the rest of his career (even after serving as president), had become so popular that New York elected him governor, and when McKinley ran for a second term he brought the colonel on board as his running mate. McKinley won the second term, but on September 6, 1901, was assassinated by Leon Czolgosz (see chapter 4). Theodore Roosevelt thus became the president of the United States.

President Roosevelt served the remainder of McKinley's term and was elected to a new term in 1904. As president, he implemented a number of progressive reforms, dealt with the anthracite coal strike, would be responsible for the building of the Panama Canal, won the Nobel Peace Prize for his peace talks between Russia and Japan, and built the U.S. Navy into the most powerful in the world. He decided not to run for reelection in 1908, and instead handed the Republican Party's reins to his chosen successor, William H. Taft. Taft won the election, and Theodore went on safari.

In 1912, after having watched from the sidelines for four years as Taft squandered, at least in Roosevelt's mind, his nearly eight years of progress, Roosevelt decided to do something about it. He decided he would accept the nomination to be the Republican presidential candidate. This threw the party into a quandary over whether to support the sitting president, Taft, or the former president of the United States, Theodore Roosevelt. Complicating the field was a senator from Wisconsin, Robert M. "Fighting Bob" La Follette Sr., who remained popular despite having made a very damaging speech in February of that year.[2]

The delegates met in Chicago and began their deliberations. In and among the committee meetings and the backdoor politics, it became clear that if the party nominated Taft, he was sure to lose to the Democratic Party's candidate. La Follette had little chance, and most of the delegates who had supported him switched to Roosevelt. If nominated, Roosevelt stood the best chance of winning the general election. However, the party bosses were neither willing to oppose the sitting president nor willing to endure another controversial Roosevelt term in office. They decided they would rather lose the presidency for four years than nominate Roosevelt. The delegates voted 561 for Taft, 107 for Roosevelt, and 41 for La Follette. The Republican Party had set a course for defeat.[3]

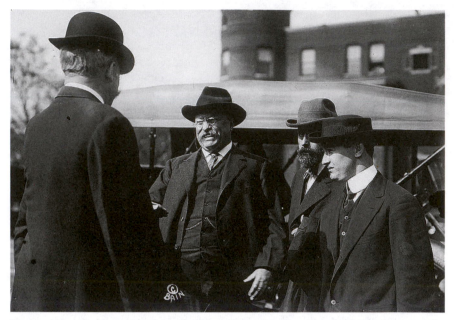

Figure 5.1.   Former President Theodore Roosevelt greeting local dignitaries as he ran for president under the Bull Moose Progressive party on October 14, 1912. (Courtesy of the Library of Congress, George Grantham Bain Collection.)

Feeling that the nomination had been stolen from him, Roosevelt accepted the nomination of the National Progressive Party at its convention in August 1912, declaring, "I think the time has come when not only men who believe in Progressive principles, but all men who believe in those elementary maxims of public and private morality which must underlie every form of successful free government[,] should join in our movement."[4] He immediately launched an aggressive campaign.

The campaign took him from city to city, and he often gave more than a dozen speeches a day. By early October he was beginning to become punchy and lose his voice.[5] In one speech, in Marquette, Michigan, a heckler mocked Roosevelt when he praised the governor, Hiram Johnson. Roosevelt turned on the man and gave him such a tongue-lashing he was said to have "tore the hide off the man's words."[6] Despite his ability to deliver such a fiery retort, by mid-October his voice was nearly gone and he was forced to take a day of rest on Sunday, October 13, in Chicago. He insisted, however, that the next day he would make the speech in Milwaukee and that "even if he could not speak, at least the audience would witness his good intentions."[7]

JOHN F. SCHRANK

John Flammang Schrank was born in Bavaria, Germany, in 1876 and moved to the United States at the age of twelve.[8] He was never very close to his parents, and had moved to New York City to live with his uncle and aunt. His new parents were respectable people who owned a profitable neighborhood saloon located at 370 East Tenth Street in the immigrant section of town. Their patrons were primarily Germans, and it was a popular meeting place on Sunday afternoons, a little German *biergarten* in America. They were kind and caring to John, and he was a well-mannered boy; everyone found him to be delightful. He liked to read, especially poetry, and even took up some writing himself.

It was only years later that Schrank revealed a dream he had around this time. On the night of September 15, 1901, the day after President McKinley was killed, he had a dream.[9] McKinley appeared to him, his assassin-inflicted wounds still visible, then spoke to John. Upon waking, John wrote, "In a dream I saw President McKinley sit up in his coffin, pointing at a man in a monk's attire in whom I recognized as Theo. Roosevelt. The dead President said, 'This is my murderer, avenge my death.'"[10] This particular revelation did not come to light until Schrank was interviewed by a panel of alienists following his arrest. During this time, Schrank is also known to have fantasized about a romance with a neighborhood girl, Elsie Ziegler. He claimed that at one point he had asked her to marry him and she agreed. Yet all of this was revealed only after 1904, the year Elsie died in a ferryboat fire in New York Harbor. Those who knew Elsie denied they had ever talked to one another, much less were engaged to be married.

John had been put to work almost right away in order to help the saloon (and family) run, something very common in the late 1800s. He did odd chores and was also taught how to tend bar and, in a sense, run the establishment. In 1910, when John was twenty-two, his aunt died. He became more responsible for running the saloon and proved to be an asset to his uncle. One year later, however, his uncle died, and at twenty-three John was left with the responsibility of running both the saloon and an apartment complex nearby.[11]

John decided it would be better for him to sell both the holdings he inherited, and the result was $25,000, the equivalent of a little over $500,000 in 2009 dollars. John Schrank never worked another day in his life. He simply lived off the proceeds from the sale. With ample free time he decided to enroll in various nightschool classes, primarily to improve his English, but also to learn more about history, government, and the Bible. He also continued to write poetry and kept a journal of thoughts that came to him, many related to politics.[12]

These interests continued to grow, and early in 1912, before the presidential campaign, Schrank composed his own treatise on what he felt were the four unwritten laws of government. He called them his "Four Pillars of Our Republic."[13] He felt that it was critical that America enforce the Monroe Doctrine, deny the American presidency to Roman Catholics, avoid wars of conquest, and limit presidents to two terms. Although Schrank's hatred for Theodore Roosevelt was primarily related to the last point, as Roosevelt was seeking a third term, Schrank also felt the president was instrumental in a "war of conquest" against Cuba when he had served as the colonel of the Rough Riders during the Spanish-American War. He had further reason to hate Roosevelt: while he was a saloonkeeper in New York, he had to endure

Roosevelt's enforcement of the blue laws, which required that all bars be closed on Sunday when Roosevelt was the police commissioner from 1895 to 1897.[14]

Despite the fact that Schrank was attempting to enhance his education and things seemed hopeful for him, his mental state began to change. He began visiting his aunt's and uncle's graves, and would often stay for hours on end, if not all day. He even moved into an apartment near the Brooklyn cemetery so that he could be closer to their graves. It was also around this time that he had a second vision. According to Schrank, he was visited on September 14, 1912, again by President McKinley. He claimed that he was writing a poem, late at night, when "someone tapped me on the shoulder and said: 'Let not a murderer take the presidential chair. Avenge my death.'"[15] This became the final trigger to his hatred for Theodore Roosevelt.

Schrank went out the next day and purchased a .38-caliber Colt police special and a box of cartridges for $14.55, then booked passage on a steamship from New York City to Charleston, South Carolina.[16] According to the newspapers, Roosevelt was to speak there. At this point, Schrank began stalking Roosevelt on the campaign trail, looking for the opportunity to answer McKinley's call. He followed Roosevelt to Augusta, Atlanta, Birmingham, Chattanooga, Nashville, Louisville, Evansville, Chicago, and finally Milwaukee.[17] He later claimed that he had the right opportunity in Chicago, but he did not want to spoil the "decent, respectable reputation" of the city.[18] It was in Milwaukee that he believed he had the greatest opportunity, obviously unconcerned for the city's reputation.

On the evening of October 14, 1912, John Schrank visited Herman Rollfink's saloon across the street from the Hotel Gilpatrick. He drank his beer and chatted amiably with the bartender, Paul Thume. Thume would later write that Schrank "asked the bar musician to play some song, something with 'stripes' in it, and then he bought each one a drink."[19] The song he had requested was "Stars and Stripes Forever." Schrank danced merrily around the bar as the music played, bought everyone one more round of drinks, and then left the bar. A few minutes later, he shot Theodore Roosevelt.

THE ASSASSINATION ATTEMPT

The concept of death was certainly nothing new to Roosevelt. While he was vice president, the story goes, he was wintering in Colorado when a cougar attacked some of his hounds, whereupon he leapt off his horse, kicked the hounds aside, and fought the cougar to death with a knife.[20] In addition, after being notified he was the president upon McKinley's death, the train that carried him to Washington, D.C., wrecked and he was nearly killed. In fact, his entire life was full of near-death incidents, but Roosevelt never allowed himself to fear death. He once wrote, "Only those are fit to live who do not fear to die."[21] Roosevelt was no stranger to death and did not fear dying, so, as biographer Edmund Morris explains, "Personally, Roosevelt was not worried about assassination."[22]

Yet if any president recognized the threat of assassination and should have been worried, it would be Theodore Roosevelt, for he had become president as the result of an assassin.[23] He also, no doubt, was quite cognizant of the history of Lincoln's assassination, and upon hearing of Garfield's assassination he wrote in his diary that it was a "Frightful calamity for America."[24] In addition, during his first term in office, on September 1, 1903, he was working late in his library when he heard a scuffle outside. Roosevelt, always aggressive, stepped out onto the piazza and heard two guards shout, "There he is" as they pursued and then wrestled with a young man in a buggy. The youth brandished a firearm, which was knocked to the ground. He was handcuffed and turned over to the local police, and when asked what he had been doing, he answered, "I came to kill the President."[25] Later, during Roosevelt's second term in office, a man walked into Roosevelt's office with a "needle-sharp blade up his sleeve," before being taken into custody by the Secret Service.[26] Despite all of these events, "Theodore Roosevelt remained officially unprotected."[27]

As president he had from time to time received protection from the Treasury Department, but he was not too confident in these agents. He once explained to Senator Henry Cabot Lodge, "Of course they [Secret Service] would not be the least use in preventing any assault upon my life. I do not believe there is any danger of such an assault."[28] As the Progressive Party candidate in 1912, despite being a former president, neither his ex-president status nor his status as a nominee provided him any protection by law. He was entirely vulnerable on the campaign trail.[29]

The presidential campaign was at its height on October 14, 1912, and Roosevelt was making about a dozen speeches a day. He had accepted the offer to speak in Milwaukee, Wisconsin, as a significant crowd of more than 9,000 was expected.[30] He had originally intended to dine privately in his railroad car, but a large civic committee begged him to have dinner with them at the Hotel Gilpatrick.[31] He agreed, checked into the hotel, took a short nap, engaged the committee in dinner, then went back up to his room to prepare for the speech.[32] Just shy of 8:00 P.M., he prepared to leave the Hotel Gilpatrick and enter the car that was awaiting him just outside the front door.[33] A large crowd had gathered outside around his car, and he exited the hotel, crossed the threshold and sidewalk, and entered the open-top car. He settled into his seat, but because of the cheers he decided to be polite and oblige the crowd. He stood up, removed his hat, and began waving. It was exactly 8:10 P.M.[34]

Approximately thirty feet away, John Schrank moved behind two people as cover, raised his Colt .38-caliber police revolver between them, and fired one shot at the former president.[35] The bullet struck Roosevelt in the chest, tearing through his overcoat, penetrating his steel spectacle case, passing through the folded manuscript that was to be his speech that night, and then passing through his shirt before entering his chest. He reeled backward, but quickly regained his balance. He coughed and put his hand to his mouth, pulled it

Figure 5.2. Photograph of former President Theodore Roosevelt's would-be assassin, John Schrank, taken in Milwaukee, Wisconsin, shortly before the assassination attempt on October 14, 1912. (Courtesy of the Library of Congress, George Grantham Bain Collection.)

away, and looked for any trace of blood. Seeing no red, he assumed the gunshot would not be fatal. He looked at his aide, Harry Cochems, and said quietly, "He pinked me, Harry."[36]

One of Roosevelt's staff, Elbert E. Martin, "a former New Hampshire farm boy, coal stoker, and football player,"[37] jumped from the car, charged the assailant, and forced him to the ground. Assisting were Captain A. O. Girard, a former Rough Rider and presidential bodyguard, and several police officers.[38] Meanwhile, as the crowd recognized what had happened, and seeing that the would-be assassin had been subdued, they began yelling, "Kill him! Kill him!"[39] Roosevelt, still standing in the car, began yelling back at the crowd, "Stand back! Don't hurt him! Bring him here! I want to look at him."[40]

Martin, having secured both the gun and assailant, brought the man to his feet and dragged him over to the car. Martin handed Roosevelt the gun and then forcibly turned the man's head toward Roosevelt and said, "Here he is. Look at him, Colonel." Roosevelt looked at the man and asked, "Why did you do it? What was your reason?"[41] Roosevelt did not wait for an answer, probably knowing he would not receive one, and told Martin to "take charge of him, and see that there is not violence done to him."[42] Martin then pulled the would-be assassin into the hotel kitchen, where he was turned over to the local police.[43]

Roosevelt did not believe he was wounded. One of the secretaries and Roosevelt's personal physician, Dr. S. L. Terrell, who had pushed his way through the crowd to come to the president's aid, encouraged Roosevelt to go to the hospital. Roosevelt, determined as ever and with a strong sense of duty, nearly shouted back, "You get me to that speech; it may be the last I shall deliver, but I am going to deliver this one."[44] Roosevelt, most likely animated by adrenaline, did not feel injured and saw this speech as a great political opportunity despite having just been shot at.

En route to the convention hall, one of his companions exclaimed, "Look, Colonel, there's a hole in your overcoat!"[45] Roosevelt, looking down, discovered a small hole that had entered his coat. He reached inside and stuck his finger through the hole. When he pulled his hand back out, it was covered in blood. For a fleeting second he was somewhat taken aback, but he very quickly regained his composure and commented, "It looks as though I had been hit, but I don't think it is anything serious."[46]

He arrived at the hall and was quickly ushered inside through the crowds. A call went out for any physicians in the audience, and three arrived behind the curtains to examine the president.[47] The wound itself was still bleeding slightly, and he had a stain on his shirt about the size of a man's fist.[48] All three doctors concluded that the bullet had entered his right breast, but had not exited. They unanimously declared that Roosevelt should proceed immediately to the hospital. He refused. Knowing perhaps the political mileage he might generate by giving a speech immediately after having been shot, he stated rather melodramatically, "I will make this speech, or die; one or the other."[49] He then walked onto the stage.

The crowd gave out a roar as he walked to the lectern. He steadied himself by holding tightly onto the platform as the presiding officer quieted the crowd. Once calm was restored, Harry Cochems, looking very somber, stated matter-of-factly, "I have something to tell you and I hope you will receive the news with calmness. Colonel Roosevelt has been shot. He is wounded."[50] A collective gasp was heard from the audience. A heckler in the crowd "boisterously disputed the claim," shouting, "Fake!"[51] In answer to the heckler, Roosevelt stated, "No, it's no fake." He unbuttoned his vest and exposed his bloodied shirt.[52] Another collective gasp was heard from the audience, followed by a buzz of conversation. Roosevelt raised his hand, and the crowd became solemn and quiet. "Friends, I am going to ask you to be very quiet and please to excuse me from making you a very long speech," Roosevelt began. "I'll do the best I can, but you see there is a bullet in my body, but it is nothing. I'm not hurt badly."[53]

The crowd remained quiet as Roosevelt reached into his coat pocket for the manuscript he had stashed there earlier. The manuscript was fifty pages long and folded in half lengthwise. As he pulled it out, he noticed there was a hole in the middle of the manuscript, where the bullet had passed through. He would also discover that the bullet had passed through the metal case in which he carried his spectacles.[54] Several days later, reflecting back on this particular moment, he would continue his brave front by remarking, "It was nothing, nothing. I felt a little pain, but it was not serious."[55] He did, however, concede that the sight of the hole in the manuscript had startled him. "When I stretched out my arms or reached for my manuscript it made me gasp a bit, but that was all. It was quite amusing when I reached for my manuscript to see that it had a hole in it from the bullet and there was a hole in my spectacle case too."[56] Roosevelt then lifted up the manuscript for all to see and exhorted, "It takes more than that to kill a Bull Moose!"[57] He began to deliver the speech.

Several times throughout the speech Roosevelt showed signs of weakness, but he fought against it. Or rather, he fought against his aides trying to take him from the lectern. He would steady himself by gripping the lectern more firmly and stating, "Let me alone. I'm all right."[58] Occasionally, throughout the speech, he would pause, clearly ad libbing, and argue that it was the utterances of the newspapers that caused his assassination. Yet another time he claimed it was a weak-minded man who tried to assassinate him. When the doctors came on stage to urge

Figure 5.3.   Photograph of Elbert Martin, former President Theodore Roosevelt's stenographer, with the 50-page, bullet-pierced manuscript of the speech Roosevelt delivered after being struck by John Schrank's bullet on October 14, 1912. (Courtesy of the Library of Congress, George Grantham Bain Collection.)

Roosevelt to leave and go to the hospital, he refused, then turned to the crowd and added, "If these doctors don't behave themselves, I won't let them look at me at all."[59] Although his speech would normally have lasted two hours, he stopped early, at one hour and ten minutes, clearly having made his point.[60] He then left the stage, and many in the crowed pressed forward to shake the former president's hand, which caused him additional pain.

Despite the crush of well-wishers, Roosevelt was able to quickly leave the hall.[61] He was driven to the Johnston Emergency Hospital in Milwaukee, where he was rushed into the operating room and examined by the attending physicians. The examination revealed a deeper wound than anyone had anticipated, and an X-ray was ordered to determine just how far the bullet had penetrated. While they were waiting, Roosevelt began talking politics and joking around with one of the physicians. Allegedly he said, "I do not want to fall into the hands of too many doctors and have the same experience that McKinley and Garfield had."[62]

The X-ray quickly revealed the location of the bullet. It had entered his chest just to the right and below his right nipple, and was deflected by his rib and imbedded in his chest muscles. The result was a fractured fifth rib, with the bullet lodged close beside, less than one inch from his heart. Because it had passed through the coat, a metal spectacle case, 100 pages of paper, and his shirt and undershirt, the speed of the bullet had been slowed enough that it stopped at the rib and muscles, failing to pass through the ribcage and into his lung.[63]

The physicians all agreed that Roosevelt should be transferred to a larger hospital, one that could better care for his needs. At 12:45 A.M., Roosevelt left the Milwaukee hospital and boarded the train for Chicago. An ambulance was waiting for him when he arrived. Seeing the ambulance and ever mindful of the press, Roosevelt stated, "I'll not go to a hospital lying in that thing. I'll walk to it and I'll walk from it to the hospital. I'm not a weakling to be crippled by a flesh wound."[64] He did just that, and then checked into Chicago's Mercy Hospital. It was there that the doctors made the decision not to try to remove the bullet, due to its location, and instead gave him a shot of tetanus antitoxin and monitored the wound for signs of infection.

THE AFTERMATH

John Schrank was immediately taken into custody and within five minutes of the shooting was on his way to the central police station in Milwaukee.[65] Papers that were found on his person demonstrated that he had been following Roosevelt across the country looking for the opportunity to assassinate him. A rough diary demonstrated that Schrank believed the ghost of President McKinley had appeared to him and told him that Roosevelt was the one who murdered him.[66] As mentioned, he stated that McKinley had shown up one night as a ghost and told him, "Let not a murderer take the presidential chair. Avenge my death."[67] In another entry, Schrank challenged Roosevelt for seeking a third term in office, something he felt was entirely inappropriate: "Any man looking for a third term ought to be shot."[68] Other pieces of paper had a list of the nine hotels he had stayed at while tracking Roosevelt on the campaign trail.[69]

Schrank was taken to a Milwaukee District Court on October 15. When asked by the judge how he would plead, Schrank replied very matter-of-factly, "I am guilty."[70] The judge believed him to be sane, bound him over to the November term, and fixed his bail at $7,500, which was later raised to $15,000.

On November 13, 1912, Schrank appeared in municipal court before Judge August C. Backus. At this preliminary hearing, he was again asked for his plea, and he replied, "Why, guilty. I did not mean to kill a citizen, Judge; I shot Theodore Roosevelt because he was a menace to the country. He should not have a third term. I did not want him to have one. I shot him as a warning that men must not try to have more than two terms as President."[71] Schrank explained that he was not trying to kill Roosevelt as a citizen, as a former president, or as the head of the Progressive Party; rather, he continued, "I shot Roosevelt as a warning to other third termers."[72] It was apparent to all present that John Schrank was mentally unstable, but to ensure he was not bluffing, the judge ordered that Schrank undergo an examination by a commission of five "alienists," a common term for doctors who treated mental disorders during this time period. The five alienists interviewed Schrank and declared in a report on November 22 that he was, in fact, insane. The judge then declared him insane. Interestingly, he disagreed with the verdict, but thanked the doctors, shook their hands, and told them they had done the best they could. The judge then committed Schrank to an insane asylum for an indefinite period of time.

Preparing to go to the prison hospital in Waupon, Wisconsin, Schrank thanked the sheriff and his jailers and added, "I hope I haven't caused you much trouble."[73] Then, on the way to the prison, where he would remain until his natural death, the train was passing through a forested area. The guards were talking about hunting, and they asked Schrank if he liked to hunt. He replied, quite dryly, "Only Bull Moose."[74] Some time after arriving at the hospital and adjusting to his surroundings, he fired off a letter saying that he wanted his pistol and the bullet to be donated to and put on display by the New-York Historical Society. When someone told him that the bullet was still in Theodore Roosevelt, he became agitated and shouted, "That is my bullet!"[75]

Despite these sinister outbursts, Schrank remained a model patient, often being referred to as "Uncle John" by the other patients and staff. The only complaint most people had about John Schrank was his distaste for bathing. Often his clothes became so odoriferous that they had to be burned and he was forced to bathe. When told in 1919 that Theodore Roosevelt had died, Schrank replied he was sorry to learn of his death.[76] His ire was, however, raised when Franklin D. Roosevelt, a cousin of Theodore, ran for a third term, but for the most part he retained a pleasant disposition. Perhaps it is ironic that he died in the hospital on September 15, 1943, the same year in which F.D.R. announced that he was running for a fourth term in office and the same day that he had received his vision in 1901. No one ever visited John Schrank in prison, and in the end, his body was turned over to the Marquette University Medical School for autopsy practice.[77]

On the evening that Roosevelt was shot, his wife, Edith, attended a performance of Johann Strauss's operetta *Die Fledermaus* in New York City.[78] She was notified by Oliver Roosevelt, a cousin, as to what had happened and was shocked by the news. She asked Oliver to confirm that he was not hurt, and upon his return he explained that he had been "scratched but had kept on with his speech."[79] Because of this, and so as not to appear rude or cause a stir, she remained until the end of the play. Then she was taken to the headquarters of the Progressive Party, where she waited for further news of her husband's condition, and learned that he had delivered his speech and had been taken to the hospital. At around midnight, she went to stay with Theodore's cousin, Laura Roosevelt.

The next morning she was told that her husband was at Mercy Hospital in Chicago and that he was resting comfortably. She also received the telegraph that Roosevelt had dictated on his way to the Milwaukee hospital, which read, "I very earnestly beg you not to come out. I am not nearly as hurt as I have been again and again from a fall from my horse."[80] He assured her that the campaign would go on. Edith's response to this missive was to say, "That's just the sort of thing that was said when Mr. McKinley was shot." She packed her bags and boarded the first train for Chicago.

She was accompanied on the trip by their son Ted, their daughter Ethel, and the Roosevelts' personal physician, Dr. Alexander Lambert. Upon her arrival, she found Roosevelt in the hospital bed with his breathing labored as a result of the broken rib. In addition, his side was causing him pain. The entire area was beginning to turn black and blue.[81]

Theodore Roosevelt remained in the hospital for nearly a week. Edith remained at his side and took control of his care, sleeping in a furnished room next to his.[82] While in bed, Roosevelt continued to orchestrate his campaign by highlighting his continued capacity despite the attempt on his life.[83] His surgeon released a statement that said, "Colonel Roosevelt has a phenomenal development of the chest. It is largely due to the fact that he is one of the most powerful men I have ever seen laid on an operating table. The bullet lodged in the massive muscles of the chest instead of penetrating the lung."[84] Dr. Alexander Lambert also issued his own statement after examining his patient: "The folded manuscript and heavy steel spectacle case checked and deflected the bullet so that it passed up at such an angle that it went outside the ribs and into the muscles. If this deflection had not occurred and the bullet gone through the arch of the aorta or auricles of the heart, Colonel Roosevelt would not have lived 60 seconds."[85]

Senator Albert Beveridge of Indiana, hearing of the assassination attempt while in Chicago, visited Roosevelt the next day. Roosevelt provided him with a dictated message that he asked Beveridge to deliver, which he did so in Louisville, Kentucky, the next day. The message stated:

It matters little about me, but it matters all about the cause we fight for. If one soldier who happens to carry the flag is stricken, another will take it from his hands and carry it on. One after another the standard bearers may be laid low, but the standard itself can never fail. You know that personally I did not want ever to be a candidate for office again. And you know that only the call that came to the men of the 60's made me answer it in our day as they did more nobly in their day. And now, as then, it is not important whether one leader lives or dies; it is important only that the cause shall live and win. Tell the people not to worry about me, for if I go down another will take my place. Always the cause is there, and it is the cause for which the people care, for it is the people's cause.[86]

Although Roosevelt was clearly using the assassination attempt to gain political mileage, his two opponents, Taft and Woodrow Wilson, sent messages of sympathy to Roosevelt. Taft wrote that he was shocked "to hear of the outrageous and deplorable assault made on you, and I earnestly hope and pray that your recovery may be speedy and without suffering."[87] Both Taft and Wilson told the public that they would refrain from any public statements, effectively ceasing their campaigns, until Roosevelt was released from hospital. Roosevelt, seeing this more as a sign of weakness and an acknowledgment that he was somehow incapacitated (which he was), drafted a wholly political response which was published two days after he had entered the hospital. It read, in part:

I cannot too strongly emphasize the fact upon which we Progressives insist, that the welfare of any one man in the fight wholly is immaterial compared to the great and fundamental issues involved in the triumph of the principles for which our cause stands. If I had been killed the fight would have gone on exactly the same.. . . So far as my opponents are concerned, whatever could with truth and propriety have been said against me and my cause before I was shot can with equal truth and equal propriety be said against me now, and it should be so said; and the things that cannot be said now are merely the things that ought not to have been said before. This is not a contest about any man; it is a contest concerning principles.[88]

Theodore Roosevelt remained in the hospital until October 21, one full week, and then returned to his home in Oyster Bay. He remained at Sagamore Hill, quietly recovering, cared for only by his wife.[89] It is said that within days he began to recover and his appetite came back, and "soon the chicken bones were 'stacked like cordwood' around his plate, which disgusted Edith."[90] One of his servants would remark that "the bullet was never made could kill a man that can eat as much fried chicken as that and live."[91] Ten days later, he gave his first speech since the assassination attempt.

On October 31, 1912, in Madison Square Garden in New York City, he spoke before a crowd of 15,000 people.[92] This time he was protected by agents privately hired from the Burns Detective Agency, as well as over a thousand police officers.[93] He gave a typically fiery Roosevelt speech, and to show that he was recovered, he often and repeatedly pounded the lectern. He was well received, and many remarked that he appeared to be in good health and that the indomitable Roosevelt energy was back.

Several days later, on Election Day, the results began to pour in, and what was suspected came true: Roosevelt had split the vote and Woodrow Wilson was the winner. Wilson had captured 41.8 percent of the popular vote, Roosevelt had received 27.4 percent, while the incumbent president, Taft, had captured 23.2 percent. Had Roosevelt not run, it is believed that Taft would have captured a majority of the popular vote. Although the "Bull Moose" Party had made the greatest showing to date of any new party in history, it would become clear that what had carried the Progressive Party was simply Theodore Roosevelt himself.

The loss of the election sent Roosevelt into a quandary as to where to go with his life. He became somewhat more reflective, and many of his letters over the next year, before embarking on his voyage through the Amazon on the River of Doubt,[94] dealt with his reaction to the assassination attempt. One such letter explained:

I doubt if any man has had a greater volume of obliquity poured upon him than I have had during the past nine months, and I have been assailed with an injustice so gross as to be fairly humorous. But there is a good deal in Emerson's law of compensation, and to offset this I have been praised in connection with the shooting with quite as extravagant a disregard of my deserts. The bullet passed through the manuscript of my speech and my iron spectacle case, and only went three or four inches into my chest, breaking a rib and lodging against it. I never saw my assailant, as it was dark and he was mixed with the dense crowd standing beside the automobile, and as I was standing unsteadily I half fell back for a second. As I stood up I coughed and at once put my hands to my lips to see if there was any blood. There was none, so that as the bullet was in the chest I felt the chances were twenty to one that it was not fatal.[95]

He also wrote on several occasions concerning his would-be assassin, John Schrank, never referring to him by name. In one letter he wrote:

Just one word about the madman who shot me. He was not really a madman at all; he was a man of the same disordered brain which most criminals, and a great many non-criminals[,] have. I very gravely question if he has a more unsound brain than Eugene Debs. He simply represents a different stratum of life and of temperament, which if not more violent is yet more accustomed to brutal physical expression. He had quite enough sense to avoid shooting me in any Southern State, where he would have been lynched, and he waited until he got into a State where there was no death penalty. I have not the slightest feeling against him; I have a very strong feeling against the people who, by their ceaseless and intemperate abuse, excited him to the action, and against the mushy people who would excuse him and all the other criminals once the crime has been committed.[96]

This was a common theme with Theodore Roosevelt throughout his life. He fully advocated the use of the death penalty for murder; what he argued against were the "emotional men and women"[97] who were against it because they only considered the fate of the one sentenced to die. He once wrote that these people took into consideration "neither his victim nor the many millions of unknown individuals who would in the long run be harmed by what they ask."[98] However, he did believe that criminals could be rehabilitated; after being punished, if a criminal showed "a sincere desire to lead a decent and upright life, he should be given the chance, he should be helped and not hindered; and if he makes good, he should receive that respect from others which so often aids in creating self-respect—the most invaluable of all possessions."[99] In some ways, this balance of punishment and rehabilitation may explain what he wrote in another letter in regard to his not wanting Schrank to be harmed after attempting the assassination:

I would not have objected to the man's being killed at the very instant, but I did not deem it wise or proper that he should be killed before my eyes if I was going to recover, so I immediately stopped the men who had begun to worry him, and had him brought to me so that I might see if I recognized him; but I did not.[100]

Finally, in another letter, Roosevelt's bravado reached a high point with regard to the attempt on his life when he wrote,

I did not care a rap for being shot. It is a trade risk, which every prominent public man ought to accept as a matter of course. For eleven years I have been prepared any day to be shot; and if any one of the officers of my regiment had abandoned the battle merely because he received a wound that did nothing worse than break a rib, I should never have trusted that officer again. I would have expected him to keep on in the fight as long as he could stand; and what I expect lieutenants to do I expect *a fortiori*, a leader to do.[101]

The bullet was never extracted from Roosevelt's chest. It was deemed safer to just leave it alone. He carried the bullet with him to his grave in 1919. It apparently never bothered him, as he would note to a friend in March 1913 that "I do not mind it any more than if it were in my waistcoat pocket."[102]

CONCLUSION

Theodore Roosevelt, who had become the twenty-sixth president as the result of an assassin's bullet, became the fifth president to be the victim of an assassination attempt. He was also the first ex-president and first presidential party nominee to have his life put at risk, and he was the first president to be shot and survive. Roosevelt recovered from the wound and went on to one of his greatest adventures, the exploration of the River of Doubt in the Amazon jungle,[103] before dying in his beloved home of Sagamore Hill in Oyster Bay, New York, on January 6, 1919.

John F. Schrank, after having been declared mentally unfit in a Milwaukee court of law, was confined to a mental hospital for the rest of his life. He became a model mental patient, but still harbored resentment for Theodore Roosevelt for having sought a third term. Ironically, before dying on September 15, 1943, Schrank would live to witness Theodore's cousin become president for a third term and announce his intent to secure a fourth term.

In the wake of Roosevelt's assassination attempt, the Secret Service protection of the president continued much as it had before. Congress considered providing Secret Service protection to presidential nominees, but that would have to wait until the assassination of another presidential contender, Robert Kennedy, in 1968.[104]

6

Franklin D. Roosevelt

INTRODUCTION

Franklin Delano Roosevelt was enjoying the few weeks he had to himself between the election of November 1932 and his inauguration day, set for March 4, 1933. Roosevelt was relaxing on Vincent Astor's private yacht before officially becoming the nation's leader.[1] After a farewell dinner on the yacht with some close friends, Roosevelt climbed into a green Buick convertible for a short public rally at Miami's Bay Front Park before heading back to Washington. That February 15 was a beautiful, clear night in Miami—perfect for a short public rally for the future president.

That same night, an unemployed bricklayer who was staying temporarily in Miami carried a .32-caliber pistol that he purchased at a local pawn shop to the Bay Front Park and joined an excited crowd of 20,000 citizens there to meet the president-elect. The park was lit up with red, white, and blue floodlights while a drum-and-bugle corps played patriotic songs. After a short, impromptu speech, five shots rang out. Five people were quickly wounded, and the gunman apprehended. His target not only was unharmed but would go on to be elected president three more times.

FRANKLIN ROOSEVELT

Franklin Delano Roosevelt was born on January 30, 1882, in New York. He grew up in a very wealthy family, but was also often sick as a child, contracting both typhoid fever and scarlet fever. His parents frequently took their son overseas as a young boy.[2] Through his travels, Franklin learned both French and German, and acquired a lifelong love of the sea.

F.D.R. attended Harvard University, graduating in three years. While there, he was president of the undergraduate newspaper, the *Crimson*. But he did not stand out as an intellectual student. His grades maintained a mediocre C average,[3] making some suggest that if it were today, F.D.R. might have some difficulty gaining admission to the university.

Franklin graduated from Harvard in 1904 with success in social and extra-curricular activities.[4] He fell in love with his fifth cousin, Eleanor Roosevelt, and they were married on March 17, 1905. She was the niece of President Theodore Roosevelt, who gave her away during the wedding ceremony.[5] During their lives together, Franklin and Eleanor had six children (one girl and five boys), five of whom reached adulthood.[6]

Franklin attended Columbia Law School but did not graduate. Nonetheless, he passed the New York bar examination in 1906.[7] In 1910, he ran for the New York State Senate. He campaigned strenuously, touring rural areas, which helped him win the campaign. He then won reelection in 1912, despite having contracted typhoid fever. He served in the New York Senate from 1911 to 1913.[8]

During the 1912 campaign, Roosevelt supported Woodrow Wilson's bid for the presidency. In 1913, after Wilson became president, he appointed Roosevelt to be the assistant secretary of the Navy, the same position once held by Roosevelt's famous uncle.[9] In that position, F.D.R. was responsible for managing the operation of U.S. navy yards, negotiating labor contracts with civilian workers, and purchasing naval supplies. He had to deal with procurement, supply, and both civilian and land-bound personnel.[10] He served in that position from 1913 to 1920.

In August 1914, F.D.R. decided to run in the primary for the New York Democratic nomination for the U.S. Senate. Despite heavy campaigning, he lost the campaign and returned to his navy job.[11]

In 1920, F.D.R. became the Democratic nominee for vice president, but the Democrats lost the election.[12] Because the Republicans won, F.D.R. lost his job as assistant secretary of the Navy. He returned to New York, became vice president of the Fidelity and Deposit Company, and took up the practice of law again in the firm of Emmet, Marvin and Roosevelt.

In early August 1921, F.D.R. was struck with polio (poliomyelitis) from the waist down and never walked again without assistance. It happened while he was visiting Campobello, the Roosevelt's vacation home off the coast of Maine.[13] After a day of working outside, Roosevelt felt weak, but nonetheless invited his family to run with him to his favorite swimming place. They went swimming in the Bay of Fundy in extremely cold water. They then ran home, even though a horse-drawn carriage was available for the return trip.[14]

When F.D.R. returned to the house, he was too tired to get out of his bathing suit, so he sat in his wet suit while he read the mail that had just arrived. After about an hour, he started to shiver and went to bed, wrapped in blankets. He had had no appetite for dinner. He was very tired and suffered some aches in his legs, which he thought was lumbago. The next morning, the pains in his legs were worse, even extending to his back. He was too weak to leave bed.[15]

Doctors were called to the home immediately. One doctor said F.D.R. had a bad cold, whereas another said he had a blood clot in the spinal cord that was starting to dissolve.[16] But his condition continued to deteriorate and he developed a high fever. Dr. Robert S. Lovett of Boston was the first to recognize the signs of poliomyelitis, which causes permanent damage to nerves and paralyzes arms, legs, or lungs. Within days, Roosevelt was paralyzed from the waist down, unable to walk or stand by himself. From 1924 to 1928, Roosevelt worked tirelessly to recover the use of his legs. He exercised faithfully with special equipment, but to no avail. He began using steel braces that weighed seven pounds each.[17] This enabled him to walk for short distances. Eventually, F.D.R. arranged for a car to be modified with hand controls so he could drive by himself.

F.D.R. discovered a dilapidated resort in Georgia called Warm Springs, where the water had a natural temperature of 89° Fahrenheit. Swimming in the warm water seemed to improve his condition. The warmth helped relax his muscles, and the water helped bear his weight.[18] F.D.R. spent many hours there, swimming in the pool, exercising, relaxing, and helping other people who were also suffering from the effects of polio.

Roosevelt purchased the resort in 1926. He spent $200,000 for the pool, the run-down hotel, and the surrounding land that housed a few cottages.[19] On February 1, 1927, he formed the Georgia Warm Springs Foundation, ultimately putting another $200,000 into it, or more than two-thirds of his remaining wealth. He employed an orthopedic surgeon and a team of physiotherapists; built a second covered pool; remodeled the hotel and its surrounding buildings, increasing their capacity to sixty-one patients; and built a cottage for himself (where he eventually died).

By 1924, F.D.R. was healthy enough to return to politics. He gave a speech nominating New York Governor Al Smith for president.[20] Then in September 1926, he delivered the keynote speech at the New York Democratic state convention. People listening to Roosevelt's speech were so impressed with him that they tried to nominate him to be a U.S. senator, but he resisted the efforts.

Two years later, in 1928, Roosevelt decided to run for New York governor. He fought a vigorous campaign in an attempt to convince voters that he was healthy enough to do the job despite his disability. The outgoing governor, Al Smith, who had been elected to the Senate, wanted Roosevelt to replace him. Smith told voters, "A governor does not have to be an acrobat. We do not elect him for his ability to do a double back-flip or a handspring."[21] Roosevelt won the campaign, taking office in 1929. During his reelection campaign, Roosevelt toured the state, giving campaign speeches in major cities. He amazed people with his stamina and energy, considering his almost useless legs.[22] He was reelected to be the governor in 1930 by 725,000 votes. He served as the governor of New York from 1929 to 1933.[23] As governor, Roosevelt advocated repeal of the Eighteenth Amendment (Prohibition), proposing to replace it with state controls and local options.

In 1932, Roosevelt became the frontrunner for the Democratic nomination for the presidency. He campaigned throughout the country and won the election with 22,821,857 votes to incumbent Herbert Hoover's 15,761,845.[24] He had overcome his paralysis to be elected president of the United States, but before becoming president would have to survive another near catastrophe, an assassination attempt on his life.

GIUSEPPE ZANGARA

Giuseppe Zangara was born in Ferruzzano, Calabria, Italy. His mother died when he was only two years old. To help make ends meet, his father put Zangara to work at the age of eight.[25] Zangara began to dislike children from wealthy families who could go to school instead of work. As a young man, Zangara served in the Italian Army for five years during World War I, doing a variety of menial jobs in his home village before immigrating with his uncle to the United States in 1923.

In the United States, Zangara settled in Paterson, New Jersey, and on September 11, 1929, became a naturalized citizen. He found a job as a bricklayer. He was not a very big man, only five feet one inch tall and 105 pounds. He was also sickly. For many years, he suffered severe pain in his abdomen and constantly told everyone that his stomach hurt.[26] The pains were sometimes attributed to adhesions of the gall bladder. In 1926, Zangara was diagnosed with appendicitis, and he had an appendectomy.

Besides his health concerns, Zangara also had increasing mental delusions. He blamed authority figures for his stomach pain and began to believe that the president was supernaturally responsible for his discomfort. Rather than blame an individual leader, Zangara hated all presidents and kings equally. At the same time, he was also becoming very outspoken and impatient with other people.

Because of his physical and mental conditions, it became increasingly difficult for Zangara to have many friends or hold down a job. He continued to push people away and became a very lonely man.

He continued to hate the rich and powerful[27] and envied those who had more than he did. He resented people who had more opportunities, especially with regard to education or other ways of bettering themselves.[28] He was slowly becoming an anarchist and considered assassination a desirable response to government in general. He had assassination in mind for many years and sought the assassination of "all capitalist presidents and kings."[29] He considered killing King Victor Emmanuel of Italy in 1923. He then began plotting to assassinate U.S. President Herbert Hoover during his term in office (1929–1933), but F.D.R. was elected to replace Hoover before Zangara could act on his plan—and Roosevelt happened to be in the city at the right time.[30] Zangara was not out to hurt F.D.R.

specifically, but instead any president. To carry out his planned assassinations, Zangara bought a revolver at a pawnshop on North Miami Avenue for $8.

THE ASSASSINATION ATTEMPT

Roosevelt was elected to the presidency in November 1932, but he would not become president until Inauguration Day, March 4, 1933. In the meantime, he decided to take a vacation and relax before taking office. The vacation included a cruise on Vincent Astor's yacht, the *Nourmahal*.[31] On February 15, 1933, Astor hosted a farewell dinner for Roosevelt on his yacht. After a brief press conference, Roosevelt planned to leave the yacht at 9:00 P.M. in a green Buick convertible for a short reception at Miami's Bay Front Park, and then take an overnight train to New York.[32]

Of course, F.D.R. was unaware that an anarchist with mental issues by the name of Zangara was also in Miami at that time, working an occasional odd job and living off his savings. Zangara had tried betting on the dog races, but had lost $200 instead. Zangara arrived at Bay Front Park only a half hour before F.D.R.'s speech, so he did not get to stand or sit in the front row. He tried to push his way to the front, but was told that women and children were sitting there. Instead, Zangara was forced to sit in the third row, less than ten yards from the back of Roosevelt's car.[33] Standing to his front and right was Lillian Cross, a diminutive forty-eight-year-old housewife. Behind them was Thomas Armour, a forty-six-year-old Miami carpenter.

Also attending the speech that night was Mayor Anton Cermak of Chicago. Cermak was on a mission of penance with F.D.R. because he did not support Roosevelt at the Democratic National Convention in his own city. Instead, Cermak had backed Al Smith, and even organized a movement against F.D.R. Cermak had come to Miami to make peace with Roosevelt. Cermak hoped not only to mend fences but also to win federal help for his bankrupt school system.[34]

F.D.R. was to give his speech from the back of his open car. Because of his paralyzed legs, Roosevelt often spoke from the rear seat of his open touring car rather than walking to a platform and standing in front of a podium for the duration of a speech. At Bay Front Park that night, F.D.R. was scheduled to address the annual encampment of the American Legion.[35]

The car pulled into the park and stopped in a driveway area. About 20,000 people were assembled, including many dignitaries. The amphitheater at the park was illuminated in red, white, and blue floodlights. An American Legion drum-and-bugle corps played patriotic songs. Local radio and media covered the event.

F.D.R.'s security detail helped him to sit on the back of the open car with his feet on the back seat.[36] The mayor of Miami introduced him to the cheering crowd, and he spoke a few words into the microphone that someone had handed to him. Roosevelt remained in his car. Behind him, on a stage, were dignitaries including elected officials from Miami, some of F.D.R.'s advisors, and Mayor Cermak. In his speech, F.D.R. recalled his many visits to Florida, telling listeners that he had a splendid twelve days of fishing and swimming. He talked about how much weight he gained on vacation and promised the crowd that he would be back next year. In all, F.D.R. spoke less than one minute; the speech totaled only 132 words.[37]

When he was finished, he slid back into his seat, smiled for the crowd, and chatted with reporters. He waved for Cermak to come talk to him.[38] Mayor Cermak approached, and he and Roosevelt shook hands cordially. They agreed that they would meet on his railway car about an hour later. Another man appeared with a long telegram for Roosevelt. People started to leave, and Zangara and Lillian Cross both jumped onto a bench and stood on their tiptoes for a better view of the president-elect.

Suddenly, from a distance of no more than forty feet from the president-elect, five shots rang out in quick succession. Zangara shouted, "Too many people are starving to death," as he fired a .32-caliber revolver five times at Roosevelt.[39] Roosevelt immediately scrunched down into his seat, trying to make himself a smaller target, then sat immobile and unflinching, his jaw set, ready for whatever might follow. The driver of the car accelerated as he tried to remove F.D.R. from danger.

Most bystanders ducked after the first shot, which gave Zangara a clear view of Roosevelt's head. But just at the critical moment when Zangara attempted to fire again, Lillian Cross hit his arm with her handbag and spoiled his aim. She shoved his arm upward, forcing him to jump down and forward in order to get away from her.[40] Another bystander, Mr. Armour, also said he grabbed the assassin's arm so hard that he broke it. Later, Zangara claimed the chair he was on moved and spoiled his aim.[41]

Zangara fired all five bullets at Roosevelt's car, missing him by inches.[42] In all, four people were wounded. A woman standing behind F.D.R. was hit twice in the abdomen. A New York policeman assigned to protect Roosevelt was in critical condition with a head wound, and the wife of the president of the Florida Light and Power Company suffered an abdominal wound. Blood also spurted from the hand of a nearby Secret Service agent.

The most critically wounded, however, was Mayor Cermak. A shot had penetrated his rib cage, and he collapsed to the ground. Roosevelt noticed that Cermak had been wounded, shouted for the car to stop, and directed that Cermak be helped into the car beside him. He told Cermak to keep quiet, and said, "It won't hurt if you keep quiet."[43] He did not think Cermak would live. Once Cermak was in the car, the driver sped off to Jackson Memorial Hospital. Roosevelt held Cermak with his left arm, felt for his pulse with his right hand, and when the mayor became conscious, encouraged him and continually urged him to conserve his strength and say nothing.

Meanwhile, the crowd yelled, "Stop that man!"[44] and wrestled Zangara to the pavement. Within moments, he was handcuffed and held down by three policemen. The crowd began to assault him, and some of his clothes were torn off. A trailing car conveyed the injured policeman as well as the apprehended gunman away from

Figure 6.1. Chicago Mayor Anton Cermak on February 15, 1933, after being struck by a bullet from Gisuseppe Zangara's pistol that was meant for President-Elect Franklin Delano Roosevelt at Miami, Florida's Bay Front Park. Cermak would die from complications two days after F.D.R. was inaugurated as the 32nd president of the United States. (Courtesy of the Library of Congress.)

the crime scene. Zangara had been forced onto the luggage rack with two policemen sitting on him and another present on the running board.[45]

THE AFTERMATH

Roosevelt stayed at the hospital with Cermak for about two hours until he was brought out of the emergency room and his condition stabilized. He spoke with him for several minutes and then visited the other shooting victims. He stayed overnight in Miami, visiting the victims again the next morning. Cermak bravely said to Roosevelt, "I'm glad it was me instead of you."[46] After they briefly discussed the issues that Cermak wanted to discuss with the president-elect, Roosevelt left Miami on his train at 10:15 A.M. He sent a telegram of thanks when he learned of Mrs. Cross's role, then never mentioned the episode again.[47] His Secret Service detail later said that Roosevelt did not seem to be affected by the shooting, but remained easygoing, confident, and poised, even sleeping soundly that night.

After the shooting, Roosevelt called his wife, who was in New York at the time. Eleanor nonchalantly told the press, "These things are to be expected."[48] Roosevelt's reaction to the incident brought forth a national surge of confidence in him. Many people had been unsure what to expect of the man who was to become president a few weeks later, especially because he had a visible disability. It was clear that F.D.R. lacked physical fear, and his courage caused the country to rally behind him. The events in Miami showed that the man elected to be the next president would easily cradle a wounded man in his arms and reassure him that he would be fine, even as it became clear that he may not. Roosevelt's compassion and concern for those who had been injured impressed all observers and had a reassuring effect on the American public. Simply put, his calm during the ordeal aroused admiration for his demonstration of courage.[49]

For a few days, Cermak battled colitis, pneumonia, and gangrene. He was able to listen to Roosevelt's inaugural address on the radio on March 4, but died two days later of peritonitis.[50] It was nineteen days after the shooting. He was the only fatality. All of the other victims survived.

After the shooting, Zangara was taken to the Dade County Courthouse jail where he gave his name as Joseph Zangara and gave a sworn statement confessing to the shooting. Sheriff Dan Hardie of the Dade County Sheriff's Office conducted the interview. Zangara explained that he had come over from Italy on September 1, 1923, and had lived in New Jersey working as a bricklayer. He explained that he had planned to kill the president years before, and that he had considered killing the king of Italy. He explained he never had

Figure 6.2. President-Elect Franklin D. Roosevelt (R) and President Herbert Hoover (L) on March 4, 1933, riding together to the U.S. Capitol for the inauguration of Roosevelt, two weeks after an assassination attempt on his life. (Courtesy of the Library of Congress.)

the chance to kill the king, but in the papers he had learned that the president-elect was to be in town giving a speech and he thought he might have the opportunity. At one point he explained about his desire to kill, "I have the gun in my hand. I kill kings and presidents first and next all capitalists."[51] Zangara stated that he wanted to kill F.D.R. because he blamed the president-elect, all rich people, and all capitalists for his chronic stomach pain. He stressed several times that he had only wanted to kill the president and that he had acted alone.

When it came to the court proceedings, Zangara pleaded guilty, and the judge declined to question him. Zangara's defense attorney pleaded with the judge to allow Zangara to take the witness stand in order to tell his own story in the belief that it might lessen the sentence the judge would give Zangara. Judge E. C. Collins relented and Zangara took the stand. Basic questions of his birth, parents, and occupation were asked, and Zangara answered them matter-of-factly. When asked if he played games, Zangara responded by saying, "No. Me sick all the time. I play sometimes shuffleboard in the park."[52] When asked if he had ever been in jail, Zangara answered, "No," and when asked if he had planned the shooting, he again answered, "No." He further stated that he decided to commit the shooting when "I got it in my mind capitalist hurt people. They are to blame for my stomach hurting. My stomach was hurting bad. It was like I was on fire. It burns my mind, I act like a drunken man. It came in my mind when I was suffering."[53] It was clear by the many contradictions in Zangara's testimony that he had both physical and mental problems, but his testimony was still cogent and he understood what he had done.

More importantly, however, when asked if it was on the day of the shooting that he planned to kill Mr. Roosevelt, Zangara did not dispute the accusation and simply stated, "Yes, yes, I guess so. I see it in the papers it is coming."[54] When asked if he knew Mayor Cermak, Zangara replied, "No, not at all. I just went there to kill the president. I am sorry I shot somebody else. I want to shoot the president because capitalists is because I am sick."[55] Therefore, there was little doubt that Zangara was there to assassinate President-Elect Franklin D. Roosevelt, despite others' beliefs that Cermak was truly the intended target or that it was just a random act of violence.[56] In the end, when asked if he was sorry that he had tried to kill Roosevelt, Zangara replied, "No, no, no. I am sorry only because I did not kill. I am sorry about nothing. Put me in the electric chair."[57] It was a line he would often repeat until his wish came true.

Zangara was then sentenced for four counts of assault with the intent to kill. The first charge was for the assault with the intent to kill the president-elect. For that particular assassination attempt, Judge Collins stated, "It is the sentence of this court that you Giuseppe Zangara, alias Joseph Zangara, be confined in the state penitentiary at hard labor for a term of 20 years."[58] In the end, he would receive twenty additional years for each of the other three shootings, with the charges for the shooting of Anton Cermak still pending Cermak's final outcome.

As Zangara was led out of the courtroom, Zangara told the judge, "Four times twenty is eighty. Oh, judge, don't be stingy. Give me more. Give me a hundred years."[59] The judge, aware that Cermak might not survive his wounds, replied, "Maybe there will be more later."[60] After Cermak's death, Zangara was indicted for first-degree murder, and because Zangara had intended to commit murder, it was irrelevant that his intended target was not the man he killed. Zangara pleaded guilty to the charges and was sentenced to death. After hearing the decision for his sentence, Zangara lashed out by shouting, "You give me electric chair. I no afraid of that chair! You one of capitalists. You is crook man too. Put me in electric chair. I no care!"[61]

Under Florida law, a convicted murderer could not share cell space with another prisoner before his execution, but another convicted murderer was already awaiting execution at the same prison. Zangara's sentence required prison officials to expand their waiting area, and the "death cell" became "death row." Zangara complained about the absence of photographers to record his execution and became incensed when he learned that no newsreel cameras would be filming his final moments. After spending only ten days on death row, Zangara went fearlessly to the electric chair on March 20, 1933, in the Florida State Penitentiary in Raiford, Florida.[62] Before the execution, he was heard to have shouted for prison officials to push the button.[63]

F.D.R. was personally opposed to the death penalty but said nothing to influence the sentencing.[64] Later, Roosevelt wrote, "I heard what I thought was a firecracker; then several more."[65] Roosevelt believed that with a name like Zangara, he might well have been a Chicago gangster aiming at Cermak. Otherwise, he asked, why didn't Zangara shoot at him when he was speaking, when he would have been a much easier target?[66]

In fact, some conspiracy theorists, even today, believe that Zangara was a hitman who had been hired by Chicago organized crime figure Frank Nitti as a diversion for a second shooter, who never fired a shot and was never seen. Cermak was an enemy of Chicago organized crime, and Nitti wanted him dead. It was also said that Cermak was blamed for an attack on Nitti earlier in Chicago in which Nitti was wounded by Chicago police. Cermak had left Chicago to escape retaliation by Nitti's gunmen. Thus, Zangara's primary target was never President-Elect Roosevelt. The conspiracy theorists point out that Zangara was one of the Italian Army's best marksmen before coming to the United States. While this was true, his marksmanship was with a rifle, not a .32 pistol and there was never any solid evidence that Zangara killed Cermak for organized crime.[67]

The Federal Bureau of Investigation case file on the assassination attempt of President-Elect Roosevelt would remain open for a number of years, and even as late as 1950 continued to be supplemented with letters from prominent citizens and sources suggesting Zangara had mafia ties and had not acted alone. The records show that investigations were conducted in both Philadelphia and Chicago in order to verify these connections. No evidence was uncovered to even suggest that Zangara had ever visited Chicago or Philadelphia, nor did it appear that he had family or associates living in either city. The report also concluded that his intended target had been, from the beginning, President-Elect Roosevelt and not Mayor Cermak.[68]

CONCLUSION

In the end, with five shots, Giuseppe Zangara, a thirty-two-year-old unemployed Italian bricklayer from New Jersey, killed the mayor of Chicago, critically wounded two other people, and lightly wounded two more.[69] All evidence suggests that Zangara was attempting to assassinate President-Elect Roosevelt, for which he would receive a sentence of twenty years in prison, but it was the eventual death of Mayor Cermak that would earn Zangara the electric chair. A little over one month after the shooting, Zangara was executed.

Roosevelt, who was not hit in the assassination attempt, went on to become a successful president during twelve of the most difficult years in American history.[70] He was the architect of the New Deal, the man who rescued the nation from the Great Depression, and the victor in World War II. He was the only U.S. president ever elected four times. The man who could "do little more than wiggle his toes was to become the longest serving of all presidents and the dominant American political personality of the twentieth century."[71]

Today, although Anton Cermak has become a footnote to history, Bay Front Park in Miami, the scene of the assassination attempt, features a plaque in honor of him. On it, one can read his most famous words, "I am glad it was me instead of you." His crypt in the Bohemian National Cemetery in Chicago, Illinois, bears the same inscription.

7

Harry S Truman

INTRODUCTION

November 1, 1950, was an unusually warm day in Washington, D.C. President Truman and his family were temporarily living in the Blair House while the White House was undergoing repairs. Because of the heat, the front door of the Blair House was wide open, as were the windows of the second-floor bedroom where Truman was taking his usual afternoon nap. He was awakened by the sound of gunshots just outside his window.

Truman looked out the window to see what was happening. He may have made eye contact with his would-be assassins, but guards yelled, "Get back!" After the assassination attempt, Truman said, "A president has to expect these things," and continued with the events scheduled for the remainder of the afternoon.[1]

HARRY S TRUMAN

Harry S Truman was born on May 8, 1884, in Lamar, Missouri. When he was six years old, Harry got glasses, which prevented him from playing sports and quickly set him apart from the other kids.[2] At the age of nine or ten, Harry caught diphtheria and was sick for many months.[3] During that time, he had to quit school, but continued to study at home in order to keep up with the other children. He studied so hard at home that when he returned to school, he was allowed to skip the third grade altogether.[4] Throughout his school years, Truman was a diligent student, reportedly reading every book in the public library.[5]

After high school, Truman applied to the U.S. Military Academy at West Point but was not accepted because he had poor eyesight.[6] Harry returned home to help run the family farm and joined many social groups. He applied for membership in the Masonic Lodge, the American Legion, the Elks, the Eagles, and the International Acquaintance League.[7]

When World War I began, Truman enlisted in the Missouri National Guard, and served as a second lieutenant in the 129th Field Artillery, eventually earning the rank of captain.[8] He spent eight months in the winter of 1917–1918 training at Camp Doniphan, Oklahoma, before embarking for France in April 1918.[9] He led his men through numerous bloody battles, perfecting his leadership skills and building a strong reputation for himself.

When he returned home to the farm in 1919, he married his childhood sweetheart, Elizabeth "Bess" Wallace, and opened a men's clothing business with a friend in 1920 called Truman and Jacobson. The store became a success and turned a profit for two years, but failed during the postwar recession in 1921.[10]

After the store closed, Truman was seeking new employment. He was approached by the Pendergast family who asked him to run for political office. During the war, Truman had become friendly with Jim Pendergast, a fellow officer in the 129th Field Artillery.[11] Pendergast was the nephew of the Kansas City "politician" Thomas Pendergast. Over the years, the Pendergast family had created a notorious political machine and had become a powerful organization that promoted gambling, prostitution, narcotics, racketeering, and bootlegging in Kansas City.[12] Tom became the boss of the family, and by the 1930s, his power had become as great as or possibly greater than that of any political boss in the country.

The Pendergast family was interested in expanding its power outside of Kansas City. To do that, Tom was looking for a loyal lieutenant to serve in the rural part of the county. He also wanted a man who would stand up and say what he thought. Truman fit the bill, so Jim and Tom Pendergast offered the job to him. Truman was not in the inner circle of the boss's lieutenants, but nonetheless accepted their offer at once, with no hesitation.[13]

This by no means implies that Truman had connections to organized crime. In Kansas at that time, any Democrat who aspired to public office had to deal with the Pendergast family. Pendergast was a powerful politician whose organization never lacked funds to get its candidates elected. If Truman wanted to serve as an elected official, he had to have contact with the Pendergast family. Even though he was affiliated with the Pendergast family, it is said that Truman refused to take bribes or do anything illegal to win votes to stay in office. But without the Pendergast backing, Truman never could have won office on the county court. In that sense, Pendergast helped Truman's career. The relationship between them was subtle, but it made Truman vulnerable to criticism once he arrived on the national political scene.[14]

With the support of the Pendergast family, Truman ran for judge of the Eastern District county court of Jackson County, Missouri, in 1922. During the campaign, Truman's army friends filled his audiences and created an enthusiasm that the candidate sometimes lacked himself. They applauded Major Harry loudly. The support from his army friends was crucial for his victory.[15] Truman won the election and served in Jackson County from 1922 until 1924. As a county court judge, he managed the county's property and finances.[16] Despite the name, it was an administrative office rather than a judicial one. Truman was a model administrator in the county. He foresaw the need for road building because of increasing numbers of automobiles and trucks, and insisted on good concrete roads.[17]

In 1924, things appeared to be going well, but Truman was not reelected to the county court judgeship. He returned to politics in 1926, being elected presiding judge of Jackson County.[18] Here he had jurisdiction over the county highway department. He oversaw the building and maintenance of county roads, bridges, and other public works. He was in charge of government money for construction projects and was credited for saving taxpayers money in the process. He established a reputation for honesty and hard work. He served two four-year terms, from January 1927 until January 1935.[19]

Truman was also president of the Missouri County Judge Association. Holding such a prominent position helped Truman in his political career. He developed relationships with 342 county judges who were influential in local Democratic Party organizations. Thus, they were well acquainted with Truman's excellent record.

At the same time, Truman attended law school at night. In October 1923, he enrolled in Kansas City Law School. He attended the program for two years, but had to quit after his sophomore year.[20]

At one point, Truman considered joining the Ku Klux Klan to gain political support, without realizing that the group was committed to preserving the power of white Protestants. When asked not to appoint any Jews or Catholics to office, he resigned on the spot. With this action he made many enemies in the Klan, and they worked hard to defeat him in later political races.[21]

In 1934, Truman became Pendergast's candidate for U.S. Senate. Throughout the campaign, Truman was on the road from morning to night, traveling to all 114 counties in the state, giving about fourteen speeches a day. He won the election, but received criticism from some voters who thought that his victory was due to Pendergast's help.[22] Truman served as a U.S. senator from 1935 until 1945.

Over the years, it was difficult for Truman to shake off the widely held notion that he was merely Pendergast's stooge. The two men appeared together at the 1936 Democratic National Convention, which only served to feed the rumors. But Truman went about his business and kept in close touch with his constituents. The country was in the middle of the Depression, and many people were out of work. Thousands of businesses went bankrupt. Throughout it all, Truman worked hard for the people and gained their respect. He was known for his honesty, fairness, and no-nonsense approach to solving problems.

Truman's run for reelection to the U.S. Senate in 1940 was a grueling contest, partly because Tom Pendergast had lost his power and was replaced by one of his antagonists, Lloyd C. Stark, the governor of Missouri since 1937.[23]

In the primary, because Pendergast's machine was in shambles, Truman was on his own. It was the toughest campaign of his career, but he succeeded in winning the office once more.

As a senator, Truman was responsible for drafting the Civil Aeronautics Act of 1938 and was co-sponsor of the Transportation Act of 1940, major enactments and remarkable achievements for a freshman senator. He also spent a lot of time investigating railroads.[24]

During his second term, Truman became one of the Senate's most important members. He was the chair of a committee to investigate all activities involving national defense, the Senate Special Committee to Investigate the National Defense Program. It became known as the Truman Commission.[25]

By this time, World War II had begun, and Truman traveled across the nation in his car, visiting factories that made weapons and other war supplies. During these travels, he found careless spending and became greatly concerned about government waste.

In 1944, the Democrats chose President Franklin D. Roosevelt to run for a fourth term, but sought a new vice presidential candidate. Many in the Democratic Party thought that the vice president at the time, Henry A. Wallace, had some radical views that might offend some voters. When Truman's name was brought up as a possible replacement candidate, many Democrats liked Truman's moderate views and thought they would appeal to most voters. They saw him as a candidate who would not divide the party and give ammunition to the Republicans. On the other hand, some Democrats were opposed to Truman because of his connections to the Pendergast machine.

Truman was happy in the Senate and feared that he could not accomplish as much in the vice president's job; thus, he was not interested in the position.[26] Nonetheless, he agreed to run with Roosevelt. The pair ran a successful campaign and won.

As vice president, Truman made no important decisions. The president met with Truman only twice and rarely asked for his advice. Truman was not consulted or informed about key issues. But by that time Roosevelt was a very sick man, and he died suddenly on April 12, 1945. Truman had been vice president for only eighty-two days when he became president. U.S. Supreme Court Chief Justice Harlan F. Stone administered the oath of office to Truman in the White House Cabinet Room. He was sixty years old.

Truman was not prepared to be president, nor did he want to be president.[27] Many Americans did not feel he was qualified to fill Roosevelt's shoes. At first, Truman felt overwhelmed. He had no experience in relations with Britain or Russia, no firsthand knowledge of Winston Churchill or Josef Stalin. He did not know the right people to help him. He had no background in foreign policy, nor any experts or experienced advisors to call upon for assistance.[28] He barely even knew Secretary of State Edward R. Stettinius Jr.

At the time, World War II was still going on. Truman worried about the number of people dying each day and promised the American public he would work for peace. Germany surrendered on May 7, 1945, a few weeks after Truman became president. The war in Europe was over, but the continent lay in ruins.

But in Asia, America was still at war with Japan. Two weeks after Germany surrendered, Truman learned of a top-secret initiative called the Manhattan Project, in which the government was making an atomic bomb.[29] Within only months of taking office, Truman had to decide whether to use nuclear weapons against Japan. This was possibly the most fateful decision made by any president in the country's history.[30] After careful consideration, Truman decided to use the atomic bomb in Japan on August 6, 1945, in Hiroshima. The city was destroyed, and 75,000 people were killed instantly. When there was still no word of surrender from the Japanese government, Truman used another bomb three days later that destroyed Nagasaki. This time, 40,000 people were killed. Japan formally surrendered on September 2, 1945, bringing an end to World War II.

In other actions, world leaders helped to form the United Nations to work for world peace. Truman led the United States in helping to create the UN, drafting its charter at the San Francisco conference in 1945. It met for the first time in London in October 1946. Truman also chose to join the North Atlantic Treaty Organization (NATO) with Canada and ten Western European nations in a defense pact so that if any country was attacked, all others would respond. Truman believed that there was no point in supporting Europe economically and then having it fall to a military attack from the Eastern European satellite nations or the Soviet Union.[31]

Truman also faced other problems in Europe. World War II ruined many countries. Truman feared the Soviet Union would try to control Greece and Turkey if the two countries did not get help from America. He announced the Truman Doctrine on March 12, 1945, a broad program to assist nations in danger of communist subversion. He asked Congress for $250 million for Greece and $150 million for Turkey, and was given $300 million for Greece and $100 million for Turkey.[32]

Additionally, Truman supported the Berlin Airlift. In 1948, Berlin faced a Soviet blockade. Soviet guards stopped all traffic and shipments into the city and cut off electricity. The people of Berlin were in desperate need of vital supplies, and turned to the West for help. Over the course of 270,000 flights, the United States and Britain carried over 2 million tons of supplies to the people of Berlin. The shipments included necessities such as dehydrated eggs and potatoes, meat, chocolate, and even Volkswagen Beetles for the police.[33]

Truman also devised the Marshall Plan, also known as the European Recovery Program, which was named after Secretary of State George C. Marshall, who had succeeded Stettinius in 1947. Economic aid would be distributed throughout Western Europe over four years to provide the foundation for the recovery of Europe's war-shattered nations. Marshall offered aid to all the countries of Europe, but the Russians would have no part of it. Between 1948 and 1952, Marshall Plan grants and credits totaled $13 billion for reconstruction projects, which put the European economy on the path to unprecedented prosperity.[34]

As president, Truman was genuinely concerned about the mistreatment of America's minority citizens and worked diligently to gain more rights for them. He was the first American president to speak before the National Association for the Advancement of Colored People (NAACP). On June 29, 1947, he spoke to the annual convention of the organization and said that "we can no longer afford the luxury of a leisurely attack upon prejudice and discrimination."[35] Truman's ambitious civil rights proposals protected black Americans in industries with federal contracts and forced reform of treatment of blacks in the military services. He called for state and federal action against lynching and the poll tax and for the end to inequality in education and employment. During Truman's presidency, progress was also made in building public housing for minorities.[36]

In 1946, multiple strikes crippled the country, forcing presidential action. Over a million workers were on strike, resulting in shortages of food, housing, and clothing. Congress passed the Taft-Hartley Act in 1947, which outlawed industry-wide strikes, closed shops, and mass picketing, and allowed the president to obtain injunctions in strikes involving interstate commerce, public utilities, and communications. The law was passed over Truman's veto. The labor troubles were embarrassing to the president, who had previously been friendly to labor. He also signed the G.I. Bill of Rights into law to help returning servicemen and -women make the difficult transition to civilian life more smoothly.

During the Truman administration the country faced the Red Scare, a time of deep public concern over alleged communist infiltration of the government. It centered on the case of Alger Hiss, a former State Department official who was accused of membership in a communist espionage ring. Hiss was later convicted of perjury. Truman established a Temporary Commission on Employee Loyalty to facilitate the removal of security risks from sensitive federal jobs. In 1951, Julius and Ethel Rosenberg were convicted of passing atomic secrets to the Soviets; they were later executed. In February 1950, Republican Senator Joseph McCarthy of Wisconsin claimed to have a list of 205 names of known communists in the State Department. He failed to produce a shred of evidence to substantiate the charge, but he continued to lash out against communists in the executive branch.[37] In the end, however, the Red Scare resulted in accusations of political wrongdoing and mistrust in the highest levels of the U.S. government, including officials at the Justice, Treasury, and State departments.

President Truman had no choice but to deal with the Korean War from 1950 to 1953. The immediate cause of the war was the invasion of South Korea by North Korean communist forces in June 1950. Truman won a UN mandate to expel the North Koreans from the southern part of the country. Truman was concerned about the Soviet Union taking control of more countries. He sent U.S. soldiers to help UN forces defend South Korea. Many Americans died, and there was great public controversy over the United States' involvement in the war.

In 1948, when Truman ran for president, many Democrats did not think he would win and encouraged Dwight Eisenhower to run. But Truman gave more than 300 speeches, often blaming Congress for America's problems. Enough voters supported Truman so that he won the election. Truman faced many difficult issues during his elected term, but one he did not anticipate was an attempt to assassinate him.

GRISELIO TORRESOLA AND OSCAR COLLAZO

Harry Truman was popular in Puerto Rico. He had done more for the country than any previous president. He favored the right of the Puerto Rican people to determine their political relationship with the United States and had said so publicly several times.[38] He named the first native Puerto Rican as governor of the island, extended Social Security to the people who lived there, and backed a liberal form of government for them. Because of his support, Congress passed laws that permitted Puerto Ricans to elect their own governor and other executive officers and create a constitution, giving the people control over their local affairs.[39]

But these actions were not enough to satisfy a small number of fanatics in Puerto Rico who wanted to become an independent nation. In the 1940s, the Nationalist Party of Puerto Rico (NPRR), which had only about 1,500 members, was increasingly angered by what they viewed as great injustices toward their country, and they wanted freedom and independence.[40] Nationalists preached violent revolution as a way to increase support for their cause, and according to an FBI report, the NPPR became especially noted for its violence. Much of the violence was directly related to the group's leaders, including Pedro Albizu Campos. For a short time during the mid-1930s, while Campos had been in prison, violence in Puerto Rico stopped.[41]

One follower of Campos was Griselio Torresola, a young man from a dedicated nationalist family in Puerto Rico. He was born in 1925 and had a happy childhood in Puerto Rico. He was a good athlete, a loyal friend, and generally a popular kid. He moved to New York in 1948. Two of his siblings had been involved in a failed insurrection in the Puerto Rican capital of San Juan only three days before the attempt on Truman's life.[42]

Another Campos follower was Oscar Collazo. He had been born in a small town called Florida in central Puerto Rico on January 20, 1914, the youngest of fourteen children. The family lived on a forty-acre farm, where his father oversaw fifty workers. Their major crop was coffee. When Oscar was five, his father sold the farm, then died. Oscar went to live with an older brother who had a small grocery store. He moved to New York in 1931 and became a metal polisher, but returned to Puerto Rico in 1932, where he got more involved with the nationalist movement. He returned periodically to New York. He was angry that Puerto Ricans were being discriminated against in New York and that the United States was ruling his native island.

Both Torresola and Collazo were living in New York, but they shared the cause of the Puerto Rican nationalists.[43] Both men had strong ties to their communities, had strong families and good childhoods, and were full of dreams. Neither man had a criminal record in the United States. They had met in New York City and became good friends. On October 28, 1950, they received the news that the Jayuya Uprising, led by Puerto Rican Nationalist Leader Blanca Canales, had failed. In this revolt against the United States, the NPPR attempted to seize the government by armed force, but the insurrection was quickly suppressed.[44] Torresola's sister had been shot and captured by government officials, and his brother Elio had been arrested. Collazo and Torresola then decided to assassinate President Truman with the intention of bringing world attention to the cause of Puerto Rican independence.[45] Collazo later said they attacked Truman because he was a symbol of the system.[46]

THE ASSASSINATION ATTEMPT

Torresola owned a German Luger and was skilled in using guns, but Collazo was not.[47] He did not own a gun, and had never even fired a pistol before. Torresola purchased a German Walther P-38 for Collazo for $35. Both guns were service automatics of the Third Reich, brilliantly designed, and though one was new and one old in design, both were highly efficient lethal weapons. They were better guns than American policemen had, firing a high-power 9 mm cartridge that had extremely powerful ballistics and steel-jacket bullets. The weapons could be loaded quickly with magazines that held seven rounds, while police revolvers had to be loaded one round at a time and held only six rounds. Between them, the would-be assassins had sixty-nine rounds of ammunition.[48]

Torresola and Collazo traveled to Washington, D.C., from New York on October 31, 1950. The clerk at their hotel later said that Collazo looked like a divinity student.[49] The following morning the men took a tour of the city because they wanted to see the Capitol. After their tour, they hailed a taxi in order to see the White House. They learned from the cab driver that Truman was not in the White House at the time, but in the Blair House because of remodeling in the presidential home. The men briefly visited the house, and decided it was vulnerable to attack. After lunch they went back to their hotel, and Torresola gave Collazo a lesson in how to use the gun.[50]

Torresola and Collazo decided to take another casual stroll by the Blair House for a last-minute check to see if anything was different from before. Nothing was out of the ordinary, and nobody was on special guard duty.[51] Capitol Police Officer Private Donald T. Birdzell was stationed at the bottom of the front steps, just under the canopy, facing the street. Two more uniformed White House guards were in two white guard booths on the sidewalk to Birdzell's left and right, about thirty yards apart. Private Joseph Davidson and Secret Service Agent Floyd Boring were in the East Booth, and Private Leslie Coffelt in the other. A fourth White House policeman, Joseph Downs, protected the basement door.

On November 1, Truman started his day with his usual 10:00 A.M. staff meeting. He then met with Delos W. Rentzel, chairman of the Civil Aeronautics Board, followed by Nelson A. Rockefeller, the head of Standard Oil and of the International Development Advisory Board.[52] He then had a disquieting meeting in which it had been "clearly established" that the forces now opposing UN troops in North Korea included 15,000–20,000 Chinese communist soldiers. Next he went to the White House Rose Garden for a ceremony to give a medal to Marine Colonel Justice Marion Chambers, who had performed heroically on Iwo Jima, and then met with W. Stuart Symington, the chairman of the National Security Resources Board.[53]

At 1:00 P.M., Truman went back to the Blair House for a quiet lunch with Bess and her mother, and then went upstairs for his usual nap.[54] He was scheduled to leave for Arlington Cemetery at 2:50 P.M. to speak at the unveiling of a statue of British Field Marshal Sir John Dill, a member of the Combined Chiefs of Staff during World War II, who had died in Washington as a result of his wartime service.[55]

The day was unseasonably warm. It was 85° Fahrenheit in the shade, the hottest November day on record for Washington, D.C.[56] Because of the heat, Truman undressed and stretched out on the four-poster bed in his underwear, the window open. Downstairs, the front door stood open to the street, the screen door latched. Except for the heat, the afternoon seemed typical. People walked by the Blair House and beneath the president's window. Streetcars and automobiles drove along the street.

At about 2:00 P.M., Torresola and Collazo approached the Blair House from opposite directions with the intent of entering the house and killing President Truman. Their plan was to meet at the steps to the Blair House, overpower the Secret Service guards, charge inside the house together, and assassinate the president.

When Collazo, who was dressed in a blue-green pinstriped suit, was about eight feet from the steps, he whipped out a handgun and began firing at Birdzell.[57] Nothing happened immediately because the pistol misfired on the first shot, but he managed to fire his weapon again just as Birdzell was turning to face him. He hit Private Birdzell in the right knee.[58] Despite the injury, Birdzell ran out into Pennsylvania Avenue to draw the fire away from the president's quarters. In Collazo's mind, this left the front door unprotected so he could enter the home and shoot the president. Unbeknownst to him, a guard with a machine gun was stationed just inside the door.[59] As Birdzell moved onto Pennsylvania Avenue, Collazo pivoted and kept firing, hitting him again. Birdzell crumpled by the streetcar tracks, about forty feet away, but turned on one knee and shot back.[60] Torresola saw Birdzell aiming at Collazo from the south side of Pennsylvania Avenue, and he shot Birdzell in the left knee. Now shot in both knees, Birdzell was no longer able to stand and should have been incapacitated, yet he kept firing at the men, his pistol braced on the pavement. Birdzell shot Collazo, who fell to the ground.

From the west sentry booth, Private Leslie Coffelt fired at the men as Collazo tried to rise.[61] Torresola, however, had reached the open door of Coffelt's guard booth, paused for a second at the window, and said something in a loud voice, apparently in an effort to divert attention from Collazo.[62] Torresola then fired four shots at Coffelt at point-blank range. Three bullets ripped into his chest and stomach. Coffelt slumped down in his chair, mortally wounded, and began slowly to bleed to death.[63] Sadly, Coffelt was not even supposed to be working that day. He had agreed to work for a friend who wanted some time off to paint his house.[64]

Collazo made a run for the front door of the Blair House, which was standing wide open. Only a screen door with a light latch was between him and the interior of the house and the president. But Secret Service Agent Floyd Boring and White House Police Officer Joseph Davidson, guards in the east booth, were on the alert. Boring and Davidson opened fire on Collazo with their service revolvers. Collazo returned fire, but soon found himself outgunned. The wounded Birdzell managed to draw his weapon and join the shootout from the street. Collazo was struck by two .38-caliber rounds in the ear and right arm. With another shot, Boring hit Collazo in the chest, and Collazo fell face down on the sidewalk, his legs spread out beside the front step, his hat still on.

Figure 7.1.   President Harry S Truman and his wife Bess (center) at the funeral of Private Leslie Coffelt, a White House policeman who was killed on November 1, 1950, protecting the president in the assassination attempt on his life at the Blair House. (Courtesy of the Harry S. Truman Library & Museum.)

Birdzell had thus prevented Collazo from turning his attention directly toward other guards.[65]

Torresola then noticed officer Joseph Downs, who had run toward the basement door of the Blair House upon hearing shots fired. Torresola was able to shoot Downs in the hip, the back, and the neck before returning fire. Downs was able to reach the basement door and get inside, closing the door behind him. This prevented Torresola from entering Blair House and assassinating Truman.

Torresola realized he was out of ammunition. He stood to the left of the steps to the Blair House and reloaded his weapon. At the same time, despite his mortal wounds, Private Coffelt got hold of his own pistol, staggered out of his guard booth, leaned against it, and aimed his revolver at Torresola, approximately thirty feet away. Coffelt managed to fire one more shot, hitting Torresola two inches above the ear on a slight upward angle and blowing out a portion of his brain. Torresola was killed instantly.[66] Officer Coffelt succumbed to his wounds in a hospital four hours later.

The gunfight involving Torresola lasted approximately twenty seconds, while the gunfight with Collazo lasted approximately thirty-eight and a half seconds.[67] In that time, twenty-seven shots were fired. One of the assassins and a guard were killed, and the other assassin and two guards wounded. Neither assassin came close to getting inside the Blair House. And even if they had, it would have made no difference, as Agent Stewart Stout had rushed to the gun cabinet in the usher's office and stood waiting at the front door with a Thompson submachine gun.[68]

Inside the Blair House, the Trumans were in the front bedrooms, resting and preparing to attend the dedication of the statue of Field Marshall Dill. Truman had awakened to the sound of gunfire and had approached the bedroom window to look outside. He could probably see Birdzell, laying on Pennsylvania Avenue, and Torresola reloading his pistol, only thirty-one feet from the window. It also means that Torresola could see the president, who would have been in Torresola's range, and he may have been able to shoot the president.[69] It is unknown whether either man saw the other. A Secret Service agent looked up, saw him, and shouted, "Get back! Get back!" ordering Truman away from the window.[70]

Upon seeing the commotion, Bess gasped, "Harry, someone's shooting our policemen." Truman quickly dressed and came downstairs. He remained perfectly calm, and within fifteen minutes was on his way out the back door with multiple Secret Service men following him. He went about his day's activities as if nothing happened, departing on schedule for the dedication of Field Marshal Dill's statue.[71] As mentioned, he later said, "A President has to expect these things."[72]

At Arlington, the several hundred people gathered for the ceremonies saw Truman step from the car. No one knew what had happened until ten minutes later, when a motorcycle messenger arrived to pick up a photographer's film and word about the events began to spread.[73] Immediately, a rumor went around the city that the president had been murdered. Those who attended the ceremony in Arlington knew that Truman was fine.

THE AFTERMATH

Birdzell lay motionless in the street, blood flowing onto the pavement from both legs. Private Coffelt was sprawled on his back beside his sentry box. Downs, who had been dragged to a basement room, was asking for a priest. Torresola was dead, lying in a heap beneath a shrub. Collazo was still alive. Officers Birdzell and Downs eventually recovered from their wounds and returned to their jobs.[74]

Coffelt died of his wounds in the hospital. When Truman heard that Private Coffelt died, he became extremely upset. He said that the guard who had been killed never had a fair chance.[75]

In 1951, Coffelt's widow, Cressie, was asked by the president and the secretary of state to go to Puerto Rico, where she received condolences and expressions of sorrow from various Puerto Rican leaders and crowds. She was awarded a gold medal from the Puerto Rican police and $4,816.59 collected by schoolchildren.[76] Mrs. Coffelt responded with a speech absolving the island's people of blame for the acts of Collazo and Torresola. A plaque at the Blair House commemorates Coffelt's sacrifice, heroism, and fidelity to his duty and his country. The day room for the U.S. Secret Service's Uniformed Division at the Blair House is named for Coffelt as well.

Even though Truman said, "A President has to expect these things," changes were made in the president's security. When he went for a walk the next morning, he looked casual, but there were at least a dozen more Secret Service men in addition to the four immediately beside him. Some officers walked well ahead of him and across the street. Others were more heavily armed, following in a slow-moving automobile.[77] The president could no longer walk from the Blair House to the White House. The presidential limousine was armored and supplied with running boards where agents could ride. Public access was limited at the Blair House for the remainder of the time the Trumans lived there. Police guards at the Blair House were doubled.[78]

Truman publicly insisted that he had never been in danger. The only thing one need worry about, he said, was bad luck—and that was something he never had. But he said the bloodbath was unnecessary. The gunmen had been fools. Truman's plan to attend the ceremony at Arlington had been in the morning paper. The assassins had only to have waited another twenty minutes, until he came out of the Blair House, to have a clear shot at him.[79]

The surviving attacker, Oscar Collazo, was convicted of four counts, including the murder of Coffelt, by a jury of ten women and two men. He was sentenced to die in the electric chair. As a goodwill gesture to the people of Puerto Rico, Truman commuted the sentence to life imprisonment in 1952.

He explained his choice by saying that Puerto Rico had no death penalty.[80] Collazo served twenty-nine years in prison, most at the federal penitentiary in Leavenworth, Kansas, where he was a model inmate, mastering different languages, reading voluminously, corresponding with family members and friends, and helping other inmates. Throughout his term in prison, Collazo never renounced his nationalist beliefs. In 1950, he said the order to execute Truman was given by the leader of the Nationalist Party. There were to be four men involved, but only he and Torresola showed up.[81]

In 1979, Collazo was pardoned by President Jimmy Carter and released from prison.[82] After the pardon, he returned to Puerto Rico, where he was greeted as a hero by the small band of nationalists still left. He died in 1994. His wife, Rosa, had also been arrested by the FBI on suspicion of having conspired with her husband in the attempt, and spent eight months in federal prison. Upon her release from prison, Rosa continued to work with the Nationalist Party.

In 1952, Truman decided not to run for reelection and Dwight Eisenhower was elected president. Truman retired to Independence, Missouri, where he wrote a book about his life called *Mr. Citizen*. He also wrote his memoirs. The first volume was called *Year of Decisions* (1955), then *Years of Trial and Hope* (1956). He also wrote a book entitled *Truman Speaks* (1960). He traveled to Europe and received an honorary degree from Oxford University.

Some note that the most remarkable thing about this assassination attempt was how quickly the events surrounding it were forgotten. Most people today do not remember it or know about it. The attack on Truman was the first assault on a president in his Washington residence, but the assassins did not even penetrate the outermost defenses. In an office building nearby, a Secret Service man with a clear view of the Blair House was watching the events. He was assigned to shoot any attacker who made it to the front door of the house. Even if the would-be assassins had gotten past the front door, they would have been confronted by another security agent who was positioned just inside the entrance with a submachine gun. There was also an agent on the stairway, one in front of Truman's door, and undisclosed others in surrounding rooms. It was estimated that the assassins would have had to shoot their way past at least twenty agents before reaching the president.[83]

There were other attempts, or rumors of attempts, on Truman's life. In one of the most serious, the mayor of a large city reported that his police had received a tip that someone would try to kill Truman with a high-powered rifle as he crossed the field at the Army-Navy football game. It was customary for the president to sit on the Army side of the field during one half and on the Navy side of the field during the other half. Truman insisted that he was going to walk across the field, so the Secret Service doubled their usual precautions. Men were stationed at every conceivable point in the stadium where a rifleman might position himself. Truman strode across the field, smiling and waving to the crowd, completely unbothered by the incident.[84]

An earlier incident had occurred in the summer of 1947, when the so-called Stern gang of Palestine terrorists tried to assassinate Truman through the mail.

Numerous cream-colored envelopes, about eight by six inches, arrived via the mail at the White House. Each one was addressed to the president and other staff members. Inside each of them was a smaller envelope with the words "Private and Confidential." Inside that second envelope was powdered gelignite, a pencil battery, and a detonator that was rigged to explode when the envelope was opened. The White House mail room personnel were alerted to the possibility that such letters might arrive, since at least eight similar letters had been sent to British government officials. When the British police exploded one of the envelopes, they concluded that it could have easily killed or maimed the person who opened it. When similar letters appeared at the White House, mail room personnel turned the letters over to the Secret Service, and they were defused by their bomb experts.[85]

CONCLUSION

During his presidency, Truman changed the direction of American policy to one of involvement and participation, with the Truman Doctrine, the Marshall Plan, the formation of NATO, and the decision to commit U.S. armed forces to fight in the Korean War. With these actions, the government altered its policies toward Europe. When he left the presidency, he marked a place for the United States in international affairs in ways that would shape the destiny of humankind for decades to come.

As president, Truman had some of the highest and lowest public approval ratings of any president, and was described as being folksy and unassuming. Over time, however, President Truman has been consistently ranked by scholars as one of the greatest U.S. presidents. The president died on December 26, 1972, in Kansas City, Missouri, at the age of eighty-eight. The official cause of death was "organic failures causing a collapse of the cardiovascular system."[86]

The protection of the president by the U.S. Secret Service was greatly enhanced, especially in the immediate aftermath of the assassination attempt while President Truman lived in Blair House. It was not, however, until after the Kennedy assassination (see chapter 8) that the methods of protecting the president would dramatically change.

—— 8 ——

John F. Kennedy

INTRODUCTION

On Friday, November 22, 1963, the attractive forty-six-year-old president, John F. Kennedy, was on a political trip to Texas to reach out to the people of that state. His beautiful and elegant wife Jackie was traveling with him, something she rarely did. She was so popular with voters that Kennedy wanted her to be there as a way to increase his appeal with the citizens of Texas. The couple arrived at Dallas's Love Field from Fort Worth at 11:38 A.M. and proceeded to a motorcade that would give thousands of Dallas residents a view of the president and first lady.

On the sixth floor of a warehouse that overlooked the motorcade's route, a young ex-marine with communist leanings and a checkered past built a sniper's nest out of cartons of books. No American president had been assassinated since Leon Czolgosz had shot and killed William McKinley more than sixty years earlier. Now Lee Harvey Oswald was about to place in his rifle's crosshairs a popular president who had already made history dealing with the Soviet Union, Cuba, civil rights, and other issues. The story of this assassination is arguably the dominant American story of the twentieth century.

JOHN FITZGERALD KENNEDY

The thirty-fifth president of the United States, John F. Kennedy, was born on May 29, 1917, in Brookline, Massachusetts, the second of nine children.[1] His father was Joseph P. Kennedy, a wealthy Irish Catholic businessman from Boston, and his mother was Rose Fitzgerald, whose father was John F. "Honey Fitz" Fitzgerald, the mayor of Boston.

Because his father was appointed by President Franklin Roosevelt to serve as an ambassador to the Court of St. James in London, Kennedy spent much time in Europe as a young man. He graduated from Harvard University and studied briefly at Stanford Business School. He greatly admired his older brother, Joe, whom his father predicted would one day become president. But Joe was killed during World War II on a bombing mission. John Kennedy also served in the war, from 1941 to 1945.[2] In the Navy, he was nearly killed when a Japanese destroyer rammed into his gunboat, the PT-109, in the Pacific Ocean. But he survived the crash and won a medal for saving his crew.[3] Kennedy rose to the rank of lieutenant and was awarded a Purple Heart and the Navy and Marine Corps Medal.

After the war, Jack worked briefly as a journalist, but quickly began a career in politics. At the age of twenty-nine, he made his first run for Congress and was elected in 1946. He was reelected in 1948 and 1950, representing the state of Massachusetts. While in the House, he served on the House Education and Labor Committee and spoke out for low-cost public housing. He supported the Truman Doctrine and the Marshall Plan.[4]

In 1952, he ran for the Senate, and served as a U.S. senator from 1953 to 1961. There he served on the Government Operations Committee, Labor and Public Welfare Committee, Foreign Relations Committee, and Joint Economic Committee.[5] During this time, Kennedy published a book called *Profiles in Courage*, alleged to be largely ghostwritten, which won a Pulitzer Prize for biography in 1957.[6]

On September 12, 1953, Kennedy was married to Jacqueline Lee Bouvier.[7] She would bring a touch of glamour to the White House, and was well liked by the public and foreign officials. Together they had two children, Caroline and John Jr.

Kennedy was elected again to the Senate in 1958. But in 1960, he ran for president on the Democratic ticket against the Republican candidate, Vice President Richard Nixon. Kennedy won the election by a slim margin and, at age forty-three, was the youngest man ever elected to the presidency. He proved a very popular president with the American public.

While in office, Kennedy's major foreign policy concern was the Cold War with the Soviet Union. Since Cuban leader Fidel Castro had come into office in 1959, Cuba had become increasingly friendly with the Soviet Union. The thought of having a Soviet ally so close to the Florida shore made many Americans nervous. On April 17, 1961, 1,400 Cuban exiles, trained and armed by the CIA, landed at the Bay of Pigs in Cuba to lead a revolt against Castro. But few Cubans joined them, and the promised U.S. air support never came. Castro's forces fought them for three days, at which time the surviving 1,100 soldiers surrendered.

In the end, the invasion was a disaster, and President Kennedy was forced to take the blame for a major blunder at the very beginning of his administration. In 1962, the United States paid Cuba $53 million in food and medical supplies for the release of the surviving soldiers. The invasion had been planned by the Eisenhower administration, but President Kennedy approved its execution and accepted full responsibility for its failure.[8] The invasion was a great embarrassment to Kennedy.

In October 1962, Kennedy again faced an international crisis involving Cuba and the Soviet Union. U.S. intelligence discovered that the Soviet Union was building nuclear missile bases on Cuba that were capable of hitting the eastern portion of the United States, as well as areas in Latin America. The Soviet Union argued they were only for defense purposes, but intelligence photos showed otherwise. In a televised address on October 22, Kennedy condemned the Soviet Union for lying about the nature of the bases and ordered that Cuba be quarantined. Kennedy then ordered navy ships to surround Cuba and dared the Soviets to run the blockade. Eventually, the Soviet ships turned around, and Soviet leader Nikita Khrushchev agreed to remove the missile sites in exchange for a promise from the United States that there would be no invasion of Cuba. These events, called the Cuban Missile Crisis, were the closest that the world has ever come to nuclear war.[9] Soviet warheads had never been so close to American cities.

Kennedy also had to deal with international affairs with other countries. In May 1963, government forces attacked unarmed Buddhist demonstrators in North Vietnam and conducted raids on pagodas in other cities. At this time, the number of U.S. military advisors in Vietnam increased from a few hundred to nearly 17,000, essentially bringing America into the Vietnam War.[10]

There was also a call by black Americans for increased civil rights during the Kennedy administration, and during this time the civil rights movement surged ahead. Kennedy favored equal rights for all, and he tried to appoint qualified minorities to federal jobs at high levels.[11] Kennedy also ordered troops to help integrate the University of Alabama and supported civil rights legislation in Congress. For example, he sent a civil rights bill to Congress in 1963 in which he sought to eliminate segregation in pubic facilities, give everyone with a sixth-grade education the right to vote, and end job discrimination.[12] In November 1962, President Kennedy ordered an end to discrimination in housing owned, operated, or financed by the federal government. He established the President's Committee on Equal Employment Opportunity to study the issue of discrimination in the workforce.

But many white southerners during this time still favored segregation and resented Kennedy's actions to provide civil rights. Kennedy realized it was important to move slowly in this area so the southern Democrats would not be too offended. But civil rights activists such as Martin Luther King Jr. called for more action. During the 1960 election, Kennedy said that it would take only the "stroke of a pen" to issue an executive order against racial discrimination, so African Americans overwhelmingly supported him in the election. They did, however, note that it took him twenty-two months to do that.[13]

In September 1962, Kennedy sent federal marshals to enforce a court order that admitted James Meredith, an African American, to the University of Mississippi. Governor Ross Barnett physically attempted to prevent Meredith from being admitted, and violence erupted on the campus and on the streets. Two people were killed and many others were injured. Kennedy federalized the National Guard and moved troops into the state to help stop the violence.

A culmination of factors caused Kennedy to plan a trip to Dallas, Texas, in November 1963. Kennedy's showing in Texas in the 1960 election, his support of civil rights legislation, and his Massachusetts-style liberal views all left him in a less-than-favorable position for the 1964 election, which was fast approaching. His trip to Dallas would serve, in part, to shore up his support in the Lone Star State. As President Kennedy's motorcade proceeded through Dallas, the streets were lined with people nearly the entire route.

LEE HARVEY OSWALD

Lee Harvey Oswald was a twenty-four-year-old former marine with a ninth-grade education when he shot the president. He was born in New Orleans on October 18, 1939, at the Old French Hospital. His father, Robert Edward Lee Oswald, was a life insurance agent and premium collector. He died of a heart attack at the age of forty-five, only two months before his son was born.[14] His mother, Marguerite Claverie Oswald, had married his father in 1933 and had two children from a previous marriage. They were a lower-middle-class family living in an unsafe section of the French Quarter with many bars, strip clubs, and gambling dens that were controlled by organized crime. As a single parent, Oswald's mother had to work to support her young children. She was domineering, controlling, and cold toward her children, and did not provide Lee with adequate education, leadership, or guidance. She sent her two older boys to a Catholic orphanage in Louisiana, but kept Lee at that time because he was too young to go there. He lived with his aunt, housekeepers, and babysitters.

When Lee was three, he was put into the Bethlehem Children's Home (the Evangelical Lutheran Bethlehem Orphan Asylum). The following year, when Lee was four, his mother took the kids back and moved to Dallas to be near a man she met. They married the next year. The two older boys were placed in a military academy in Mississippi, while Lee went to first grade in Fort Worth. Lee got along well with his stepfather, but his mother and stepfather had a falling out, and Lee and his mother moved back to Louisiana. When his mother reconciled with her husband, they returned to Texas. Soon his stepdad moved out and the couple was divorced in 1948.[15]

Lee moved from school to school, never staying long at any of them. He sometimes had to repeat grades, so he was older and bigger than the other students. As he got older, he often refused to go to school and got into fights with other children. He would sometimes seem to look for reasons to argue with others. He had social problems, moodiness, and declining school grades.

Lee returned to New Orleans briefly in 1950, and he stayed with his aunt Lillian Murret and her husband "Dutz" for two or three weeks.[16] It is alleged that Dutz did menial work for mob boss Carlos Marcello in New Orleans.

In 1952 the Oswalds moved to New York City, where his oldest brother, John Pic, was stationed in the military. Lee and his mother stayed there for two years. At first, they lived with Pic and his family, but one afternoon, Lee pulled a pocket knife on Pic's wife when she asked him to turn down the volume on the television. After that, Lee and his mother found their own apartment.

Lee was enrolled in junior high at the time. An IQ test showed that he was in the upper range of bright to normal intelligence.[17] But he often missed school. At one point, he was caught skipping school at the Bronx Zoo and was sent to the Youth House for Boys to be examined for emotional and physical problems. He was soon released from the facility.

In New York, Lee again failed to fit in with his classmates. He was ordered by a judge to see a psychiatrist, but instead his mother took him back to New Orleans. He tried to quit school and enroll in the U.S. Marines Corps, but they rejected him because he was underage.

Lee and his mom moved to Fort Worth in July 1956, where he enrolled in high school. He withdrew from school after only twenty-three days. But he was seventeen, and finally old enough to join the Marines. While in the Marines, he was sent to Jacksonville, Florida, and trained as a mechanic. He also went to Mississippi to learn aircraft surveillance, and then to Tennessee, where he was trained as an aviation electronics operator, learning how to maintain and repair aircraft electronics systems on the ground and while airborne.

In the Marines, Lee's marksmanship record shows that he was a sharpshooter, the middle ranking between marksman and expert. The Marines gave him a "confidential" military clearance.[18] In all, Lee served three years in the Marines, including service in Japan, where he worked on surveillance, aircraft identification, and fighter direction. While in the service, he read a lot of communist, Marxist, and socialist literature. He was discharged from the Marines on September 11, 1959, because of a hardship plea; he claimed his mother needed his financial support.

However, instead of helping his mother, Oswald, who was nineteen at the time, left the United States for the Soviet Union. It was 1959. Oswald thought the Soviets were expecting him because his tourist visa was issued so quickly. His application for the visa did not list his Marine service, but said he was a student traveler. Lee did not tell officials that he wanted to defect and become a Soviet citizen until his second day there.[19]

Although the Soviets kept Oswald under surveillance, they also recognized that he knew no secrets and could be of no help to them. They considered him to be mentally unfit.[20] At first the Soviets denied his request for citizenship and to live in their country, and it was only after officials found him in his hotel room with his wrists slashed from a suicide attempt that they relented. He spent seven days in the psychiatric ward of the hospital, then checked into the Metropole Hotel. Later that day he was contacted and told that while officials had refused to grant him citizenship, he could live in the Soviet Union as an alien resident.[21] He offered to tell Soviet officials everything he learned

Figure 8.1. The famous photo of President Kennedy's assassin, Lee Harvey Oswald, with his Russian rifle prior to the assassination. The Warren Commission later determined the rifle in the photo was the one that killed Kennedy. (Courtesy of the Library of Congress.)[22]

while he had been a radar operator during his three-year enlistment in the Marines. Lee gave interviews to correspondents for major wire services and several other reporters in which he described his love of communism.

Lee tried to renounce his American citizenship by turning in his passport to the U.S. Embassy in Moscow, but the embassy advised him to hold onto it until he had some assurance of Soviet citizenship. He never forfeited his passport or completed the necessary paperwork to do so.[22]

In January 1960, Soviet officials told him that he could live in Minsk, 450 miles southwest of Moscow. He got a job as a metal worker in a local radio and television factory and was assigned a one-room apartment. He lived reasonably well.[23] But he did not want to work in a factory and quickly grew bored in the Soviet Union. He met a young girl and asked her to marry him, but she turned him down. He decided to return to the United States, but then he met a nineteen-year-old pharmacology student named Marina Prusakova. She agreed to marry him only one month after they met. She was living with her uncle, who allegedly had links to the Soviet Ministry of Internal Affairs, an organization that controlled the Soviet secret police, and thus had links to espionage groups. Lee and Marina had a baby daughter in February 1962. On June 1, 1962, they left the Soviet Union and went to live with Oswald's brother in Fort Worth, Texas. Oswald had a series of low-paying menial jobs and allegedly abused his wife.[24]

After a time in Fort Worth, they moved to Dallas, where Lee found a job at a graphic arts company as a photographic trainee. Lee was fired from that job in April 1963 because of incompetence.[25] On January 27, 1963, Lee ordered a Smith and Wesson .38-caliber "Victory" model revolver (Commando model number 1905). In March, he ordered a 6.5-caliber Mannlicher-Carcano Italian carbine with a scope. Both weapons were sent to a post office box that was owned by A. Hidell, not Lee Harvey Oswald.

Oswald used the rifle to try to kill General Edwin Walker as he was sitting behind his desk in his dining room on April 10, 1963. Walker was a former U.S. Army officer who had resigned from the military because of his ultra-right-wing political beliefs. Oswald took a shot from near Walker's backyard fence, leaning against the general's station wagon to brace himself. From there, he was less than 100 feet away from the window, which had no covering to block his view into the brightly lit room.[26] The bullet hit Walker's hair but did not go into his head. It turns out that Oswald had planned to kill him for two months. Later that night when he returned home, he told Marina that he had shot at General Walker but was unsure if he had killed him.

Not long after the murder attempt on General Walker, Oswald went back to New Orleans to try to find work and to get away from the police. He stayed with his Aunt Lillian and Uncle Dutz Murret for a short time. They were not even aware that he had returned from the Soviet Union and that he was married with a baby. Soon he was able to rent an apartment, and Marina and the baby joined him. He found a job at the Reily Coffee Company, even though his application was full of lies. He made up references, said he had just left the Marines, and claimed that he was at the time attending college.

In New Orleans, Oswald also joined the Fair Play for Cuba Committee (FPCC), becoming his chapter's only member. In that job, he defended pro-Castro activities and distributed FPCC leaflets on the streets of New Orleans.[27] In August 1963, he told a group of anticommunist Cuban exiles that he opposed the Castro regime. One day, the exiles saw him handing out pro-Castro handbills and started a fight. Oswald was fined $10 for disturbing the peace. At that point, his discharge from the Marines was changed to dishonorable because it was discovered he obtained it under false pretenses.[28]

Oswald was fired from his job at the Reily Coffee Company, so he decided to move to Cuba. To get there, he went first to Mexico, traveling by bus.[29] He visited the Cuban Embassy, but Cuban officials refused to give him permission to enter Cuba. He also visited the Russian Embassy. After being denied entry into Cuba, he returned to Dallas on October 2. Oswald asked his wife to help him hijack a plane to Cuba. When Marina said no, Oswald proceeded to increase his muscle strength by doing knee bends and arm exercises and tearing through their apartment at night in his undershorts to practice leaps. He brought home airline schedules and a large map of the world. He planned to sit in the front row and at some point walk into the pilot's cabin with a gun and order the pilot to turn the plane around.[30]

Then in October 1963, he got a job at the Texas School Book Depository. In that company, he was a clerk who filled book orders, making $1.25 an hour. He pulled books out of boxes to match order forms. The sixth floor was being refloored, so boxes were stacked in the southeast corner, close to the windows that overlooked Dealey Plaza.

Oswald said he liked the Kennedy family, but at the same time he attributed the president's success to his family's wealth. He saw that Kennedy received many breaks that someone like Oswald never got. The Kennedys had almost everything, and Oswald nothing.[31]

A month before he shot Kennedy, Oswald became a father for the second time. They had another daughter. But this did not stop him from carrying out the assassination of President Kennedy.

THE ASSASSINATION

November 21, 1963, was the first day of a political trip to Texas for the Kennedys. They would visit San Antonio and Houston, then fly to Fort Worth to spend the night, and then travel to Dallas on November 22.

Kennedy was considering the upcoming 1964 election, and he knew that his reelection was not secure. He had lost a substantial amount of support in the southern states because of the civil rights bill and would need to make up these electoral votes. It was thought that a "nonpolitical" tour of western states would help mend some fences. There was a particular need to repair political fences in Texas, which was a critical state to Kennedy's reelection.[32] No Democrat had ever won a presidential election without winning Texas. Kennedy had also decided to come to Texas to reconcile differences between opposing factions of the Democratic Party in the state. He knew that there was a chance that a motorcade with his popular wife might sway a few voters without him even saying a word. However, Dallas was considered to be a Republican and conservative city, so many in the Kennedy team did not look forward to the trip.[33]

The president and first lady were greeted by huge, cheering crowds at San Antonio, Houston, and Fort Worth. President Kennedy gave a speech in Fort Worth. Then on November 22, the president and his party flew into Dallas's

Love Field at 11:38 A.M. As mentioned, Jackie Kennedy had never previously accompanied her husband on a political trip. He wore a blue-gray suit and blue tie; she had on a pink suit, pillbox hat, and white gloves. They spoke for about ten minutes with an enthusiastic group of supporters lining the fence, but they were on a tight schedule.

Kennedy was fully aware of the potential danger of the trip to Texas. In October, UN Ambassador Adlai Stevenson, who had been hit with a sign in Dallas, warned Kennedy that he might not be safe in Texas. On November 21, 1963, someone distributed 5,000 fliers on city streets in Dallas that featured the president's picture and read, "Wanted for Treason."[34] Twenty thousand windows overlooked the motorcade route, far too many for the Secret Service to watch.[35] That morning, the newspapers published the route of the motorcade, so the president's scheduled whereabouts became public knowledge.

A specially built presidential Lincoln Continental convertible had been flown to Texas from Washington. Kennedy got into the midnight-blue open car at the head of the motorcade. He sat in the rear seat on the right-hand side, with Mrs. Kennedy to his left. In the "jump" seat directly in front of Kennedy sat Governor John Connally, with Mrs. Connally at his left in another jump seat. A Secret Service agent was driving, and two others ran alongside. Motorcycles preceded the car, and on each side of the car and slightly behind it rode two more motorcycle police. There were supposed to be Secret Service agents on each side of the car, but they were ordered not to pull up with the limo to avoid blocking the public's view of the president. Behind the limo, another car carried more Secret Service agents, presidential aides, and Vice President Lyndon Johnson and U.S. Senator Ralph Yarborough.

A protective bubble top for the car was available to provide protection from rain. (Though it was not bulletproof, it might have slightly deflected the paths of the bullets that would soon be fired.) But the temperature was in the seventies that day, and Kennedy wanted face-to-face contact with the people, so he decided against using it. The car also had bulletproof side windows, but they were down for the trip through Dallas.[36] The possibility of an assassination attempt had been studied, but was thought to be a remote one—despite the fact that in downtown Dallas, quite often one out of every five local citizens carried a gun.[37]

The open limousine rode through the city, going only ten or eleven miles an hour. The destination was the Dallas Trade Mart, where Kennedy was to speak before 2,500 people.[38] First, the motorcade progressed through residential suburbs and light industrial zones, where only a few people lined the sidewalks. As the motorcade made its way through the streets of Dallas, the reception from the crowds along the streets was enthusiastic. Mrs. Connally looked over her shoulder toward the president, smiled, and said, "Mr. Kennedy, you can't say that Dallas doesn't love you." He responded by saying, "No, you certainly can't."[39]

In the final part of the route, the motorcade would come down Main Street and, when it reached Dealey Plaza, turn right for one block to Elm, facing the Texas School Book Depository at the top of the hill. The cars would make a left turn on Elm, pass directly in front of the depository, and go downhill. Once at the underpass, the automobile would speed up, make a right turn onto Stemmons, and head for the Trade Mart, less than three miles away.

That morning, Oswald carried a large package to work at the Texas School Book Depository building. He said the package contained curtain rods.[40] The seven-story brick building had recently been converted to a warehouse, and though it was set back from the street, the corner of the building had an unobstructed view of the motorcade route. Other employees saw Oswald go to the sixth floor right around lunchtime. At the time, the sixth floor was used for storage.[41]

At about 12:30 P.M., as the motorcade entered Dealey Plaza, shots were fired at Kennedy from the Texas School Book Depository building.[42] Some thought it was a firecracker, and others thought it was a backfire. The first shot missed Kennedy and hit the curb. One Secret Service agent thought the president said, "My God I am hit."[43] The second rifle shot ripped through the president's back and out his throat. In response, the president threw up his arms to his throat. Mrs. Kennedy saw her husband react to the shot and screamed, "What are they doing to you?"[44]

The Secret Service agent who was driving the car did not know what was going on. Because of the confusion he slowed down instead of accelerating, almost stopping the car so he could look back at the president. As he turned around, another

Figure 8.2.   As the motorcade made its way through the streets of Dallas, President and Mrs. Kennedy were seated in the backseat of the convertible. Governor and Mrs. Connally were directly in front of them in the vehicle's jump seat. (Courtesy of the Library of Congress.)

shot rang out. This bullet hit the president's skull. The right side of the back of his head was gone, and his brains spewed out. Jackie crawled out the back of the car, onto its trunk, but a Secret Service agent pushed her back into the seat.[45]

To most people it appeared that the shooter had fired a high-powered rifle from the southeast corner of the sixth floor of the School Book Depository building just off the motorcade route. Some people reported seeing someone in the window before the assassination.[46] Most of the depository employees had been outside watching the motorcade. Only a few remained inside, watching out the windows of the building. Three young employees of the depository who had been watching the motorcade from the fifth floor reported that the gunshots came from over their heads. They said they could even hear the clicking of a rifle bolt and the sound of spent cartridges hitting the floor.[47]

Other witnesses, however, reported hearing shots from other directions. Just to the west of the depository was a portion of Dealey Plaza that later became known as the grassy knoll. To the north is a slight hill. Some reported the shots came not from the depository, but from this area.

The president was rushed to Parkland Hospital in Dallas. When they got to the hospital, Jackie cradled his head in her lap. Blood and brain tissue were scattered over the seats. Jackie refused to let anyone take her husband out of the car because she did not want people to see the president's devastating wound. When a Secret Service agent took off his jacket to cover the president's head, Jackie allowed doctors to take her husband.[48] She entered the emergency room and handed the doctor part of Kennedy's brain.[49]

He was rushed into a trauma room on the ground floor of the hospital, where physicians found lingering vital signs. Eleven doctors worked on the president.[50] Even though he was virtually dead when the second bullet entered his skull, doctors still tried to save his life. They performed an emergency tracheotomy and administered blood transfusions and oxygen, but the president's heart had stopped. Even cardiac massage failed to revive him.[51] In performing the procedures, the doctors destroyed crucial evidence as to the nature of his wounds, but it was the appropriate medical procedure.

Vice President Johnson was taken into a small room in the emergency area, where he could be protected. Governor Connally was also injured. He was unconscious in the middle seat, still lying across his wife.[52] His shirt and jacket were heavily stained with blood. Connally was wounded in the chest, ribs, and arm.[53] His condition was serious but not critical.

Kennedy died about a half hour later, at around 1;00 P.M. A Roman Catholic, he was given last rites by two priests, and his body was laid in a coffin.[54] He died without ever regaining consciousness. Kennedy's body was then transferred to Andrews Air Force Base and would lie in state in a closed, flag-draped coffin in the East Room of the White House. It was then transferred to the Capitol Rotunda, where an estimated 250,000 mourners filed by, including former presidents Harry Truman and Dwight Eisenhower. There was a funeral mass on November 25 at St. Matthew's Roman Catholic Cathedral in Washington, D.C.

World leaders and royalty came to Washington for the funeral or sent condolences, including the leaders of England, France, Germany, Austria, Brussels, Rome, Lisbon (Portugal), Norway, Spain, Denmark, Finland, Sweden, Switzerland, Greece, Turkey, Canada, Peru, Buenos Aires, Venezuela, Rio de Janeiro, Chile, Mexico, Colombia, Soviet Union, Yugoslavia, and Hungary.[55]

Kennedy's body was taken by horse-drawn caisson from the Capitol and buried at Arlington National Cemetery. Later, an eternal flame was lit beside President Kennedy; it burns to this day.

THE AFTERMATH

That afternoon, only ninety-nine minutes after the assassination, U.S. District Court Judge Sarah T. Hughes administered the oath of office to Vice President Lyndon Johnson aboard Air Force One as it stood on the runway at Love Field. The coffin containing the body of the slain president was on board, located at the rear of the plane. Mrs. Kennedy stood next to Johnson as he took the oath. She refused to change her clothes and still wore the blood-stained pink suit. She said, "Let them see what they did to him."[56] Johnson chose to return to Washington that night. No one knew whether other high-level officials would be targeted. One of Johnson's first official actions was to declare November 23 a national day of mourning.

After the shooting, Oswald concealed his rifle among some crates on the sixth floor and casually departed the building. He went home, picked up a pistol, and went out again. When the book depository was searched, they came across a sniper's nest surrounded by a wall of cartons. Hidden nearby was a bolt-action rifle, an Italian-made Mannlicher-Carcano. On the floor were three spent brass rifle shells. Inside the Mannlicher-Carcano's chamber was a fourth, unfired bullet. Also found in the sniper's nest was an odd-sized paper bag, long enough to hold a rifle. When the management gathered the building's employees together, Oswald was missing. Oswald's fingerprints and palm prints matched those on the paper bag found on the sixth floor; also, he had kept the rifle wrapped in an old green and brown blanket at home, and police later discovered that fibers on the bag matched those on the blanket.[57]

A citywide manhunt for the assassin began immediately. Officer J. D. Tippit heard the description of the suspect on the radio. At 1:15 P.M., he saw Oswald hurrying along East Tenth Street. He motioned for Oswald to stop and got out of his car to question him. Oswald drew a Smith and Wesson .38-caliber revolver and fired several shots at the officer. Four shots hit Tippit. One hit him in the forehead, and one went straight through the heart. He was dead when he hit the ground.[58] Tippit did not call in on his radio that he had stopped someone, nor did he draw his gun upon exiting the car. This indicated that he was merely suspicious, not positive that he had found the suspect.

About a half hour later (two hours after the shooting), a clerk at a shoe store saw Oswald on West Jefferson Boulevard. He acted suspiciously, sneaking into the Texas Theater, three miles from the depository.[59] There were only a few people in the small theater, and he was in the third row from the back. As police surrounded him, he pulled out a revolver, and according to different accounts shouted, "This is it," or "Well, it is all over now."[60] There was a scuffle with a second policeman, M. N. McDonald. Oswald punched McDonald in the face. McDonald lurched forward just as other police rushed to subdue the gunman. The gun's hammer clicked as the man pulled the trigger, but it did not fire. A crowd had gathered. They shouted, "Let me have him," and, "We'll kill him."[61] Police grabbed the weapon and took Oswald into custody.

He was handcuffed, rushed to downtown police headquarters, and put in a fifth-floor cell, where he was interrogated for twelve hours. The officers did not take notes and no tape recordings were made of the interview, because under Texas law, a defendant's spoken statements could not be used against him in court.[62] Oswald admitted nothing and maintained that he did not shoot anyone, including Kennedy and Officer Tippit, although several witnesses identified him as the killer and his palm print was found on the weapon that was used to kill Kennedy.

At 6:35 P.M., Oswald was taken down to the third-floor homicide bureau.[63] At that time, he was under arrest only for killing Officer Tippit. He did not look surprised. He said he hadn't done anything to be ashamed of, and denied shooting the president. He denied owning a rifle, but police discovered he had ordered the gun under a fictitious name. They even found pictures of Oswald holding the gun.[64] Oswald requested an attorney, but not a local one. Instead he demanded John Abt, a New Yorker well known for defending prominent members of the Communist Party. The police wanted to know if Oswald was part of a larger conspiracy, particularly in view of his pro-communist background.

Later that afternoon, police visited the home of Oswald's estranged wife. She showed them the weapons he had. As mentioned, he had kept the Mannlicher-Carcano rifle wrapped in an old green and brown blanket, but now the blanket was empty.[65]

At the time of Kennedy's death, there was no federal statute covering the assassination of the president. In the eyes of the law, such an act was no different from any other murder unless it was committed on federal property. This meant that Oswald would be tried under the Texas statute for murder. The charge related to the Kennedy killing was made on November 23 at 1:30 A.M.[66]

Two days after his arrest (November 24), at 11:20 A.M., Oswald was transferred under custody to the county jail. Several hundred people had gathered in front of the jail to watch the transfer. Oswald was taken by elevator from the third floor to the basement of the police department. He stepped into the corridor to go past a horde of newspaper, television, and radio reporters, and was to walk down a ramp into a waiting armored truck.

As Oswald walked down the ramp, Jack Ruby, a small-time hustler and strip-club operator from Dallas, lunged from the group of newsmen and said, "You killed my president, you rat!"[67] Ruby shot Oswald one time in the stomach at point-blank range. The bullet perforated the chest cavity and went through the diaphragm, spleen, and stomach. It cut off the main intestinal artery and the aorta, and broke up the right kidney. The wound was fatal. As Ruby tried to fire a second shot, the officer backing up the car to pick up Oswald hit Ruby in the leg and knocked him off balance. Millions of shocked viewers watched it live on television. The police wrestled him to the ground and his gun was taken from him. He said, "I am Jack Ruby. You all know me."[68]

Oswald fell to the ground, clutching his side. He quickly lost consciousness and was taken to Parkland Hospital. He died in surgery at 1:07 P.M., less than two hours after the shooting.[69]

Jack Ruby, whose real name was Jacob Rubenstein, was a heavyset middle-aged man who wore a dark brown suit and snap-brim, gray felt hat. He was born in Chicago around 1911 to a very poor family. He never finished school and spent some time in foster care. He joined the Air Force and was honorably discharged in 1946. He moved to Dallas fifteen years before the assassination in order to help his sister run the Singapore Supper Club. He allegedly worked for organized crime in Chicago, managing clubs controlled by them. He also got along well with many Dallas police officers.[70] Ruby had a police record listing six minor offenses including carrying a concealed weapon. Ruby was also a paid FBI informer in 1959.[71] Some described Ruby as emotionally unstable and prone to violence. He was also heavily in debt and on the verge of financial ruin. To kill Oswald, he used a Colt .38-caliber snub-nose revolver.

Ruby said he had done everyone a favor by killing Oswald. He said that since the police could not kill Oswald, he did it for them.[72] He also said that he did not want Jackie Kennedy to have to go through the murder trial. He thought he would be seen as a national hero and set free. Ruby also said he admired President Kennedy and his family, and was distraught over the assassination. Some reported that he wept openly at the thought of Jackie Kennedy grieving with her two small children.[73]

Ruby explained that he was walking down Main Street, toward the police station, when he saw a crowd gathering around the entrance ramp to the police garage and decided to see what was going on. Ruby said that he just strolled down the ramp without anyone stopping him. When Oswald was being escorted out, Ruby was instantly infuriated by the "smirk" on his face. According to the quick-tempered Ruby, that was all it took for him to whip out his revolver and pump a bullet into Oswald's gut.

Ruby was tried for murder in the first degree. He was convicted and sentenced to the electric chair. Two years later, the Texas Court of Appeals reversed the decision, but before he could be retried, Ruby died in prison. At first, he was diagnosed with pneumonia, but the doctors realized he had cancer in his liver, brain, and lungs. He officially died of a blood clot on January 3, 1967, three years after he shot Oswald.[74]

Because there were so many questions surrounding the assassination, President Johnson appointed a bipartisan group of highly respected government officials, led by U.S. Supreme Court Chief Justice Earl Warren, to investigate the assassination. The members included two Republicans, two Democrats, and two other men who had distinguished records of public service. The purpose of the commission was to investigate the evidence and report the commission's findings and conclusions to the president and the country. The group conducted a thorough investigation that involved hearing witnesses and hiring experts to explore every facet of the events in Dallas. Gerald Ford, a member of the commission, later said, "Never has a crime been so thoroughly investigated."[75]

Ten months later, in September 1964, the Warren Commission issued an 888-page report in which they concluded that Oswald acted alone in shooting Kennedy. Further, the commission found no evidence that either Lee Harvey Oswald or Jack Ruby was part of any conspiracy to assassinate the president. Specifically, the report indicated that Lee Harvey Oswald acted alone to kill President Kennedy and Officer Tippit, and that Jack Ruby, acting alone, killed Lee Harvey Oswald. They reported that there was no credible evidence of a conspiracy. All of the shots in the Kennedy assassination came from a sixth-floor window of the Texas School Book Depository building, where a rifle owned by Oswald was discovered. Finally, the report indicated that only three shots were fired at the motorcade, one of which passed through Kennedy's neck and then probably through the chest and wrist of Governor Connally. Another shot hit Kennedy's head, while the third shot missed.[76]

The commission's conclusion that a single bullet had wounded both Kennedy and Connally was controversial. Sometimes referred to as the "magic bullet theory," it held that a single bullet penetrated Kennedy's neck, transited the muscle layers, and exited at his throat. It then entered Connally's back, shattered his fifth rib, and exited below the right nipple. From there it entered Connally's right wrist, exiting at the palm and finally lodging in his left thigh. The bullet finally fell out and was found on Connally's stretcher at Parkland Hospital.[77]

The magic bullet theory and the Warren Report were both criticized. The report had many flaws and was said to be incomplete and inaccurate. For example, the commission did not use its own independent investigators to gather evidence but instead relied heavily on Secret Service and FBI agents for assistance. Both agencies had reason to downplay or hide material that might prove embarrassing. Thus, promising leads were never followed up and credible testimony was ignored. It also seemed clear to some that the commission had either neglected or only hastily examined the photographic record of the assassination.[78]

Further, critics complained that the information in the report was disorganized and confusing. It had no index to its exhibits. The final conclusions in the report seemed to be based on a selective examination of the evidence.[79] They blamed the report's inaccuracies on pressure put on the commission by President Johnson, who wanted the report issued before the 1964 presidential election.

Even today, many Americans remain suspicious and believe there is much more to the assassination than what the commission reported. Numerous conspiracy theories exist concerning the involvement of organized crime, the CIA, the South Vietnamese, or even Vice President Johnson.[80] Many Americans believe that the

Soviet Union or Cuba was involved because of Oswald's pro-communist sympathies.[81] Hundreds of men and different groups have been identified as the ones who killed Kennedy or were somehow involved in the assassination, including agents of the FBI, Secret Service, and CIA. Others accused of involvement include wealthy civic leaders in Dallas, the Catholic Church, Mayor Richard Daley of Chicago, exiled czarist Russians, the U.S. Defense Intelligence Agency, Poland, Red China, East Germany, and the Republican Party of Omaha.[82]

In 1979, the House Select Committee on Assassinations reinvestigated Kennedy's death. Its intensive two-year probe relied heavily on complex acoustical analysis, technology that did not exist when the first commission met. According to the final report of the second commission, Oswald fired three shots from the book depository: two hit their targets, and one missed. This included the fatal shot to Kennedy's brain, as the Warren Report had concluded.[83] The panel also agreed that Oswald had killed Tippit.

Further, medical experts testified that the bullet that passed through Kennedy's neck also struck Governor Connally and caused all of his wounds. Neutron activation analysis tests performed on bullet fragments taken from Connally's wrist and the bullet that fell off his stretcher at the hospital supported the Warren Commission's single-bullet theory.[84]

But, unlike the report of the first commission, the analysis of a police tape recording of sounds picked up on the scene by a motorcycle patrolman's radio indicated that there was a 95 percent chance that a fourth shot had been fired from the grassy knoll in front of the presidential motorcade. Thus, the committee concluded that a conspiracy was "likely."[85]

Moreover, the committee discovered that Oswald had contacts with Carlos Marcello, crime boss of New Orleans, and concluded that organized crime figures "probably" were involved in the conspiracy to assassinate the president. So the committee concluded that although Oswald shot Kennedy, there had been a second gunman who was probably a hit man for organized crime.[86]

The FBI dismissed the second committee's findings as "invalid," and maintained its original conclusion that Oswald acted alone.[87] Another study in 1982, by the National Research Council, also disputed the committee's acoustical analysis. The committee's chief counsel, G. Robert Blakely, outlined a strong case against organized crime figures Carlos Marcello and Santo Trafficante as the possible masterminds behind the assassination. However, Blakely contends that once Oswald was arrested, organized crime hired Ruby to kill him.[88]

Exactly what happened in those seconds in Dallas has never been settled to most people's satisfaction. There are still no clear and definitive answers to critical questions. The theory of one shooter with one gun but three shots is not widely accepted today. We are no closer to a consensus about the circumstances of JFK's assassination.[89]

After Kennedy's assassination, security procedures were tightened for presidents. Motorcycle escorts were reinstated, and from then on, presidents would be flanked by Secret Service wherever they went.

Another result of Kennedy's assassination was that people became disillusioned with government. Many believe that the truth of the day's events was hidden by certain people in government. The preservation of trust between the citizens and their government leaders is vital, and if the trust erodes, democracy can crumble. The investigation of this event and the hiding of evidence served to erode the trust people had in their government officials.[90]

CONCLUSION

Almost everyone who was alive at the time of Kennedy's assassination remembers where they were when they heard the news of it. The event came to symbolize the end of hope and the beginning of a more violent time in our country. Kennedy had been successful in touching the idealism of others, especially young people. Kennedy's assassination evoked despair and rage in those who admired him,[91] apparently so much so that Jack Ruby would assassinate the assassin, thus confounding any investigation into Lee Harvey Oswald's motives.

Although each presidential assassination and attempted assassination had altered the way in which the U.S. Secret Service protected the president and his family, the assassination of President Kennedy would be the catalyst for a complete overhaul of the protective duties of the U.S. Secret Service. Much of the overhaul would be as a result of the Warren Commission's investigation into the protection of Kennedy on that day in November 1963.

—— 9 ——

Gerald R. Ford

INTRODUCTION

On September 5, 1975, President Gerald Ford was scheduled to meet with California Governor Jerry Brown in Sacramento to discuss the problem of violent crime. Seventeen days later, President Ford was in California again, this time to give a television interview at the St. Francis Hotel in San Francisco.

These trips to California would be remembered as nothing more than presidential business-as-usual were it not for the fact that in both cases, the president's life was threatened by would-be assassins. Both were women with unusual backgrounds, and both had motives related to the radical politics of the day. Fortunately for President Ford, neither was capable of completing the job they had set for themselves.

GERALD FORD

Gerald Ford was born in Omaha, Nebraska, on July 14, 1913, and was given the name Leslie Lynch King Jr. after his biological father.[1] His parents divorced and Ford moved with his mother to Michigan, where she married Gerald Rudolf Ford. He adopted her son, who was renamed Gerald R. Ford Jr.[2] As a child Ford was athletic and hardworking, becoming an Eagle Scout. He enrolled at the University of Michigan in Ann Arbor in 1931, where he majored in both economics and political science. After graduation, Ford accepted a job at Yellowstone National Park in Wyoming, and also became a model for *Look* magazine.[3] He was also offered a position as assistant football coach and freshman boxing coach at Yale University.[4]

At the same time, he applied to Yale Law School. He was turned down, but later accepted. He graduated in June 1941, passed the bar exam in Michigan, and started a law firm with a friend in Grand Rapids, Michigan.[5] When Japan attacked Pearl Harbor, Ford enlisted in the Navy Reserves at age twenty-nine.[6] He became a physical fitness instructor at a base in North Carolina, and then the athletic director on the U.S.S. *Monterey*, an aircraft carrier. A short time later, Ford requested sea duty and was assigned as a gunnery division officer on the U.S.S. *Monterey*. While there he took part in most of the major wartime operations in the South Pacific. Because of his outstanding performance, he was promoted to lieutenant commander.[7]

When Ford was discharged from the Navy in 1946, he decided to go home and return to practicing law in a nationally prestigious law firm.[8] He met and married Elizabeth (Betty) Bloomer in 1948. At the same time, Ford was running on the Republican ticket for a seat in the U.S. House of Representatives. One of the issues for the candidates was the Marshall Plan to rebuild Europe. While the Democratic candidate opposed the plan, Ford recognized that the United States needed to help restore the economies of both its allies and its former foes to promote a lasting peace. He ran on this issue and won the election, becoming a congressman from Michigan at age thirty-five.[9]

While in Congress, Ford established moderate political positions, giving equal support to both liberal and conservative issues. He served on the House Appropriations Committee and the Defense Appropriations Subcommittee, where he was ranking minority member.[10] He became known for his expertise in military affairs and fought hard for a strong national defense budget to ensure a powerful American military presence around the world. He quickly developed a reputation as an honest, fair, and decent man. He was easygoing and popular with both Republicans and Democrats.[11]

Ford soon developed a friendship with Richard M. Nixon of California, another Republican. The two men often spent time together socially, discussing local political issues and how they would deal with national policy if they had the chance to decide it.[12]

In the early 1960s, Ford became chairman of the House Republican Conference. In early 1965, he was elected minority leader, a position he held until becoming vice president. After the assassination of President John F. Kennedy, Ford was appointed to the Warren Commission to investigate the assassination.

Ford was reelected to a thirteenth term in 1972, but had decided that he would run only one more time in 1974 and then retire from politics.[13] But soon after Ford was reelected, President Nixon's vice president, Spiro T. Agnew, was forced to resign to avoid prosecution on bribery and corruption charges related to actions when he was governor of Maryland. With the vice presidency open, Nixon nominated his friend and colleague Gerald Ford to fill the vacancy. Nixon chose Ford because he was well liked by both Republicans and Democrats on Capitol Hill, and because there was not even a hint of personal or political controversy. Ford had a reputation for honesty and integrity that Nixon thought would help to restore public confidence in the federal government. Nixon knew he would easily be confirmed, and he was.[14] Ford was sworn in as vice president on December 6, 1973.

Throughout most of the Watergate affair, Ford believed that Nixon was innocent of the charges against him, and he often publicly defended Nixon against the growing attacks. As the events of Watergate and Nixon's involvement in it became clear, Ford was caught by surprise.[15] During this time, Ford's pleasant and upbeat personality contrasted sharply with Nixon's dark side, which was made worse by the growing suspicion of his involvement in Watergate.

Nixon resigned from the presidency on August 9, 1974, and Ford immediately took the oath of office. The ceremony took place in the East Room of the White House at noon. Ford never sought the position, but became the thirty-eighth president of the United States, and the first to serve without being elected as either president or vice president.

On September 8, about a month after becoming president, Ford announced that he decided to grant a full pardon to Nixon for any crimes that he might have committed while in office. He justified the pardon by saying that he strongly believed that the nation needed to be spared the spectacle of a former president standing trial. He believed that the country needed to put the events of Watergate behind it and move forward with other things that needed to be done. There was also concern about Nixon's health. The former president had a serious attack of phlebitis and was very sick. However, Ford was criticized for the pardon, with some claiming that Nixon was trying to short-circuit the judicial process. Many strongly believed that Nixon should be criminally charged and face the consequences of his actions, even if it meant time in jail. Years later, it was said that Ford's presidency never recovered from the pardon.[16]

As president, Ford faced a difficult political environment and the daunting challenge of restoring public trust in government. Ford took office without having adequate time to prepare for these and other issues. Overall, his presidency did not produce any major political policies, but his low-key moderation seemed to be just what the United States needed.

Some of the political issues Ford inherited revolved around the economy. The country was experiencing the worst inflation and highest unemployment since the Great Depression. The uncontrolled economic concerns caused extreme difficulties for businesses and workers alike. An Arab oil embargo in 1973 hiked energy prices rapidly. Within a year, gasoline prices jumped 70 percent. The Ford administration created a campaign called Whip Inflation Now (WIN), which involved a request for legislation from Congress relating to farming, energy supplies, unemployment, and increased taxes. It was a request to Americans to stop wasting money and resources, especially fuel and food.[17] Despite attempts by Ford to alleviate the problems, the recession deepened in 1974–1975 and forced him to abandon the program.[18] The recession replaced inflation as a primary concern for the White House. In response, the president proposed tax cuts and reductions in domestic spending. He also approved the creation of federal jobs for the unemployed and established a Council on Wage and Price Stability. But the nation's problems demonstrated to many that Ford was not able to confront a serious issue.

Another problem Ford faced was campaign finance. In 1974, Ford backed campaign reform laws, a reaction to the campaign finance abuses of the Nixon administration. The bill, signed by Ford in October 1974, established public funding for presidential campaigns and strict limits on individual contributions to campaigns as well as campaign expenditures. Funds for the public funding program would be derived from a $1 check-off box on federal income tax returns.[19]

In January 1975, Ford established a commission to investigate alleged abuses of power by the CIA, after disclosures implicated the agency during the investigation into the Watergate scandal. In its final report, the Rockefeller Commission confirmed that unlawful acts had been committed by the CIA, including infiltrating dissident groups, mail tampering, testing mind-altering drugs on unsuspecting citizens, and physically abusing and confining foreign defectors.[20]

Also in 1975, Ford at first refused to lend federal funds to financially strapped New York City. But by November of that year, after the city itself raised taxes and cut spending, Ford signed legislation extending $2.3 billion in short-term loans, enabling New York to avoid default.

Ford traveled to Japan, being the first U.S. president to go there. He was able to discuss many issues with Japanese officials, and left the country with a better understanding of issues that were important to leaders of both countries. He then traveled to South Korea to meet with its president and visit U.S. troops. He also met with the Soviet leader, Leonid Brezhnev, which eventually led to a symbolic joint U.S.-USSR manned space mission in 1975.

In a measure that angered many, in September 1974 Ford offered a conditional amnesty to all draft dodgers and deserters of the Vietnam War. Those who accepted the offer were required to perform two years of public service and swear an oath of allegiance to the United States. War veterans' groups were opposed to the offer.

Ford ran for reelection in 1976, but lost to Democrat Jimmy Carter, partly because of his pardon of Nixon and in part because of his own limitations as a leader. While serving as president, there were two assassination attempts on Ford in the span of a few weeks. Both would-be assassins were women. Ford survived both attempts.

LYNETTE FROMME

Lynette "Squeaky" Fromme was in her mid-twenties when she tried to assassinate the president. She was devoted to Charles Manson and believed that by shooting the president, she could bring attention to Manson's cause.

Lynette grew up in California. Her father served briefly in the Air Force, receiving an honorable discharge after only a few months. After leaving the service, he knew he wanted to build airplanes, so he found a job at Northrop Corporation in California and moved his family there. As a child, Lynette was a member of the Lariats, a group of children who sang and danced. The group performed for Lawrence Welk, Dinah Shore, and Art Linkletter, and at Disneyland.[21]

In junior high school, Lynette was voted "Personality Plus."[22] But her father punished her frequently and harshly, often for no reason. Either she ran away from home or he kicked her out of the home when she was a teenager. Soon she met Charles Manson and became a devoted follower of his group.

Lynette also developed a lengthy FBI record. She was arrested several times on charges ranging from drug possession to trespassing. She was also charged with attempted murder in 1971, and spent ninety days in jail after "spiking" the hamburger of a witness who was going to testify against Manson with the hallucinogenic drug LSD in an attempt to prevent that witness from testifying.[23] The case ended with a plea bargain, and she was sentenced to three months of probation. Lynette was also arrested for robbery at a 7-11 convenience store, but the charges were dismissed.[24]

Although Lynette was not involved in the Tate and LaBianca murders, the two cases of multiple killings for which Manson and his cohorts were responsible, she supported Manson during his trial. She was sometimes referred to as the leader of the Manson Family in Charles Manson's absence. During that time, she also became romantically involved with Manson's attorney, Paul Fitzgerald.[25]

During the trial, Lynette became obsessed with clearing Manson's name because she saw him as a Christ figure. Lynette became a "Manson nun." As such, she dressed in a red robe and lived her life in devotion to the "ranch," the Spahn Ranch in southern California where the members of the "family" had lived as a model to the world. They also lived as a warning to the world about the environmental and spiritual pollution of the Earth. Lynette believed that the Tate-LaBianca murders were directly related to those issues. She thought that other Manson family members had found enough courage to commit acts that brought attention to their cause, and Lynette believed it was her turn to prove herself worthy of the family. If she did something like the Tate murders, it would capture the imagination of the world.[26] She thought she could do so by threatening the president. She would stand trial and Manson would be called as a witness, giving him a platform to proclaim his message to the world.[27] She originally said that she had no plans to shoot the president, but "just wanted to get some attention for a new trial for Charlie and the girls."[28]

As Fromme prepared for the attack on President Ford, she realized her gun would not fit in her purse. Fromme owned a leather holster for the gun, but decided not to use it because she thought that people might see it. So she got an elastic belt, threaded it through the holster's belt loop, and wrapped it around her left calf. She had to wrap it three times until it was tight enough to prevent too much of the belt from dangling.[29] Even though the gun still showed under her dress, it did not show under her red robe, which she intended to wear. The robe was a red ceremonial gown to wear when she went about her work cleaning the

Earth, which is what she thought she was going to do when she eventually decided to go so far as to shoot Ford. She also wore a red bandana.[30]

THE FIRST ASSASSINATION ATTEMPT

On the morning of September 5, 1975, in Sacramento, California, Ford was going to a meeting with California Governor Jerry Brown and was set to give a speech to the legislature. He was also to meet privately with Republican politicians and give an interview to a television reporter from Los Angeles before returning to Washington. Ironically, he was in California to discuss the problems of violent crime. The newspapers in the area had published Ford's itinerary in detail.

At 7:25 A.M., Ford gave a speech to the annual Sacramento Host Breakfast. The breakfast was held at the Earl Warren Community Convention Center, just three blocks away from the Senator Hotel, where Ford was staying. Even though it was so close, Ford was driven there. Uniformed police were located on the roofs of the hotel, the convention center, and most of the area's other buildings.

When Ford arrived at the convention center, he did not seem to notice about fifty protesters, probably because he entered the building through the rear entrance. Those in attendance at the breakfast included some of the state's top elected and judicial officers, the San Francisco–based diplomatic corps, and the heads of many of California's largest firms. During his speech, Ford mentioned that he was proud that the federal government had issued almost no regulations in the area of firearms. That meant that under both federal and state law, just about anyone could own virtually any sort of firearm.[31]

After the breakfast, Ford returned to the hotel for a short break. After that, he was scheduled to go to the capitol building for a thirty-minute meeting with Governor Brown. He could cross the street in his armored limousine and enter the capitol building through the legislature's private underground parking garage. Instead, he decided to walk the short distance. He left the hotel at around 9:55 A.M., three minutes behind schedule. It was a nice day, about 82° Fahrenheit.[32]

An aide ran ahead to position the press pools so they could photograph Ford as he encountered the crowd. The public would only be able to see Ford during the walk from the hotel, a time of about two minutes.[33] Being seen by the press and the public in this manner was the primary reason Ford decided to walk rather than drive. He was wearing a blue suit and red, white, and blue tie, and was surrounded by agents representing the Secret Service, Sacramento Police Department, and California Highway Patrol.[34]

There was some concern for the president's safety because earlier in the day a woman had called Secret Service agents in Sacramento with information that she had had a vision of Air Force One crashing. The airplane, which had the word "trouble" written across it, crashed to the ground. She said her vision was a warning of trouble from heaven. She also said she had had visions of Kennedy's assassination.[35] After a brief investigation, security felt this woman's premonitions to be unfounded.

Crowds lining the streets cheered for him, and Ford walked forward, shaking their outstretched hands. He noticed a small, thin, odd-looking young woman about two feet away, wearing a long red dress and red turban, keeping pace with him from behind the ropes. She appeared to want to shake his hand. He thought she wanted to reach out to him, even though he had already passed her by, so he turned back toward her.[36]

He was about a hundred yards from the rear entrance to the capitol building, when someone yelled, "Gun," and another, "Forty-Five."[37] Fromme had pulled out a pistol and pointed it at Ford at a range of two feet.[38] Secret Service Agent Larry Buendorf saw the gun and grabbed the weapon with his right hand, cutting himself. He forced the weapon down, seized Fromme's free arm with his left hand, swung her around, and marched her forward through the crowd, away from the president. All the while, Fromme was yelling, "It didn't go off."[39] Police then pushed her to the ground, flat on her back,[40] and took the weapon from her. Fromme argued with the Secret Service agent, saying, "You shouldn't be protecting him, he's not a public servant."[41] After removing the weapon from her grasp, they put her in a car and locked the doors.

Other Secret Service agents formed a huddle around Ford and pushed him down to his knees. When Fromme had been scurried away, security rushed

Figure 9.1.   U.S. Secret Service agents rush President Ford toward the California State Capitol following the attempt on the president's life by Lynette "Squeaky" Fromme, September 5, 1975. (Courtesy of the Gerald R. Ford Library.)

Ford to the capitol building, knocking down photographers on the way. Ford's face was drained of color, but he signaled to the press that he was okay, even though he was shaken and could barely speak.[42] He told the crowd, "Everything is all right."[43] Ford did not even mention the assassination attempt at his meeting with the governor.[44]

Luckily for Ford, the gun had failed to fire. It was discovered later that the weapon's bullet chamber was empty. The gun had not been fired in some time, and the bore was filled with dust.[45] There were four rounds in the weapon's magazine. Fromme had achieved the distinction of being the first woman to try to kill a president of the United States.[46]

THE AFTERMATH

After the assassination attempt, Ford took a few minutes to compose himself, then continued his scheduled meetings with Governor Brown and Brown's chief of staff, Gray Davis. They were not even aware of the shooting, and (as mentioned) Ford said nothing about it. They learned of the events about thirty minutes into the meeting, when a White House aide appeared with a report for the president. Ford was determined to continue with his schedule as normally as possible.

After Ford met with Brown and Davis, he went on with the planned calls on legislative leaders. At 11:34 A.M., he gave a speech to the legislators from California. As he spoke, a woman called the United Press International (UPI) bureau in San Francisco and said that a sixty-pound bomb had been placed in the capitol and would explode at 11:55 A.M., right in the middle of Ford's speech. Security officers searched the building, but Ford ignored the threat. He finished his speech a minute behind schedule at 12:06 P.M.[47]

Then at 12:18 P.M., another woman called a television station in Sacramento to say that a "dude" was at "Sixteenth and J streets" with a shotgun and that he was going to shoot the president. There was no man there.[48]

When Ford finished his speech, he returned to the Senator Hotel, this time by armored limousine. At 12:46 P.M., he made a statement to the press about the events. He praised the Secret Service agents and thanked Californians for being so friendly and hospitable. He then promised to continue to have personal contact with Americans, despite the assassination attempt. He flew back to Washington that afternoon.

Many Americans sent telegrams, letters, greeting cards, and gifts, and made telephone calls expressing concern for Ford. He even received one from former president Nixon. Some world leaders sent notes as well, including UN Secretary-General Kurt Waldheim, Soviet Premier Leonid Brezhnev, the Taiwanese ambassador, President Park Chung Hee of South Korea, Shah Reza Pahlavi of Iran, the presidents of Liberia and Tunisia, and the Vatican.[49]

Meanwhile, Fromme was taken to police headquarters, complaining that her handcuffs were too tight.[50] She gave her name as "Mrs. X" and lied about her address. She told police that "we are killing our children" and that the children were becoming angry. She complained that the country was rich but that the young people could not get the things they needed and that people needed to get in touch with the Earth.[51] Fromme was tested for drug use, and no traces of illegal drugs or alcohol were found.

Fromme's state of mind was key to the prosecution. Under federal rules at the time, the government had the burden of proving a defendant's sanity if the accused raised an insanity defense. Under California law, however, the burden fell on the defendant to prove her insanity, but Fromme refused to speak to a psychiatrist.[52]

Fromme was charged with attempted assassination, and her bail was set at $1 million.[53] The trial was set for November 4, 1975. The president was subpoenaed to appear at the trial. The judge ordered that Ford could testify on videotape within ten days, and that he could do it at a place of his choosing. Ford agreed to testify against Fromme. He testified on November 1 for nineteen minutes. Fromme considered her own trial to be a farce. Since Manson was not called as a witness, she refused to cooperate.

When the trial was completed, the jury deliberated for nineteen and a half hours over three days before finding Fromme guilty. For many hours, the jury was stuck on the absence of a bullet in the firing chamber. The defense argued that if there was no cartridge in the chamber, the gun was not a weapon. Some thought the jury would have preferred to continue deliberating, but it was Thanksgiving and they wanted to go home.[54]

Fromme was sentenced to life imprisonment with no parole.[55] She was the first person tried under the special statute enacted in 1965 after the assassination of President Kennedy, which made attempted assassination of the president a federal offense punishable by life imprisonment. At first it was unclear if she would be prosecuted under state or federal law, but she was ultimately tried in a U.S. district court.[56]

Later, Fromme sent Ford a letter saying that she did not regret trying to kill him. The letter was dated December 30, 1975, and was sent while she was in jail.[57]

The night Fromme was found guilty, a man scaled a fence at the White House and crept fifty yards into the grounds before setting off an alarm. He then crossed the tennis courts, crawled to a driveway, and approached Ford's daughter Susan, who was unloading camera equipment from a car. A guard spotted the man and grabbed him. The man said his motive was to seek attention for a loved one he felt had been unjustly convicted of drug smuggling. The man was charged with unlawful entry and released.[58]

In late December 1987, Fromme heard that Manson was dying from cancer, and so she escaped from the federal women's prison in Alderson, West Virginia, where she was being held, to go see him. To escape the prison, she had to scale an eight-foot barbed-wire fence. She was captured two days later, on Christmas Day, only a few miles from the prison.[59] Two prison employees driving down a rural road saw Fromme walking out of the woods near a fishing camp. They pulled over and Fromme, who was soaking wet from the rain, got in the car. She was dressed in two pairs of pants, a green overcoat, and a crocheted hat.[60] The judge added fifteen months onto Fromme's life term and fined her $400 for the escape.

Many thought the assassination attempt underscored the need for gun control, but the White House announced that the encounter would have no effect on the president's opposition to gun control. But even a new law would not have prevented the second assassination attempt on Ford's life.

SARA JANE MOORE

The second would-be assassin in Gerald Ford's presidency was a gray-haired, forty-five-year-old bookkeeper from Charleston, West Virginia.[61] Sara Jane Moore, sometimes called Sally, was raised in a middle-class family. She was the second daughter to Olaf and Ruth Kahn, one of five children. She grew up in a rural area where there was plenty of room to run and play.

Moore's father was a violinist until he was injured while serving in the Marines.[62] When discharged from the military, he worked for DuPont as a mechanical engineer. Her mother, Ruth, was also a violinist, with the Charleston Symphony Orchestra. Every child in the family took music and dance lessons, and everyone played at least one instrument.

Ruth was a perfectionist who was rarely satisfied with the children's performances. She had high standards and would inspect their work, often redoing it. Olaf was strict as well. He kept to himself and was not very involved with his children's lives. As a child, Moore was a straight-A student and a talented violinist, actor, and artist. Despite all of this, Moore never seemed to fit in. She was isolated from others and would often tell strange stories to other children. She did not have any friends.[63]

In the fall of 1946, when Moore was sixteen, she left for school and did not come home. Her parents searched frantically, but there was no trace of her. Three days later, she returned home but would not tell anyone where she had been. Her mother explained the disappearance as a bout with amnesia.[64]

When she graduated from high school, Moore decided to pursue a career in medicine and did well for the first semester. But instead of signing up for a second semester, she quit school and joined the Women's Army Corps (WAC), and was selected for the Officer Candidate School. But she began to suffer from fainting spells, one of which occurred on the National Mall in Washington, D.C. When she regained consciousness, she claimed to not know who she was. Nurses treating her found photos of herself stuffed in the bodice of her dress.[65]

Sara left the WACs and divorced a marine she had married previously, only to marry a second military man. She became pregnant and had a son in 1951. She was again pregnant in December 1952, and had a daughter in 1953. Moore's husband filed for divorce, claiming she was a poor mother and wife.

They were divorced in 1954, but reconciled later that year. They had a third child in 1954 who was severely disabled. The child, a girl, was institutionalized for a short time before being cared for by a family who offered foster care to mentally disabled children.[66]

In October 1955, Moore filed for divorce from her husband. She was pregnant again, and gave birth in 1955 to another son. At this time, she was a single mother with three children under the age of six. After arranging for her children to go to her parents' house, Moore disappeared and her mother, Ruth, was left to raise the children by herself after her father, Olaf, died of a heart attack.

During this time, Moore covered her tracks well, and no one knew where she was. She may have taken classes at UCLA, where she met John Aalberg, a sound recorder and special effects expert who had been nominated for nine Academy Awards. Moore called him the love of her life. They were married in 1965, but one month later she left him. By then, she was pregnant again, and had her fifth child in March 1966.

In December 1967, Moore married Willard J. Carmel Jr., a physician. She got involved in many political causes and divorced Carmel in September 1971. She had started to support the radical youth politics of the time, joining such groups as the Students for a Democratic Society (SDS). Moore drove to many radical political events in the San Francisco Bay area and became known as a peripheral figure in radical movements of the time. Moore worked at a free clinic and marched in support of Cesar Chávez.

One day, Moore read that the Symbionese Liberation Army (SLA) had kidnapped Patty Hearst and that her kidnappers wanted money for a food program to help feed the poor. Patty's father, Randolph Hearst, donated $2 million for the People in Need (PIN) program. Moore wanted to work for PIN, and convinced the agency to give her a job. She worked hard for the agency.

At one point, Moore was approached by the FBI about becoming an informant for them, and she agreed.[67] The FBI was hoping that Moore's contacts and leads would help them find Patty Hearst.[68] About a week after becoming an FBI informant, Moore was fired from PIN. She started working for the United Prisoners' Union (UPU) and started attending a political study group in San Francisco. The group read a lot about socialism, and Moore became interested in the ideas. But she soon started to feel guilty about betraying the people who had become her friends. When she believed the group was growing suspicious of her, she confided in one of them about her secret role as an informer. When her radical friends found out that she was an FBI informer, they wanted nothing more to do with her. Moore even received death threats. Without her left-wing contacts, Moore was useless to the FBI and they dropped her, too.[69]

When Moore heard about Fromme's attack on President Ford, she thought she could also get back in the good graces of her friends by assassinating the president. Knowing that she would be caught, she considered her act to be a personal sacrifice. By shooting Ford, Moore hoped to impress radical friends with whom she was no longer in a close relationship.[70]

The day before Moore tried to assassinate the president, she was arrested for carrying an unloaded, illegal .44-caliber revolver and two boxes of ammunition. The weapon was confiscated by an inspector in the San Francisco Police Department, Jack O'Shea, and Moore was cited for carrying a concealed weapon, a misdemeanor under state law, and released.[71] O'Shea warned Secret Service agents that Moore could be another Fromme. After that warning, two agents were sent to interview her but found no grounds for arrest. Apparently the fact that she was an informer for the police and a federal agency caused the Secret Service to let her go. The next day, Moore tried to kill the president.[72]

THE SECOND ASSASSINATION ATTEMPT

On Saturday, September 20, the *San Francisco Chronicle* published details about Ford's visit to the Bay area. The morning of Ford's visit, Moore made several phone calls. She tried to call Agent Martin Haskell at the Secret Service, but he was not in the office. She then called Bert Worthington at the FBI, but he also was not in. She called Jack O'Shea at the San Francisco Police Department and told him she was going to Stanford to "test the security" and see if it worked equally for those on the left as for those on the right. O'Shea realized that she was going to be where Ford was speaking. He was immediately alarmed and called the FBI, Secret Service, and Bureau of Alcohol, Tobacco and Firearms (ATF). Moore then called Mark Fernwood, a gun dealer, and arranged to purchase a .38 -caliber Smith and Wesson revolver.[73]

On September 22, Ford visited San Francisco. It was only seventeen days after Fromme's assassination attempt on his life.[74] Ford was scheduled to give a television interview to a local station in the St. Francis Hotel. That day, Moore drove to the St. Francis Hotel and waited for Ford to appear. Her presence went unnoticed. Instead, security agents were focused on protesters hoisting placards with such messages as "Release Patty Hearst" and "Arrest Gerald Ford."[75] Moore had the .38-caliber revolver in her purse.

At about 3:30 P.M., Ford finished the interview. He was to leave the hotel and go straight to the airport and return to Washington. Outside the hotel, people waited to get a glimpse of him. At first, a presidential aide walked out the door. Moore pulled her gun halfway out of her purse, but then realized the person leaving the hotel was not the president. Ford then emerged from a side entrance and waved to the crowd as he entered a limo to go to the airport. Moore raised her gun to shoulder height in her right hand, bracing it with her left.[76] A single shot rang out. When he heard the shot, Ford dropped down immediately. Two Secret Service agents flung Ford into the limousine and to the floor, and then jumped in after him. The motorcade immediately drove away from the hotel.[77] Moore had fired her weapon at the president from about forty feet away, missing him by five feet.[78]

This time, the president's life was saved by Marine Corps veteran Oliver Sipple. Sipple saw Moore point the pistol at Ford and struck her hand as she fired,

Figure 9.2. President Ford winces at the sound of gunfire at the moment of the assassination attempt by Sara Jane Moore in San Francisco, California, on September 22, 1975. (Courtesy of the Gerald R. Ford Library.)

deflecting her aim. The bullet struck the wall of the hotel to Ford's right and ricocheted, struck the curb to Ford's left, and bounced up and hit a taxi driver in the groin.[79] Moore attempted to fire a second time, but Sipple's actions prevented her from doing so. After Sipple pushed Moore's hand to the side, a San Francisco police officer grabbed the cylinder of the gun and pushed it down toward the ground. Moore did not want to let the gun go, but the officer finally got it, yelling, "Here it is."[80] The police put handcuffs on Moore to subdue her.

THE AFTERMATH

Moore was taken inside the St. Francis Hotel and her handcuffs were taken off. She refused to answer any questions until they promised her son would be safe. They told her that he had been picked up from school and placed in protective custody. Moore said she knew she fired too high to hit the president. She also said if the president had not come out of the hotel when he did, she would have had to leave to pick up her son. But she also said if she had her .44 with her, she would have shot him.[81] Moore admitted she acted alone.

About 4:30 P.M., Moore was taken to jail. Upon her arrest she said, "I'm no Squeaky Fromme."[82] She explained that at first, she had no intention of killing the president, but instead it was an ultimate protest against the system.[83] She said that her purpose for shooting the president was to unite the Bay Area's radical community to "forge some kind of unity between the rage that led to the formation of the SLA combined with theoreticians."[84]

During her trial, Moore did not participate in the legal proceedings and would not answer questions. Although she resisted being labeled insane or incompetent, she agreed to a full psychiatric evaluation. None of the psychiatrists who evaluated her came to the same diagnosis. Each attributed her behavior to a different personality disorder. Nonetheless, they all agreed that she was sane and competent to stand trial.[85]

At first, Moore entered a plea of not guilty, even though her actions were undeniable. She had been seen by many shooting the president, and was even caught on film. Later, she wanted to change her plea to guilty. When the judge ruled that she was mentally competent to change her plea, no trial was scheduled. At her sentencing hearing, Moore received life imprisonment. She was sent to the Federal Correctional Institution at Terminal Island in California, known to some as the "country club" of federal institutions.

Upon arriving at the prison, Moore immediately got involved with two issues within the prison. The first issue that concerned Moore was that the male prisoners could see directly into the women's rooms, and the second was that women had more restrictions on their movements in the prison than did male inmates. Moore arranged for a personal sit-in where she refused to move until the issues were addressed. The prison administration eventually made changes to both policies.[86] A year after her conviction, Moore gave an interview to *Playboy* magazine in which she said that most people told her they wished she would have killed Ford. She was angry with Fromme because if she had not tried to assassinate Ford earlier, he probably would have come to the street to shake hands and she would have had a better chance to shoot him.[87]

A few years later, Moore was sent to a prison in West Virginia. The federal prison system had built a new facility, and they were moving high-risk people from all over the country to the new prison. Moore's daughter went to see her, but Moore denied having a daughter and refused to see her.

Although Moore's shot failed to unite the radical movement, it did result in security changes for the president. After the assassination attempt, President Ford called for hiring 150 new Secret Service agents at a cost of $13.5 million. Additionally, Secret Service protection was extended over other major presidential candidates.[88]

On February 5, 1979, it was discovered that Moore and another inmate were missing at bed count. They had climbed over the twelve-foot prison fence that was topped with barbed wire. They walked in the woods until eighteen-year-old David Ross saw them walking along the road. He drove them to Lewisburg, and the women took a taxi to the next town. A local police officer knew it was too cold for either locals or tourists to be out walking, so he asked their names. He called a security guard, and they arrested them. They were absent from the prison for less than four hours. Moore was found guilty of escape, and two years were added to her life sentence. She was also given a $5,000 fine. On December 31, 2007,

Moore was released from prison to five years of supervised parole. At the time, she was seventy-seven years old.

CONCLUSION

Even though two people tried to assassinate him, Ford refused to cancel future public appearances. He ran for reelection in 1976 but did not have a strong campaign organization. A serious challenge for the Republican nomination came from the former governor of California, Ronald Reagan. Ford won a narrow victory over Reagan, and he chose Senator Robert J. Dole of Kansas as his running mate. He ran against Jimmy Carter, the Democratic governor of Georgia. It was a close race, but Ford lost the presidency.

Sometimes called the "accidental" president, Ford was the first person to serve as vice president and president without being elected to either office. Even though he served as president for just two and a half years, Ford led the nation in a calm, reassuring manner, helping to restore faith in government and ease political conflict. People generally trusted him.

Ford died in his home on July 14, 2006, at the age of ninety-three. After funeral services at the National Cathedral in Washington, D.C., he was buried at his presidential museum in Grand Rapids, Michigan.

Fromme served time in the federal women's prison in Alderson, West Virginia, for her crime. In 1985, she became eligible for parole, but did not apply and remained in prison. In 1987, she escaped from the prison, but was located two days later suffering from the elements. On August 15, 2009, at the age of sixty, Fromme was paroled from the Federal Medical Center Carswell, a prison-hospital complex in Fort Worth, Texas.

Oddly enough, Sara Jane Moore's imprisonment somewhat mirrored Fromme's.

Moore was also held in the federal women's prison in Alderson, West Virginia, and in 1979 she attempted to escape. Moore, however, was recaptured within four hours, not two days. On December 31, 2007, at the age of seventy-seven, Moore was released from prison after serving thirty-two years of her life sentence.

— 10 —

Ronald Reagan

INTRODUCTION

On March 30, 1981, sixty-nine days into his presidency, Ronald Reagan spoke at a meeting of AFL-CIO representatives at the Hilton Hotel in Washington, D.C.[1] Though Reagan and organized labor were not on the best of terms, the president could not have known that addressing labor leaders would be the least of his challenges on that blustery March afternoon.

The speech completed, Reagan exited the hotel. A crowd waited, hoping to get a glimpse of the president as he made his way from the hotel to the presidential limousine. Among them was a disturbed young man yearning to profess his love for an inaccessible woman in a dramatic fashion. This intersection of personalities would put to the test the agents who protect the president, the doctors who care for him, the leaders and appointees who support him, and the will of the president himself to survive.

RONALD REAGAN

Ronald Reagan was born on February 6, 1911, in Tampico, Illinois, to his parents John Edward "Jack" Reagan and Nelle Wilson Reagan.[2] Jack Reagan was a shoe salesman, plying his trade in Tampico at the time of Ronald Reagan's birth, then in Monmouth, Galesburg, and Chicago, before finally returning to Tampico in 1919, where they lived above the H.C. Pitney Variety Store. Very early on, Ronald Reagan was given the nickname "Dutch" by his father because of the combination of his chubby features, Dutch-boy haircut, and clothes, making him altogether look like the "Fat little Dutch boy" seen in the advertisements of the day (Dutch Boy Paints). That nickname remained with him through his childhood and into his adult life among his close friends.

The Pitney Store closed in 1920, so the Reagans moved once again, this time to Dixon, Illinois. Although Reagan's family had a Catholic background (Jack and Nelle were married in a Catholic ceremony in 1904), Dutch was baptized into the Disciples of Christ Presbyterian faith in 1922. At Dixon High School, Dutch developed a wide variety of interests, ranging from swimming and football to acting and storytelling. His first job drew upon his swimming skills when he became a lifeguard at the Rock River in Lowell Park, near Dixon, in 1926. Reagan would always cherish the memory of the seventy-seven lives he saved while serving as a lifeguard.[3]

Upon graduating from high school, Dutch attended Eureka College, where he majored in economics and sociology. He was active in sports and played football for Eureka. He also joined the Tau Kappa Epsilon fraternity. Although he enjoyed his time at Eureka and would remember it fondly, in many ways it was a stopping point along the way, for his great desire was to move on and become a sports announcer. After graduating in 1932 with a bachelor's degree, he did just that.

Dutch drove to Iowa and auditioned for a job with several small-town radio stations.[4] Initially he had little success, but did manage to secure a job announcing the home football games for the University of Iowa Hawkeyes. That led to a position with WOC in Davenport, and then on to WHO in Des Moines, where he became an announcer for Chicago Cubs baseball games.

While on a road trip with the Cubs in California, Reagan heard about an opportunity to take a screen test to potentially become a Hollywood actor.[5] He took the screen test and signed a seven-year contract with Warner Brothers Studios. His career was largely relegated to the "B" movies of the late 1930s, where it was not so much the quality as the quantity of films that mattered. They would churn out movies in a matter of months, typically filming in a period of two to four weeks. His first movie was the 1937 film *Love Is in the Air*. While working on the 1938 film *Brother Rat*, he met actress Jane Wyman, who he married on January 26, 1940.[6] They had three children: Maureen; Christine, who died shortly after birth; and Michael, who they adopted.

Reagan made nearly thirty movies over the next several years. His role in *Knute Rockne, All American*, earned him the lifelong nickname of "the Gipper." *King's Row*, in 1942, is considered the movie that made Reagan a star, but two months later he enlisted in the war effort and was never able to capitalize on that status.

The military, however, decided to capitalize on his stardom, although not right away. Initially Reagan enlisted in the Army Enlisted Reserve on April 29, 1937, and he was assigned the rank of private in Troop B of the 322nd Cavalry in Des Moines, Iowa. The following month, because he was a college graduate, he was appointed to the rank of second lieutenant in the Officers Reserve Corps, and again assigned to the 322nd Cavalry. He was then ordered to active-duty service, but because of his severe nearsightedness he was assigned to limited duties at Fort Mason, California, as a liaison officer. That position gave him the opportunity to request an assignment to the Army Air Force as a public relations officer, and he was eventually assigned to the 18th AAF Base Unit in Culver City, California, and promoted to the rank of first lieutenant.

Reagan was once again making movies, only this time they were training films for newly drafted recruits. He worked on the Provisional Task Show Unit in Burbank, California, producing, by war's end, over 400 training films. While working on these films he was promoted to the rank of captain, and then given duty in New York City, where he participated in the sixth War Loan Drive. He returned to Fort MacArthur, California, in late 1945, and was separated from active duty on December 9, 1945.

Reagan attempted to get back into the film industry but had a difficult time landing roles. He was, however, elected to the board of directors of the Screen Actors Guild (SAG). He became president of SAG in 1947 and was reelected every year through 1952, and once more in 1959. He led SAG through numerous labor-management disputes and the investigations of the House Un-American Activities Committee. Although he was still tied to the film industry, his terms as SAG president sparked his interest in politics. This led to conflicts between Reagan and his wife, resulting in their divorce in 1948.

Ironically, as part of his role as president of SAG, he treated the new medium of television warily, but when hired to host *General Electric Theater*, which proved to be quite successful, he became a strong proponent of television. As part of his job, he would tour the General Electric plants and give motivational speeches. This furthered his interests in politics, and he learned the skills necessary for mounting a campaign. In 1949, he met Nancy Davis, who supported his desire to go into politics. They married on March 4, 1952, and had two children: Patti, born that year, and Ron, born in 1958.

Although he had been a registered Democrat and admirer of Franklin D. Roosevelt, like so many of the Great Depression generation, Reagan found himself moving toward the Republican Party in the 1950s.[7] This was due in part to the speeches Reagan was writing for his General Electric plant tours. Eventually the speeches became too political for GE and they fired Reagan in 1962. At that point, Reagan formally switched parties and set about working for Barry Goldwater's 1964 Republican bid for president. Although Goldwater lost to Johnson in a landslide, Reagan's speeches on Goldwater's behalf launched his political career.

In 1966, the Republican Party nominated Reagan to run for governor of California, and he defeated two-term Governor Edmund G. "Pat" Brown.[8] Reagan was sworn in on January 3, 1967, and led California through a tumultuous period. He managed a difficult deficit by freezing government hires and raising taxes in order to balance the budget. He had to deal with numerous protest movements across California, calling out the National Guard to quell protests at the University of California, Berkeley, in May 1969. He was reelected in 1970, and began to entertain a run for the presidency.

In 1976, he attempted such a run against the incumbent Gerald Ford, but the Republican Party, by a narrow margin, decided to remain with its incumbent. Reagan then set his sights on the 1980 presidential campaign, this time easily winning the nomination of the Republican Party. The campaign against President Jimmy Carter was largely a response to a mixture of events that Carter seemed unable to deal with successfully: the Iran Hostage Crisis, double-digit inflation, high unemployment, high deficits, and a weak national defense in the wake of the Vietnam War.[9] Reagan won the popular vote by a close majority (50.7 percent of the vote), but carried forty-four states for 489 electoral votes to Carter's 49, a landslide victory. Ronald Reagan, the former actor, was now president of the United States.

Reagan, just shy of seventy years old, was the oldest man elected to the office of the presidency.[10] In his first inaugural speech, he attempted to turn around the country's economic and social malaise and argued, "Government is not the solution to our problems; government is the problem."[11] Within hours of this speech, he was able to announce that the fifty-two hostages in Iran, who had been in captivity for 444 days, were released. Further, he set about restoring the American economy through a series of tax cuts and rebuilding the U.S. military.

Sixty-nine days into his presidency, he was slated to give a speech to the Building and Construction Trades National Conference of the AFL-CIO in the Washington Hilton's ballroom.[12] He arrived at approximately 1:45 P.M. and gave his speech. As he recorded later in his diary, "Speech not riotously received—still it was successful."[13] He then left the hotel from the side entrance, where a crowd waited for a chance to see the president.

JOHN HINCKLEY

John Hinckley was born John Warnock Hinckley Jr. on May 29, 1955, in Ardmore, Oklahoma.[14] His father, John Warnock Hinckley Sr., was the owner of Hinckley Oil Company, and his mother, Jo Ann, was a stay-at-home mother. He had two older siblings: a sister, Diane, and a brother, Scott. When Hinckley was four years old, the family moved to University Park, Texas, a wealthy suburb in the Dallas–Fort Worth area. John Hinckley attended school in Dallas County, Texas, and was a well-liked boy. He excelled in sports, including both football and basketball, and joined the YMCA Indian Guides.

The family eventually moved to another suburb, Highland Park, an even more exclusive neighborhood. They had their own swimming pool and soda machine. In Highland Park, however, Hinckley's outgoing personality began to contract; he had fewer friends and stopped playing sports. Hinckley would later reflect that his high school years were greatly troubling to him as he admitted that he "was becoming more rebellious and uncommunicative."[15] He still managed to graduate from Highland Park High School in the spring of 1973. Shortly thereafter, his parents moved to Evergreen, Colorado.

In the fall of 1973, Hinckley moved to Lubbock, Texas, to begin college at Texas Tech University, where over the next seven years he would drift in and out of student status. The outgoing, skinny, smiling boy who entered college that fall eventually became a sullen and overweight recluse who sat in his apartment most days staring at the television. Once, in 1975, he moved to Los Angeles in order to become a songwriter like his idol John Lennon, but without success. He wrote to his parents, explaining his failures and begging for money. He also spoke of a girlfriend, Lynn, but she was entirely imaginary. His parents sent him the money he requested, but it ran out too fast and he was forced to move to Evergreen to live with them. This became a pattern for John Hinckley over the ensuing years—he would move out to live on his own, only to return home destitute and in need of assistance.

John Hinckley's mental instability is often associated with the premiere of the movie *Taxi Driver*, which he saw for the first time in the spring of 1976, when he was twenty-one years old. The movie starred Robert De Niro as Travis Bickle, a taxi driver who planned to assassinate a presidential candidate. The character was based on Arthur Bremer's diaries and his attempted assassination of presidential candidate George Wallace (see chapter 11). Jodie Foster played a twelve-year-old prostitute in the movie, and the actress would become the center of Hinckley's obsession. John Hinckley would see the movie an estimated fifteen times. He became infatuated with Jodie Foster and admired the character Travis Bickle.[16]

Hinckley began identifying with the movie character Bickle so much that he purchased similar clothing, ate the same foods, and drank the same alcohol. He invented a girlfriend based on a character Bickle tries to date, and when he was in Los Angeles, he wrote to his parents telling them all about her. In addition, he purchased weapons similar to those owned by Bickle, who owned one .38, two .22s, and a rifle.[17] Between August 1979 and September 1980, Hinckley purchased a .38-caliber pistol, a 6.5-caliber rifle, a .22-caliber rifle, and two .22-caliber pistols.

Around this same time, Hinckley moved to Dallas and rented an apartment by himself. He continued to be a recluse, eating junk food and gaining weight. Depressed, he moved back to Lubbock for another failed attempt at college before turning his attention to Nazi literature. In September 1979, he created an imaginary group called the American Front and published the organization's newsletter, giving himself the title of "national director." Hinckley began reading about Lee Harvey Oswald, and Oswald replaced John Lennon as his hero. He also joined the National Socialist Party of America and marched in a Nazi parade in March 1978, but the organization kicked him out as he advocated shooting minorities. As the party head later explained, "[W]hen somebody comes to us and starts advocating shooting people, it's a natural reaction: the guy's either a nut or a federal agent."[18]

Hinckley once again returned home in January 1980. He weighed 225 pounds, when his normal weight had been 160. His parents took him to the doctor, but he found no medical explanation for the dramatic weight gain and poor health. After visiting his sister in Dallas, he returned to Texas Tech for one last try at the college life, and once again it proved a disaster. That May, Hinckley picked up a copy of *People* magazine and read a story about his favorite actress, Jodie Foster.

The article reported that Jodie Foster would temporarily leave her acting career to begin working on a degree at Yale University in the fall of 1980.[19] John Hinckley decided to follow her. He told his parents that he was going to Yale University to begin a writing program. They gave him the money to enroll. Yale University had no such program. With these funds he moved to New Haven, Connecticut, and began stalking Jodie Foster. On a number of occasions, he would slip messages under her door, leave poetry for her to find, and try contacting her by phone. He apparently spoke to her on two separate occasions. Needless to say, she rebuffed his advances, and although she received numerous fan letters, the ones from Hinckley were particularly disturbing, so she gave them to the college dean. Hinckley, rebuffed, became greatly discouraged and returned to his parents' home, once again destitute.

Having failed to win over Jodie Foster, he began to consider taking action similar to that of the character Travis Bickle in order to gain her attention. He considered hijacking a plane and committing suicide, but decided that the best way would be to assassinate the president. He began trailing then-President Jimmy Carter to a number of his speaking engagements in the hope of getting close enough to fire his guns. It is believed that in September he was close enough to do so in Columbus, Ohio, but he did not fire a shot. News film shot the next month showed that Hinckley had managed to get within six feet of President Carter, but again, he did not fire his weapon.

On another such foray in late October, Hinckley was picked up by the police in Nashville, Tennessee, when he set off the metal detector at the airport. He was apparently carrying three guns on his person and was charged with several firearms violations. Although President Carter was speaking less than ten miles from the airport, no link was made between Hinckley and the president, so he never came under the watch of the U.S. Secret Service.[20] He was eventually fined and released, and his guns were confiscated. Once again broke, he returned home to his parents.

His parents again bailed him out, giving him the money he needed to get back on his feet. He used the money to buy two replacement .22-caliber handguns in Dallas, Texas. At this point Hinckley was becoming even more mentally unstable, for he wrote a letter to the FBI speaking of a plot to kidnap the actress Jodie Foster.

In 1981, with the inauguration of the new president, Ronald Reagan, John Hinckley again began considering assassinating the president in order to gain Foster's attention. He went to Washington, D.C., in hopes of finding an opportunity to assassinate the new president. It is possible that he came close to such an opportunity, but he did not pull the trigger. He returned home, but this time his parents had had enough of John's behavior and condition. His father gave him $200 and told him to go find a place to stay other than their home in Evergreen.

Rejected by his parents, Hinckley called Jodie Foster again, and recorded the conversation with her. At one point Foster told him, "I can't carry on these conversations with people I don't know."[21] After that, he decided to go make himself known to the young actress. He left his parents' home on March 24, 1981, and flew to Los Angeles. Foster was again at Yale University, so Hinckley purchased a ticket to New Haven via Washington, D.C. He arrived in Washington early on the morning of March 29, a Sunday, and checked into a hotel directly across the street from the Secret Service headquarters. The next morning he saw the president's schedule in the *Washington Star* newspaper; Reagan would be giving a speech at the Washington Hilton that afternoon.

John Hinckley then took a shower, dressed, and loaded his .22-caliber revolver with six Devastator bullets, which are designed to explode on contact. He then wrote Jodie Foster one last time:

I just cannot wait any longer to impress you. I've got to do something now to make you understand in no uncertain terms that I am doing all of this for your sake. By sacrificing my freedom and possibly my life, I hope to change your mind about me. This letter is being written an hour before I leave for the Hilton Hotel.

Jodie, I am asking you to please look into your heart and at least give me a chance with this historical deed to gain your respect and love.

I love you forever.[22]

He signed the letter "John Hinckley," and left it on the desk in his hotel room.

He then went downstairs to the lobby and caught a cab to the Washington Hilton. He waited outside with the rest of the crowd that had gathered to catch a glimpse of President Reagan as he exited the hotel.

THE ASSASSINATION ATTEMPT

On March 30, 1981, sixty-nine days into his presidency, Ronald Reagan was scheduled to give a speech to AFL-CIO representatives at the Washington Hilton Hotel at 1919 Connecticut Avenue.[23] As mentioned, Reagan was not exactly on good terms with members of the labor union, but as a political concession he agreed to speak at their luncheon. The presidential motorcade departed the White House at approximately 1:45 P.M., and it consisted of three primary vehicles: the presidential limousine, the Secret Service follow-on car, and the control car. Michael Deaver, the White House deputy chief of staff, rode in the control car. A second presidential limousine was also included, in case the president's primary vehicle broke down, and it carried the White House physician. President Reagan had Secret Service protection, and was also escorted by officers from the Washington, D.C., Metropolitan Police.

The motorcade reached the hotel at approximately 1:50 P.M.[24] Surrounded by Secret Service agents, Reagan entered the hotel at the T Street entrance. He was escorted onto an elevator that delivered him to the floor below the Grand

Ballroom, where he met with several senior members of the union in a "holding room" before entering the ballroom and proceeding to the lectern.[25]

Reagan's speech was received with subdued respect by those in attendance, which was probably the best he could have hoped for.[26] Then, just prior to 2:30 P.M., President Reagan exited via the T Street door. The presidential motorcade, having turned around, was waiting for him. The areas on either side of the exit were roped off, and citizens and media were waiting to get a glimpse of or photograph the president. As he was not giving a speech to the press, there was no press-designated area.[27]

As President Reagan walked through the exit with Mike Deaver on his left, Press Secretary James Brady immediately behind him, and Special Agent Ray Shaddick behind him to his right, he was surrounded by the Secret Service. The president paused after exiting, still somewhat concealed by a concrete block wall.

Reagan stepped out from the cover of the block wall and proceeded to walk toward the limousine, where Agent Tim McCarthy was opening the rear passenger-side door. He then heard a popping sound, and he turned toward Secret Service Agent Jerry Parr and said, "What the hell's that?"[28] Parr said nothing but was already moving, clearly recognizing the distinct sound of gunfire as he practically tackled the president and pushed him toward the open car door.

Figure 10.1. President Ronald Reagan waves to the crowd upon leaving the Washington Hilton Hotel immediately before John Hinckley Jr. attempted to assassinate him on March 30, 1981. (Courtesy of the Ronald Reagan Presidential Library.)

At the same time that Reagan had cleared the concrete block wall, John Hinckley Jr. pushed forward through the crowd and drew the Rohm RG-14 .22-caliber blue steel revolver that held six Devastator bullets. He began pulling the trigger and fired all six shots in less than three seconds.[29] The first bullet struck James Brady in the head, and he collapsed immediately to the sidewalk.[30] Although Devastator bullets are designed to explode on impact, the only one that did was the one that struck Brady.[31]

The second bullet struck Metropolitan Police Officer Thomas Delahanty in the back of the neck, causing him to reel about. The third bullet went over the president's head and struck a window across the street. The fourth bullet struck Secret Service Special Agent Timothy McCarthy in the chest. After hearing the first shot, McCarthy had turned toward the sound and made himself as large a target as possible to protect the president, acting on training rather than natural instinct.[32] While others were diving for cover, McCarthy exposed himself and absorbed the fourth bullet, which would otherwise have most likely struck the president. The fifth bullet hit the window of the open door of the limousine, but ricocheted off the bulletproof glass. The sixth and final bullet ricocheted off the side of the limousine and hit the president as he was being pushed through the door and into the limousine. Hinckley, despite the fact that the gun was now empty, continued to squeeze the trigger.

The bullet struck Reagan at the "top of his seventh rib, and was deflected three inches into the lower left lung, about one inch from the heart and aorta."[33] At the moment Reagan was struck, Agent Parr was pushing Reagan into the limousine, landing on top of the president, who had struck the transmission riser between the two foot wells with his ribs. Parr shouted to the driver, Special Agent Drew Unrue, "Take off! Just take off!"[34] As Special Agent Shaddick slammed the car door shut, the limousine sped away. It had to dodge a parked police car, but was still gone within ten seconds of the first shot.[35]

While Hinckley was pulling the trigger, Special Agent Dennis McCarthy (no relation to Agent Tim McCarthy) began to react to the second shot, moving toward the sound of the gunfire.[36] He reached Hinckley about the time Hinckley was firing the last shot, at which point he tackled Hinckley. Hinckley hit the ground hard with McCarthy on top of him, followed by a metropolitan police officer and several other individuals. McCarthy was trying to get his handcuffs out to place them on Hinckley, but he was only able to get one on Hinckley's left wrist. He then yelled for the others to get off the pile. As he struggled to stand up, McCarthy noticed that one of the individuals on the pile was a civilian who had both hands around Hinckley's neck and was trying to choke the life out of him. McCarthy yelled at the man to let go, and when the man would not, McCarthy elbowed him in the jaw. Now fully in charge of his prisoner, and with the help of another agent, he began moving Hinckley toward safety.

Another citizen charged Hinckley, and McCarthy struck him hard, stopping the attack mid-assault. They made it to a police cruiser and attempted to open the door and place Hinckley in the car, but the door was locked. As they moved to the next vehicle, another citizen blocked their way and McCarthy struck him too. McCarthy would later learn that in this case he had struck another Secret Service agent. Finally, they were able to get Hinckley into a police car and leave the scene. Agent McCarthy ordered the driver, Officer Leon Swain, to go directly to the Washington Metropolitan Police headquarters.[37]

In the presidential limousine, Reagan, after landing in the rear well, let out a curse and told Agent Parr that he hurt his ribs when he landed on him. Parr commanded Unrue to proceed immediately to the White House, the securest site close by, as he began to assess any injuries to the president. It was clear that the president was in pain, which Reagan was convinced had been caused by Agent Parr. Reagan was beginning to think Parr had broken his ribs, for he said that it was the "most paralyzing pain . . . as if someone hit you with a hammer."[38]

Despite his pain, Reagan and Parr joked about their "flying entrance into the car," but Parr turned serious again when he saw the president coughing up bright, frothy red blood, a common sign of a punctured lung. Agent Parr quickly yelled at the driver, "Go to George Washington Hospital—fast!"[39]

Figure 10.2. Press Secretary James Brady and Washington Metropolitan Police Officer Thomas Delahanty lie wounded while a U.S. Secret Service agent watches over the immediate aftermath of the assassination attempt on President Ronald Reagan's life on March 30, 1981. Note that John Hinckley Jr. the would-be assassin, is subdued under the pile of people next to the Secret Service agent, a Secret Service briefcase lies open on the street after the weapon was drawn from its container, and the president's limousine is gone, having driven away. (Courtesy of the Ronald Reagan Presidential Library.)

This move no doubt saved the president's life. Dr. Joseph Giordano, the head of the trauma team that operated on Reagan that day, said later, "Jerry Parr deserves the most credit for saving the president's life. The president was very close to crashing while on the way to the White House. When Parr saw the president cough up blood, he took a beeline to the GW (George Washington University Hospital), and that saved the day."[40]

THE AFTERMATH

The president arrived at George Washington Hospital at 2:35 P.M. on March 30, 1981. Although the Secret Service had notified the hospital of the impending arrival of the president and had requested a stretcher, there was no stretcher waiting for him, and Reagan somehow forced himself to walk the forty-five feet from the limousine to the emergency room doors unassisted. A paramedic on scene noted that as he entered the emergency room, his "eyes rolled upward, and his head went back, his knees buckled and he started to collapse."[41] Reagan, falling to one knee, stated aloud, "I can't breathe."[42] The emergency room nurses who came to assist were shocked to see the president of the United States. At first they thought he was having a heart attack. They had been notified that three gunshot victims were being transported to the hospital (Reagan, Delahanty, and Tim McCarthy), but no one had mentioned that one of these was the president.

They immediately moved the president into a room and began taking his vital signs. His vitals were confusing—his pulse was slow and in some cases impossible to find. His blood pressure was extremely low. Dr. Giordano was summoned and he ordered Reagan's thousand-dollar suit be cut off. As Nurse Kathy Paul was doing this, she and Dr. Wesley Price, a surgical resident, noticed the entry wound under the president's left armpit. They realized at that moment that the president had been shot and that the bullet had entered his chest. The quickly began an IV, gave him blood, and administered oxygen by mask. Reagan began to stabilize. As he regained consciousness, Nurse Marisa Mize was holding Reagan's hand, and Reagan said, "Who's holding my hand? Who's holding my hand? Does Nancy know about us?"[43]

A few minutes later, Nancy Reagan arrived at the hospital. She was not told the true nature of her husband's admittance to the hospital until she arrived there. She entered the emergency room and went immediately to his side. Upon seeing Nancy, he lifted up his oxygen mask and whispered, "Honey, I forgot to duck,"[44] borrowing the line that Jack Dempsey delivered to his wife the night he was beaten by Gene Tunney for the heavyweight boxing championship.[45]

The doctors inflated Reagan's collapsed lung and X-rayed him to find the bullet. He was bleeding heavily, and they provided him with more blood. By the end of the day, it was reported, he had lost half of his blood.[46] When he was wheeled into the operating room, he looked around at the doctors and nurses in attendance and said, "Please tell me you're all Republicans." Dr. Giordano, a self-described liberal Democrat, replied to the president, "We're all Republicans today."[47]

President Reagan was anesthetized and the surgery began. Surgery lasted several hours because of difficulty finding the bullet, which was finally located behind his heart, only an inch away. He regained consciousness within an hour, but was unable to speak due to the effects of the anesthesia. He motioned for a pen and paper and wrote down, "All in all, I'd rather be in Philadelphia," quoting W. C. Fields's answer to the question of what he wanted written on his gravestone.[48] On another occasion, as the doctors worked over him, he wrote another note that said, "If I'd had this much attention in Hollywood, I'd have stayed there."[49] He remained under close watch overnight and was moved to the intensive care unit early the next morning. Late that evening he was moved into a secure suite, where he would remain for the rest of the week.

Over the coming weeks, Reagan continued to improve. He was able to get rid of a high fever, and the antibiotics seemed to be helping with the infection. Although many of his events were cancelled, Reagan was able to move around some before leaving the hospital on April 11. He noted in his diary later that day, after returning to the White House, "Getting shot hurts."[50] Six weeks later, while continuing to recover, but engaged in most of his duties as president, he became the oldest president to ever serve in American history. Another month went by before he held his first news conference since the shooting on June 6, 1981, seventy-nine days after he was wounded.

Immediately after the shooting, John Hinckley was taken directly to the Washington Metropolitan Police headquarters. He was placed in an empty holding cell.[51] He was searched more thoroughly, and his possessions were taken. He was then transferred to an interview room, where Detective Ed Meyers read him his rights; asked him if he understood, which Hinckley said he did; then had him sign a document to that effect. Detective Meyers asked Hinckley if he wanted to talk, and Hinckley requested a lawyer. Hinckley did not offer much information, only his name, a few bits of his background, and a vague idea as to where he had been staying in Washington, D.C. He never asked if he had hit Reagan, and he never talked about Jodie Foster. He simply answered basic questions, asked for his lawyer, and rubbed his wrists where the handcuffs had been placed tightly on him.

John Hinckley Jr. went to trial after being charged with thirteen separate offenses.[52] During the trial, the prosecution gave psychiatric evidence that Hinckley was sane at the time of the shooting, and the defense gave evidence indicating he was insane. The jury found that Hinckley was not guilty by reason of insanity, and Hinckley was confined to St. Elizabeth's Hospital in Washington, D.C. Hinckley, writing shortly after his confinement in the mental institution, noted that the shooting was "the greatest love offering in the history of the world,"[53] and that he was upset that Jodie Foster never reciprocated his love. Since then, Hinckley has been granted unsupervised visits with his parents, but is otherwise confined to St. Elizabeth's.

Police Officer Thomas Delahanty recovered from the gunshot wound he sustained, but was eventually forced to retire from the police force due to the injury.

Secret Service Agent Tim McCarthy also recovered from the gunshot wound to his chest and returned to duty as a Secret Service agent, eventually leading the Chicago division, until his retirement in October 1993. Tim McCarthy has since served as the police chief of the village of Orland Park, Illinois.[54] President Reagan's press secretary, James Brady, sustained a serious head injury and was permanently disabled, his left side paralyzed. In subsequent years, he was a strong proponent of gun-control laws.

Special Agents Jerry Parr, Ray Shaddick, Tim McCarthy, and Dennis McCarthy were all awarded the Medal of Valor, the Secret Service's highest award, for their heroic actions that day in protecting the president's life. President Reagan later wrote in his autobiography that "as I was being thrown into the limo, there, facing the camera between me and the gunman, spreadeagling himself to make as big a target as possible, was Tim McCarthy. He was shot right in the chest. Thank heaven he lived."[55]

When Hinckley was found not guilty by reason of insanity, there was a large public reaction to the laws regarding the insanity defense. As a result, the U.S. Congress made significant changes to its insanity defense statutes in the Insanity Defense Reform Act of 1984, and nearly every state followed with some type of change.[56] Several state legislatures, including Idaho, Montana, and Utah, simply abolished the defense altogether. There was also talk of changing the law in regard to the punishment for anyone attempting to assassinate the president by mandating the death penalty. Hinckley, hearing this, responded, "That wouldn't have stopped me."[57] His father asked him what would have stopped him, and Hinckley replied, "Maybe if I'd had to wait to buy a gun [or] had to fill out forms, or get a permit first, or sign in with the police, or anything complicated. I probably wouldn't have done it."[58] In 1994, the Brady Bill, which was named in honor of Reagan's press secretary and mandated a five-day waiting period for anyone wanting to purchase a firearm, was signed into law by President Bill Clinton.

The Secret Service evaluated its response to the attempt on Reagan's life and found that the protection executed was in accordance with its policies and procedures and that the agents acted properly during the assassination attempt.[59] Deficiencies were noted, however, with regard to the hospital and to the protection of the vice president. There had been no immediate Secret Service protection provided at the hospital upon Reagan's arrival, and the hospital did not have Reagan's medical records immediately available. Finally, there was no plan in place to increase the protection of the vice president in a situation in which the president was disabled.[60] The agency addressed these issues, and additional security was ordered not only for the president but also for all protectees.

When it was discovered that Hinckley had learned the president's agenda from the newspaper, the release of this particular information on a daily basis was immediately ceased by the White House.[61] Further, an important issue was raised by Herbert L. Abrams, a medical doctor and author, as to whether

Reagan's wounds and surgery were enough to have invoked the Twenty-Fifth Amendment's provisions for succession to the presidency due to Reagan's "inability" to discharge the duties of his office.[62] Indeed, this issue came up at the White House situation room during the crisis, when Secretary of State Alexander Haig claimed (wrongly) that he was "in control" while the president was disabled. This claim led ultimately to Haig's resignation.[63]

CONCLUSION

Ronald Reagan, the former movie actor and governor of California, became the fortieth president of the United States on January 20, 1981. Sixty-nine days after his inauguration, on March 30, 1981, he was shot in the chest by John Hinckley Jr., a mentally unstable man who had become infatuated with the actress Jodie Foster in the movie *Taxi Driver* and attempted to win her love by assassinating the president. Reagan survived, the bullet having been surgically removed from just behind his heart, and became the oldest man to serve as president of the United States. As of this writing, Reagan is the last president to have been wounded by an assassin. In his later years, he suffered from Alzheimer's disease, and he died on June 5, 2004.

John Hinckley Jr. was found not guilty by reason of insanity and sentenced to confinement at St. Elizabeth's Mental Institution in Washington, D.C., where he resides to this day. He has never expressed remorse for his actions.

The U.S. Secret Service conducted a complete investigation into how effectively they responded on that blustery March day outside of the Washington Hilton, and made a number of modifications. Changes were made to the procedures for obtaining medical assistance for the president, enhancing the protection of the president at the hospital, and ensuring that the vice president, the next individual in succession to the president, has enhanced protection in such an event.

—— 11 ——

Other Assassination Attempts

The presidential assassinations and attempted assassinations that have been detailed so far have resulted in the death of the president, the injury of the president, or an event that placed the president's life in immediate jeopardy. There are other cases of assassination attempts in American history that have not quite risen to these same levels, but were believed to have been either planned attacks or attempted attacks aimed at the president's life. While it is not known how many threats the U.S. Secret Service manages to thwart each year, there are some cases that have reached the news media and have been reported on widely so that we have an understanding of the circumstances surrounding these other assassination attempts on the lives of the presidents.

The earliest of these attempts is what has come to be known as the Baltimore Plot, in which newly elected Abraham Lincoln, while making his way from Illinois to Washington, D.C., for his inauguration, is believed to have been under threat of assassination had he continued with his plans for a train stop in Baltimore, Maryland. Because Lincoln's advisors recommended he avoid the city of Baltimore and proceed to Washington, D.C., at night under the cover of darkness, it is believed he avoided a possible assassination attempt, if not an actual assassination.

The next such assassination attempt, oddly enough, was on President John F. Kennedy. Both Lincoln and Kennedy faced the threat of assassination early in their administrations, only to be assassinated by others later in their tenure in office. A number of these types of attempts then seem to expand; President Nixon faced two separate threats, Carter one, George H. W. Bush one, Clinton two, George W. Bush three, and President Barack Obama, while still the Democratic nominee in 2008, two. Each of these assassination attempts, the assassin, and the circumstances surrounding them will be reviewed in this chapter, thus completing all of the known assassinations and attempted assassinations on U.S. presidents.

ABRAHAM LINCOLN AND THE BALTIMORE PLOT

The Baltimore Plot is considered to have been the first conspiracy to assassinate a president in the United States.[1] Abraham Lincoln was set to be sworn into office on March 4, 1861. To honor some of the states that helped elect him, Lincoln planned to depart Springfield, Illinois, cross eight states, and stop in seventy cities before arriving in Washington, D.C. Lincoln's plans were public knowledge, and newspapers reported on his stops. Lincoln was to make a stop in Baltimore, Maryland, on February 23, 1861, despite the fact that the city and its government were sympathetic to the southern cause.[2]

Lincoln left Springfield, Illinois, on February 11, 1861, and at every stop along the way he was greeted by dignitaries and large throngs of crowds. He had a large and growing entourage with him along the journey, but he had no formal protection. Elmer E. Ellsworth was given charge to carry Lincoln through the crowds at each stop, and Edwin V. Sumner, the senior military officer on the train, took it upon himself to organize Lincoln's overall security. The security, however, was extremely limited, as they would discover on February 16, 1861, when Lincoln arrived in Buffalo, New York. Despite military escorts and police officers, the crowd of supporters pushing forward to catch a glimpse of Lincoln resulted in injuries to some of his party, including Major David Hunter. Lincoln narrowly escaped the crush of the crowd, but the vulnerability of the president on this whistle-stop tour was clear.[3]

At about this same time, the renowned private investigator Allan Pinkerton had been hired by the railroads to investigate rumors that the railroad lines entering Baltimore were going to be destroyed in advance of Lincoln's arrival. He and several of his operatives, including Kate Warne, the first female detective, began working the case. Pinkerton himself discovered in Baltimore that there was a conspiracy afoot to attack Lincoln's carriage after it left the Camden Street Railroad Station and proceeded through the streets of Baltimore. Police protection could not be relied upon, for it was believed that the police commissioner was complicit in the attempt and that his officers were ordered to let marked agitators through the police lines, thus allowing the assassins to approach the carriage. Once the attack was finished, they would disappear back into the crowds, having assassinated Lincoln before he had even taken the oath of office.

Pinkerton made every attempt to get word to Lincoln about the possible assassination attempt. He managed to do so through one of Lincoln's aides, Ward Hill Lamson, and Lincoln considered the information. Not too long after the receipt of that news, Frederick Seward, the son of Senator William Seward, arrived at one of the planned train stops with information for Lincoln directly from his father. Seward relayed that the New York police had also discovered evidence of the

Baltimore plot. Satisfied that Seward's information was independent of Pinkerton's, Lincoln had the corroborating evidence he needed to believe that the plot was real.

Pinkerton's plan was to have Lincoln travel from his stop in Philadelphia, Pennsylvania, and take another train directly into Washington, D.C. Lincoln balked at the plan because he was scheduled to give a speech in Harrisburg, Pennsylvania; eventually, he agreed to leave Harrisburg after a visit on February 22. Pinkerton had the telegraph lines between Baltimore and Harrisburg cut, preventing any communication of Lincoln's movement. That evening, Lincoln boarded a special train that arrived in Baltimore late at night, at which point he had to transfer between the President and Camden Street Train Stations. The exchange was a success, with Lincoln having been slightly disguised with hat and cloak. Pinkerton then sent a telegram to the vice president of the Pennsylvania Railroad stating, "Plums [Pinkerton] delivered nuts [Lincoln] safely."[4]

There was never an investigation into the legitimacy of the Baltimore plot, nor was anyone ever brought to justice for the conspiracy to assassinate the president-elect. In the immediate aftermath, Lincoln was ridiculed for having avoided Baltimore by entering Washington, D.C., under the cover of darkness.

Figure 11.1. Artist Thomas Nast's illustration of the crowd at Baltimore waiting for Mr. Lincoln, the president-elect, to arrive on February 23, 1861. The mob was to serve as a cover for the assassination of Lincoln; however, Lincoln was smuggled into Washington, D.C., overnight and never arrived in Baltimore as planned. (Courtesy of the Library of Congress.)

Some have suggested that Pinkerton had simply inflated some of the rumors he heard to aggrandize himself and endear himself to the incoming president. Research supporting the conspiracy theory has often focused on Cipriano Ferrandini, a hairdresser from Corsica who was a member of an organization focused on "southern rights."[5] More recent research suggests that the conspiracy was real and that Baltimore Mayor George William Brown and City Marshall George Proctor Kane may have been complicit in it.[6]

JOHN F. KENNEDY AND RICHARD PAVLICK

John F. Kennedy, like Lincoln, had an assassin plotting to kill him before he could be inaugurated. In the case of President-Elect John F. Kennedy, however, it was not a conspiracy to assassinate him, but rather a lone individual, Richard Paul Pavlick, who was planning the attempt.

Pavlick was born on February 13, 1887, and was seventy-three years old at the time of the assassination attempt.[7] He was born in Belmont, New Hampshire, had no family, and had retired from a career as a postal worker. He was very outspoken, and he hated the idea of a wealthy, Catholic member of the Kennedy family becoming president of the United States. When Kennedy defeated Republican Vice President Richard M. Nixon on November 9, 1960, Pavlick turned over his property to a local youth camp, loaded his 1950 Buick with the few possessions he owned, and disappeared.

A short time later, the U.S. postmaster in Belmont began receiving postcards from Pavlick. Short notes stated that his hometown would soon hear from him and "in a big way." The postmaster, Thomas M. Murphy, noticed that the postcards had been mailed from post offices across the United States, including Georgetown, Washington, D.C.; Hyannis Port, Massachusetts; and Palm Beach, Florida, all locations of Kennedy family homes. After tracking them for almost a month, he realized that the dates and locations on the canceled stamps matched the dates and places that Kennedy had been visiting as president-elect. Murphy contacted the U.S. Secret Service, who began interviewing people who had known Pavlick. In their investigations they discovered that before Pavlick disappeared, he had purchased a number of sticks of dynamite.

On December 11, 1960, Pavlick watched as Kennedy went to Mass at St. Edward Church in Palm Beach, Florida.[8] He waited for Kennedy to exit the church, planning to drive his car into Kennedy's in hope that the ensuing fire would set off the dynamite he had stored in the trunk. When Kennedy came out with his wife and two small children, Pavlick changed his mind. Pavlick later stated, "I did not want to harm her or the children."[9]

By this time, the Secret Service had notified the Palm Beach police department to be on the lookout for Pavlick's 1950 Buick and to stop and detain him for questioning.[10] On December 15, 1960, Police Officer Lester Free spotted the car, called for backup, and then surrounded the car, placing Pavlick under arrest. When they searched the car, they found seven sticks of dynamite in the trunk. A letter was also found in Pavlick's possession that was supposed to be released after the assassination, which read in part, "I believe that the Kennedys bought the presidency and the White House and until he really became president it was my intention to remove him in the only way it was available to me."[11]

On January 20, 1961, Kennedy was inaugurated as the thirty-fifth president of the United States. One week later, Pavlick was, by order of the court, committed to a mental hospital in Springfield, Missouri. Two months later, he was indicted for threatening to kill the president-elect. On November 22, 1963, Kennedy was assassinated by Lee Harvey Oswald, and ten days later, on December 2, the charges against Pavlick were dropped. He was ordered to remain confined to a mental hospital in New Hampshire, but was released on December 13, 1966. In poor health, he lingered for another nine years, then died in the Veterans Administration hospital in Manchester, New Hampshire, on November 11, 1975. He was eighty-eight years old.

RICHARD M. NIXON AND ARTHUR BREMER

Although Arthur Bremer is primarily known for his assassination attempt on the life of George Wallace, a Democratic candidate for president in 1972, his true target had been President Richard M. Nixon.[12] Bremer was born in Milwaukee, Wisconsin, on August 21, 1950, to William Bremer, a truck driver, and Sylvia Bremer, a homemaker. Raised in a working-class family, Bremer claims that he was abused as a young child, not only by his parents but also by all of the children in the schools he attended. Although demonstrating a high intelligence quotient (106), Bremer was largely a misfit and was antisocial.[13]

After graduating from high school, Bremer moved out of his parents' house and into an apartment. He obtained a job as a busboy at the Milwaukee Athletic Club, but when he was found talking to himself, he was demoted to janitor. He quit that position, only to end up as a janitor at a high school. In the fall of 1971, he had a short relationship with a student, Joan Pemrich, who was only fifteen years of age. When she broke up with him, Bremer began to unravel.[14]

He was arrested on November 18, 1971, for carrying a concealed handgun and parking in a no-parking zone. A court-appointed psychiatrist determined that Bremer was a schizophrenic. After undergoing psychotherapy and paying a fine, Bremer was released. In February of the next year, he quit his job and on March 1 began writing a hate-filled diary in which he stated that he was going to assassinate someone, either Richard Nixon or George Wallace.[15]

On April 10, 1972, Bremer traveled to Ottawa, Canada, and booked a room at the Lord Elgin Hotel.[16] Nixon arrived four days later and made an appearance at Parliament Hill. Bremer was present that day, wearing a business suit and armed with a revolver, intending to assassinate the president. Owing to the work of the Secret Service and the local police, however, Bremer was never able to get close enough to fire his gun. His only opportunity came when the presidential motorcade drove by him, but Bremer decided not to fire. He was unsure if the bullets would penetrate the glass. He eventually returned home to Milwaukee and reassessed his plans.

On May 4, 1972, Bremer decided it would not be possible to assassinate President Nixon, so he set his sights on George Wallace. He offered to work on the Wallace campaign in the hopes of getting near the candidate, and he attended a number of rallies, but he never was able to get close enough to Wallace. Bremer then traveled to Maryland in order to be near Wallace's campaign headquarters in Silver Spring.

On May 15, 1972, Bremer attended an appearance by George Wallace at the Laurel Shopping Center.[17] There were over 1,000 people present, and Wallace, against the advice of his Secret Service protection, entered the crowd and began shaking hands. At approximately 4 P.M., only a few minutes after Wallace's speech had ended, Bremer moved forward, pulled out a .38 revolver, and fired all six rounds.[18] George Wallace was struck four times and crumpled to the ground. He was losing blood fast from the bullets that entered his abdomen and chest, and one bullet lodged in his spine. Three other individuals were also wounded: Alabama State Trooper Captain E. C. Dothard, who was one of Wallace's personal bodyguards; Dora Thompson, a Wallace campaign volunteer; and Nick Zarvos, a U.S. Secret Service agent assigned to protect Wallace.

Bremer was convicted of the assassination attempt on August 4, 1972, and was sentenced to sixty-three years in prison. On appeal, the sentence was later reduced to fifty-three years. Bremer's diary was published the next year and became the inspiration for the movie *Taxi Driver*, which would inspire John Hinckley Jr. to try to assassinate President Ronald Reagan (see chapter 10). Bremer served thirty-five years of his sentence and was released on November 9, 2007. He remains relatively confined to a halfway house in Maryland. George Wallace was paralyzed by the attack and confined to a wheelchair for the rest of his life. Wallace died on September 13, 1998.

RICHARD M. NIXON AND SAMUEL BYCK

The other significant attempt on President Nixon's life came just after 7 A.M. on the morning of February 22, 1974. Samuel Byck, "a burly, middle-age man,"[19] entered the Baltimore-Washington International (BWI) Airport with a briefcase in hand and walked to the front of the line at Gate C. The people in line were waiting to board Delta Flight 523 bound for Atlanta, Georgia. A security guard stood nearby, his back turned to the passenger line. Byck pulled a .22-caliber pistol from underneath his raincoat and fired twice into the security guard's back, killing him instantly. As people began screaming and running in all directions, Byck leaped over the security chain, ran down the boarding ramp, and boarded the plane. Immediately he entered through the door of the cockpit and fired one round inside the cabin of the airplane.

He then screamed at the pilot, "Fly this plane out of here!"[20] Byck's plan was to have the pilot fly Delta Flight 523 into Washington, D.C., where he would shoot the pilot and crash the plane into the White House, killing President Nixon, a mission he personally dubbed "Operation Pandora's Box."[21]

Samuel Byck was born on January 30, 1930, and at the time of the hijacking was forty-four years old.[22] He grew up in Philadelphia with a father who had a difficult time keeping a job. Sam Byck failed to graduate from high school, never making it past the ninth grade. He attempted to find a job, but settled into the same pattern as his father, unable to maintain a job. He was known as a loner who often exhibited signs of mental illness. Although he married and had four children, Byck suffered from depression due to a number of failures in his life, which led to his wife divorcing him and taking the children away. He then lived with his mother for a while, but she too abandoned him, moving to Florida. Byck was interviewed by the U.S. Secret Service in October 1972 for making the overt statement, "Someone ought to kill President Nixon."[23] Byck's psychiatrist assured the investigating agents that Byck was mostly a talker who liked to make verbal threats but did not have the capacity to carry them out.

In the fall of 1973, Byck protested twice in front of the White House without a permit and was arrested, but in both cases the charges were dropped.[24] It was about this time that Byck began writing long rambling letters to such notable people as columnist Jack Anderson, conductor Leonard Bernstein, and Senator Abraham Ribicoff. On February 20, 1974, Byck wrote his last will and testament, writing, "I will each of my children . . . the sum of one dollar each. They have each other and they deserve each other."[25] On February 22, 1974, early in the morning, and just hours before Byck would attempt to hijack the airplane at BWI, he tape-recorded a series of rants and raves against government's alleged "corruption" and "oppression," as well as a commentary on his emotions and feelings about what he was about to do. Samuel Byck had long made verbal threats and was now on the verge of carrying these threats out.

Once Byck took control of the cabin, he ordered the pilot to fly the plane. The pilot informed Byck that he could not roll back from the gate until the ground crew removed the wheel blocks. Byck, in anger, shot the copilot in the stomach. He then turned to the pilot and screamed, "The next one will be in the head!"[26] Byck then grabbed a female passenger, dragged her into the cockpit, and shoved her into the control panel, telling her to help the pilot fly the plane. At this point, two shots from outside of the plane exploded through the windshield, causing Byck to shove the woman out of the cockpit. He then turned back into the cockpit and fired twice. One bullet struck the already wounded copilot in the eye, and the other entered the pilot's right shoulder.

The pilot then radioed ground control: "Emergency, emergency, we're all shot . . . ah . . . can you get another pilot here to the airplane . . . ah . . . this fellow has shot us both."[27] The pilot also asked that the wheel blocks be removed so the plane could taxi away from the gate, then he passed out.

Byck once again grabbed a female passenger, dragged her into the cockpit, and ordered her to fly the plane. He then fired two more shots, one into the copilot and the other into the pilot. The woman was screaming and begging Byck to let her go when two more bullets from outside the plane exploded in the cabin, shattering the cockpit windows. Byck tried to respond with more gunfire, but two more sniper shots were fired. One entered Byck's stomach, and the other his chest. He fell to the floor of the cockpit, losing his pistol along the way. He scrambled around to recover the weapon, sat up, put the gun to his temple, and fired one shot, thus stopping the carnage. The briefcase he had brought on board, which was found lying underneath him, was an improvised gasoline bomb armed with an igniter.

The U.S. Secret Service decided to downplay the incident, but it was not long after the assassination attempt that they established counterdefensive measures on the roof of the White House to protect against plots such as the one Byck attempted. In 1987, in an FAA report titled, "Troubled Passage: The Federal Aviation Administration during the Nixon-Ford Term 1973–1977," it was noted that "though Byck lacked the skill and self-control to reach his target, he had provided a chilling reminder of the potential of violence against civil aviation. Under a more relaxed security system, his suicidal rampage might have begun when the airliner was aloft."[28] Investigating the terrorist attacks of September 11, 2001, when nineteen hijackers captured four planes and crashed two into the World Trade Center in New York, one into the Pentagon in Arlington, Virginia, and the fourth into a field in Pennsylvania, the 9/11 Commission Report mentioned the Byck attempt on Nixon's life.[29]

JIMMY CARTER AND RAYMOND LEE HARVEY

On May 5, 1979, President Jimmy Carter was scheduled to give a speech at the Civic Center in Los Angeles.[30] Approximately ten minutes before Carter was to speak, Secret Service agents noticed a man who looked agitated and nervous. When they approached him, he began to walk away, at which point he was seized. A quick search revealed that the man was armed with a starter's pistol. He was then identified as Raymond Lee Harvey, an unemployed drifter, thirty-five years of age, with a long history of mental illness. They took him to a secure area for questioning and Raymond Lee Harvey began to relay a strange story that at first could not have been taken seriously.

Harvey explained that two weeks before Carter was scheduled to speak, he had met three Latino men in downtown Los Angeles. The night before the speech, he again met the three men, this time in the third-floor room of the Alan Hotel, a cheap hotel near the Los Angles Civic Center. While Harvey was drinking with them, they told him of their intent to shoot President Carter at this speech. They asked Harvey for his assistance—he was to provide a diversion from the true assassination. Harvey was to work his way to the front of the crowd, fire off the starter's pistol, and while everyone diverted their attention from the president, the Latino men would fire rifles from hidden locations and assassinate President Carter. Harvey further explained that he and one of the men, who he said was named Julio, went to the roof of the hotel and fired seven blanks from the pistol in order to make sure Harvey knew how to fire the pistol and to see how much noise it would make. He then spent the night in the same room with Julio, while the other two men, the designated shooters, slept in a room nearby.

After Harvey relayed his fanciful tale, the Secret Service began its investigation to verify Harvey's story. They managed to locate the man Harvey called Julio, and identified him as Osvaldo Espinoza-Ortiz, a twenty-one-year-old male who was an illegal alien from Mexico. At first Espinoza-Ortiz denied knowing Harvey, but later it came out that they had known each other for over a year, not just the two weeks Harvey had confessed. Espinoza-Ortiz then told the Secret Service that one of the other men was Umberto Camacho, and when they searched the hotel room in which he and the other male had stayed, they found a shotgun case along with three rounds of live ammunition. Espinoza-Ortiz also admitted that he was approximately ten feet away from Harvey when he was taken into custody.

Harvey was charged with conspiring to kill the president, and Espinoza-Ortiz was taken in as a material witness. The other two men were never found. Eventually, charges were dropped against Harvey and Espinoza-Ortiz as there was not enough evidence to obtain a conviction.

GEORGE H. W. BUSH AND THE IRAQ PLOT

In 1988, George Herbert Walker Bush was elected to the presidency after eight years as vice president under President Ronald Reagan. He entered office in January 1989, a time of relative prosperity in America and of new hope in the world with the fall of both the Berlin Wall and the Soviet Union. In late 1989 and early 1990, his administration began to face the prospect of a recession, and economic concerns remained the focus of the administration until August 1, 1990, when Iraq, under the leadership of President Saddam Hussein, invaded Kuwait, its small, oil-rich neighbor to the south on the Persian Gulf. The United States and an international coalition sent troops that fall into Saudi Arabia, initially to provide a defense from further Iraqi aggression and later to expel Iraqi forces from Kuwait. The United Nations Security Council gave its approval for the use of military force to expel Iraq, and the U.S. Congress subsequently gave the president permission to use force. In the early morning hours of January 17, 1991, American and coalition forces began the bombing of Iraq, and four weeks later, on February 24, ground forces entered both Kuwait and Iraq. After 100 hours, as the Iraqi forces retreated, President Bush ordered a cessation to hostilities. The Persian Gulf War, known as Operation Desert Storm, was over.[31]

In 1992, President Bush ran for a second term in office, but mired by a recession he was defeated by the Democratic candidate, Bill Clinton. Bush returned to

Houston, Texas, and settled into private life. Saddam Hussein, despite the Iraqi military being almost entirely crippled and his standing in the Middle East greatly diminished, remained in power. It was also said by the Central Intelligence Agency (CIA) that Saddam held a personal grudge against George Bush and that he "was heard on official Iraq media promising to hunt down and punish Bush, even after he left office."[32]

In April 1993, former President Bush was invited to Kuwait University to attend a ceremony commemorating the victory over Iraq. Bush was to be honored and recognized by the emir of Kuwait for his role in the Persian Gulf War. Bush was accompanied on the trip by "his wife, two of his sons, former Secretary of State James A. Baker III, former Chief of Staff John Sununu, and former Treasury Secretary Nicholas Brady."[33] The trip took place between April 14 and April 16, 1993, seemingly without incident. It was soon learned, however, that there had been an assassination attempt planned, with the primary target being former President Bush. The individual who had orchestrated the assassination attempt was none other than Iraq's president, Saddam Hussein.

Kuwaiti authorities learned that there was to be an attempt on former President Bush's life just about the time of the visit. Almost immediately, a Toyota Landcruiser was discovered abandoned near Kuwait University. It was loaded with 80–90 kilograms of plastic explosives connected to a detonator, as well as ten cube-shaped devices that each contained plastic explosives and detonators.[34] Kuwaiti officials and personnel from the State Department, CIA, U.S. Secret Service, and Federal Bureau of Investigation investigated the alleged assassination.

As Kuwaiti officials began rounding up potential suspects, CIA bomb technicians verified that the explosive devices were identical to two known devices originating in Iraq, particularly as they related to the remote-control firing mechanism. In addition, intelligence reports were suggesting that the Iraqi Intelligence Service (IIS), on the orders of President Saddam Hussein, was involved in the assassination plot. Two of the suspects, Wali 'Abd Al-Hadi 'Abd Al-Hasan Al-Ghazali (Al-Ghazali) and Ra'd 'Abd Al-Amir 'Abbud Al-Asadi (Al-Asadi), confessed that they had participated in the plot at the direction of the IIS. Apparently they were recruited at the last minute out of Basra, Iraq, where Al-Ghazali was a nurse from Najaf and Al-Asadi was the owner of a coffee shop in Alashar.[35] They were given the Toyota Landcruiser and told to drive it to Kuwait, park it along the Bush motorcade route, and detonate it by remote control. The FBI estimated that the explosives could potentially have caused the destruction of an area of one-quarter mile in radius.

Upon arriving in Kuwait, Al-Ghazali and Al-Asadi traveled to Kuwait University, but the high level of security made them nervous. Over the next several days, they began losing many of the weapons so they would not get caught with them in their possession. Although they had parked the Toyota Landcruiser as ordered, they had done so immediately upon their arrival; after it sat for two days along the motorcade route, Kuwaiti officials became suspicious, seized the vehicle, and discovered the explosives. The would-be assassins then stole a white Mercedes-Benz to drive back to Iraq, but it broke down and they were forced to walk toward the Iraq border. They were eventually picked up and placed under arrest.[36]

A total of seventeen individuals were taken into custody. Three were released, and of the fourteen remaining defendants, twelve were from Iraq and two were from Kuwait. Al-Ghazali and Al-Asadi pleaded guilty, while the other twelve defendants pleaded not guilty. All but one of these were eventually convicted. In addition, while the court hearings proceeded, President Bill Clinton, in retaliation for what he saw as an aggressive act by the government of Iraq, ordered the U.S. Navy to launch twenty-three Tomahawk missiles against the headquarters of the Iraqi Intelligence Service, the agency that orchestrated the attempted assassination.[37]

BILL CLINTON AND FRANK CORDER

On September 11, 1994, a thirty-eight-year-old man by the name of Frank Eugene Corder, who had little skill in piloting an aircraft, became highly intoxicated and stole a small Cessna 150L airplane from the Aldino Airport in Maryland.[38] He managed to get the aircraft off the ground and turned toward Washington, D.C. He entered restricted airspace and aimed the plane directly at the White House. He was about to accomplish what Samuel Byck had failed to do, albeit with a much smaller plane.

Frank Corder was born in Perry Point, Maryland, on May 26, 1956, to William Eugene Corder, an aircraft mechanic, and Dorothy Corder, a stay-at-home mother. Frank did not do well in school and dropped out of Aberdeen High School during the eleventh grade.[39] He enlisted in the Army and was stationed at Fort Knox, Kentucky, and Fort Carson, Colorado, where, like his father, he worked as a mechanic. There were no reports of any problems with Frank during his military service, and he was honorably discharged in 1975 as a private first class. He then went to work as a truck driver, a job he would hold for approximately seventeen years.

Frank Corder began to unravel somewhat in the early 1990s, abusing both alcohol and drugs.[40] Out of work and with a growing habit, he was arrested for theft on April 15, 1993. Later that year he was arrested for possession and dealing drugs, and was admitted to a 90-day drug rehabilitation center. After being released in February 1994, he lived with his third wife, Lydia, in a motel in Aberdeen. With no job and a serious addiction, his life was spinning out of control. Lydia then left him, and Frank became depressed and suicidal.

After drinking at a bar with a friend, his friend dropped him off at the Aldino Airport, where he stole the keys to a Cessna airplane. He had enough flight experience to take off and pilot the plane. He headed north and was first spotted by FAA radar at 1:06 A.M. over York, Pennsylvania. He then managed to head the plane toward Washington, D.C., entering restricted airspace at

1:48 A.M. At an altitude of 2,700 feet he began to rapidly drop the plane's altitude and steer it toward the south wall of the White House. He misjudged somewhat, and at 1:49 A.M. on September 12, 1994, he crashed the plane into the South Lawn, skidded across the lawn, and came to rest against the White House wall. Corder died on impact from "massive blunt-force injuries."[41]

There was never any conclusive proof as to whether Frank Corder intended to kill President Clinton. The investigation later concluded that the crash was intentional—the airplane's wing flaps were up and the throttle was full forward, neither indicating a pilot trying to perform an emergency landing.[42] Even if Corder had intended to assassinate the president, he failed miserably, for Clinton was not even in the White House at the time. The mansion was undergoing construction at the time, and the First Family was living across the street at the Blair House. There was, however, no way for Corder to have known that; the Secret Service, for security reasons, had decided not to share that information with the public, having learned that lesson after the assassination attempt against President Truman at that house (see chapter 7).

BILL CLINTON AND FRANCISCO DURAN

Less than six weeks later, President Clinton once again became the target of a would-be assassin, Francisco Martin Duran, who fired an assault weapon at the White House on October 29, 1994. Duran was twenty-six years old at the time, having been born on September 8, 1968, in Albuquerque, New Mexico.[43] Like Corder before him, Duran had had a difficult childhood. He dropped out of high school and was arrested on several occasions for minor crimes. In the wake of Operation Desert Storm, he decided to enlist in the U.S. Army. However, unlike Corder, Duran received a dishonorable discharge from the military in 1993, primarily due to his conviction of aggravated assault with a vehicle. This felony conviction caused him to have difficulty finding a job afterward. He moved to Widefield, Colorado, with his wife Ingrid after the discharge. There, Duran drifted in and out of odd jobs, began abusing alcohol, and faced ever-increasing levels of depression.

In late September 1994, Duran left home and did not return. His wife became concerned and contacted the El Paso County Sheriff's Office on October 1 to file a missing persons report. Ingrid received a call on October 15, 1994, from Francisco stating that he was preparing to do something drastic and that he would be killed in the "assault" he was planning. He refused to tell her where he was or what he was planning, but after the conversation, she became so concerned that she contacted the FBI. As there was no mention of the president being the target of Duran's anger, the FBI did not forward the information on to the Secret Service. In a later investigation, it turned out that Duran had stated to several people that he "intended to kill President Clinton"; however, no one took the threat seriously, and no law enforcement agency was ever contacted about these threats.

On Saturday, October 29, 1994, at approximately 2:55 P.M., Duran stood on the south sidewalk of Pennsylvania Avenue in front of the White House.[44] He suddenly pulled a Chinese-make SKS semiautomatic rifle from under his long black trench coat and pointed the weapon between the iron bars of the fence toward the White House. He fired several rounds, then pulled the rifle from between the bars. He ran east along the sidewalk, firing toward the White House as he ran. When the magazine was empty, Duran stopped to reload. At this point a tourist, Harry Michael Rakosky, tackled Duran. Two other citizens, Kenneth Alan Davis and Robert Edward Haines, ran to assist Rakosky in subduing Duran.

During this time, immediately after the shots were fired, members of the Uniformed Division of the Secret Service, which protects the White House grounds and perimeter, drew their weapons and began running toward Duran. In addition, an emergency response team (ERT) officer, who happened to be patrolling along the north grounds when Duran opened fire, ran toward Duran with his weapon drawn. All of these individuals held their fire as the three citizens tackled Duran. The uniformed Secret Service members made their way around the fence, while the ERT officer leaped over. They placed handcuffs on Duran and ordered the citizens to move away. One of the three citizens was heard to say to the officers, "Thanks for not shooting me." Francisco Martin Duran replied, "I wish you had shot me."[45]

In the case of Corder, President Clinton and his family had been living in the Blair House while the White House was undergoing repair. In the case of Duran, President Clinton was actually at home in the family residence of the White House, which is located on the north side. President Clinton was watching a football game and only became aware of the assassination attempt after the fact. It was later learned that Duran had fired twenty-nine rounds, eleven of which struck the White House façade. One penetrated the window of the Press Briefing Room in the West Wing. Despite the fact that there were several individuals standing around, presumably uniformed Secret Service, in the direction of Duran's gunfire, no one was harmed in the attempt.

Duran was charged with a number of crimes, the most serious being the attempted murder of the president of the United States. In addition, he was charged with four counts of assaulting a federal officer (the four Secret Service officers who were standing in the line of fire). Further, he was charged with the illegal possession of a firearm by a convicted felon, the use of an assault weapon during the commission of a crime of violence, destruction of U.S. property (the White House), and the interstate transportation of a firearm with the intent to commit a felony. Duran pleaded not guilty, and the defense attempted to demonstrate that this was by reason of insanity. The evidence for insanity seemed wholly contrived and far-fetched, including the statement that Duran was trying to save the world by destroying an alien mist and that he was convinced by the conservative talk show host Chuck Baker to cleanse the government through an armed revolution. The defense failed to make its case, and at the end of the two-week trial, Duran was found guilty and sentenced to forty years in prison.

The Corder and Duran attacks, not to mention an additional four isolated events including some White House fence jumpers,[46] caused Secretary of Treasury Lloyd Bentsen to call for a "thorough and comprehensive" investigation.[47] While the review was ordered after the Corder incident, the Duran attack initiated a much wider review of the protection of the president and his family, as well as the policies and procedures of the U.S. Secret Service. Although the complete report was classified, a portion was developed for public consumption. Despite the impact that the review had on various policies and procedures for protecting the president, most of the media and public attention was focused on the efficacy of one recommendation: converting Pennsylvania Avenue to a pedestrian mall in front of the White House, thus banning all motor vehicle traffic.

GEORGE W. BUSH AND ROBERT PICKETT

On February 7, 2001, less than a month after his inauguration, President George W. Bush became the target of a would-be assassin, in a manner similar to Duran's attempt on President Clinton's life. In this case, however, the outcome would be very different.

The would-be assassin, Robert Pickett, was forty-seven years old and had been born and raised in Evansville, Indiana.[48] After graduating from high school, he went to a local college to obtain a degree in accounting. He allegedly turned down a commission to West Point in 1972 because the cadets were plotting against him, and instead went to work at the Internal Revenue Service. He also allegedly blew the whistle on a supervisor who was violating regulations, which made him a source of contempt within the agency. Pickett claimed he was then harassed and threatened so often that he began suffering mental health problems. There is no information to corroborate these claims. In any case, he ended up in and out of mental institutions five times, twice because he had threatened suicide. It is for this last reason that he was fired by the Internal Revenue Service in 1988.

The next decade was a quiet one for Pickett. He went to work as a certified public accountant for the Evansville accounting firm his father had worked for. He lived with his parents in the 1990s, but after they died he lived by himself. In February 2000, he went to a local pawn shop and purchased a Taurus .38 Special revolver, a small five-shot, concealable handgun. Pickett, in his background check, claimed he had never been admitted to a mental institution. There is no record that he used the gun until approximately one year later. On February 2, 2001, he wrote a letter to Charles Rossotti, the IRS commissioner, stating that Rossotti was guilty of murder because his predecessors had made decisions that killed an innocent man. The letter included additional rants in the same vein. It was discovered later that he had written similar letters to both Presidents Clinton and George H.W. Bush, but the letters were about his grievances over being fired by the Internal Revenue Service. Neither president was the focus of his discontent.

Several days later, Pickett left for Washington, D.C. On February 7, 2001, at approximately 11:26 A.M., he approached the White House fence, pulled out the .38 Special, and began firing. President Bush was in fact at home in the White House, where he was working out in the weight room on the upper floor of the residence. Pickett fired several shots, but because there were trees and bushes between the sidewalk and the White House, there was never any threat to the president. Pickett then proceeded to a security barrier near the fence line, sat down on the barrier, and held the gun pointing downward. Unlike the case of Duran, however, no citizens managed to stop Pickett, but the U.S. Secret Service and Park Police quickly confronted Pickett and ordered him to drop the weapon. He refused. Ten minutes into the stand-off, Pickett brought the weapon up, waved it in the air, pointed it at his mouth, waved it in the air again, then brought the weapon down. At this point, a uniformed Secret Service officer shot him in the right knee, moved forward, and secured the weapon.

An ambulance was summoned and Pickett was taken to George Washington University Hospital, where he underwent surgery to remove fragments of both the bullet and bone. He remained in the hospital for medical reasons and to undergo a psychiatric evaluation. The next week, he was charged with assault on a federal officer, as he had threatened the officers present when he fired his gun and threatened to fire the gun. In June 2001, when his case came before the federal courts, he pleaded under the Alford Doctrine, acknowledging there was enough evidence to convict him, but not admitting he was entirely guilty. Robert Pickett was sentenced to three years in prison and three years of probation, and he was ordered to pay a $200 fine.[49]

GEORGE W. BUSH AND SEPTEMBER 11

Any discussion of President George W. Bush would be remiss if it did not include the terrorist attacks of September 11, 2001, as his presidency and that event have become historically entwined. Whether there is any truth to the speculation that Bush was a target of the terrorist attacks, and they were therefore an assassination attempt, is not known. The release of classified documents may someday shed light on this possibility, but at this point there are only speculation, rumors, and circumstantial evidence.

What is known is that on the morning of September 11, 2001, President Bush was staying at the Colony Beach and Tennis Resort on Longboat Key, Florida. He arose early, around 6:00 A.M., to go for his morning run. One story that has circulated and appears to have originated with the Longboat Key's local newspaper is that a van with several Middle Eastern–looking men arrived at the resort and claimed they were there for a poolside interview with the president.[50] They were turned away by the Secret Service as they did not have an appointment. The U.S. Secret Service has denied this story, and it has not been otherwise verified.

After his morning run, shower, and breakfast, President Bush was driven to the Emma E. Booker Elementary School in Sarasota, Florida. He met with a class of second graders. While reading them a story, he was notified that a plane had flown into the World Trade Center, and by all accounts it was believed to have been a strange accident. When the second plane flew into the World Trade Center, the president was again alerted and the trip to the classroom was finished. Bush was quickly transported to Air Force One, which then took off for Louisiana, then Nebraska, and finally Washington, D.C.

There were nineteen hijackers that morning taking four separate planes: American Airlines Flight 11, United Airlines Flight 175, American Airlines Flight 77, and United Airlines Flight 93.[51] At 8:46 A.M., Flight 11 was crashed into the World Trade Center's North Tower, followed by Flight 175, which hit the South Tower at 9:03 A.M. Another group of hijackers then flew Flight 77 into the Pentagon at 9:37 A.M. It is not sure if the Pentagon had been the intended target or a secondary target due to the fact that one of the terrorists was apparently having a difficult time piloting the plane. The hijackers of fourth and final flight, Flight 93, met with resistance from passengers who had learned of the other planes' fates and decided to fight back. Although they managed to prevent the plane from hitting its intended target, they were not able to wrest full control of the plane, and it crashed into a rural field near Shanksville, Pennsylvania, at 10:03 A.M. The intended target for Flight 93 is believed to have been the U.S. Capitol or the White House. Coupled with the fact that the intended target for Flight 77 was probably the same, with the Pentagon as a secondary target, there is a strong chance that one of the two planes was intended for the White House and, hence, the president. In this case, although the events of 9/11 were clearly a terrorist attack, if the intended target was the White House, then 9/11 may also have been an attempt to assassinate President Bush.

GEORGE W. BUSH AND VLADIMIR ARUTYUNIAN

On May 10, 2005, President Bush was in Tbilisi, Georgia, giving a speech in the Freedom Square.[52] Vladimir Arutyunian moved through the crowd, edging his way to the front, where he stopped and pulled something from his coat pocket. He threw the object—a hand grenade—toward the podium. Seated behind Bush were Georgian President Mikhail Saakashvili and his wife Sandra E. Roelofs, along with President Bush's wife, Laura. The grenade fell short of the podium, scattering the crowd. It did not detonate, however; though it was a live RGD-5 hand grenade and Arutyunian did pull the pin, a red tartan handkerchief wrapped around the grenade to conceal it had prevented the firing pin from deploying fast enough to detonate the grenade. In addition, because the grenade had hit a young girl in the crowd, it softened the blow of the grenade before it struck the ground.

The Federal Bureau of Investigation immediately began working with the Interior Ministry in Georgia, and after examining photographs from that day, they focused their attention on one suspect. A reward was offered for his identification and for information leading to his arrest. The actual identification was achieved when photos showed a man taking pictures in the direction of the attack; the photos taken by that man, a professor from Boise, Idaho, led investigators to Vladimir Arutyunian.

Arutyunian became the primary suspect in the attempted assassination, and officials from the Interior Ministry went to his apartment to take him into custody in July 2005. Arutyunian opened fire when the Interior Ministry Agents (police officers) attempted to enter his apartment, killing one agent. DNA samples collected from Arutyunian matched DNA samples obtained from the handkerchief. In the hospital after being injured during the arrest, Arutyunian stated that he had thrown the grenade in hopes of killing President Bush. He was convicted in court on January 11, 2006, and was sentenced to life in prison.

BARACK OBAMA AND TWO SEPARATE PLOTS

The presidential election of 2008 was off to an early start, beginning as early as the spring of 2007. One of the candidates for the Democratic nomination was Senator Barack Obama of Illinois. He received a death threat in late 2007 primarily because he was a black man running for president. Although the U.S. Secret Service up to that point only provided protection for the Democratic and Republican nominees, they decided to provide protection earlier due to the threats.

As the primaries began in January 2008, the two leading contenders for the Democratic nomination for president were Obama and U.S. Senator Hillary Clinton. It was a competitive race for what could potentially be either the first female or first black president of the United States. Obama managed to pull ahead and was thus set to receive his party's nomination at the Democratic National Convention in Denver, Colorado.

When it was learned that a black man was to be nominated as the Democratic Candidate for president, Tharin Gartrell, age twenty-eight, his cousin Shawn Robert Adolf, thirty-three, and their friend Nathan Johnson, thirty-two, agreed that a black man should not become president. They decided to go to Denver to kill Senator Barack Obama before he could receive the Democratic nomination. They checked into the Hyatt Regency Tech Center hotel under the mistaken belief that Senator Obama was to be lodged at that hotel. While at the hotel, the three men began taking methamphetamines, drinking alcohol, and voicing their racist views. A woman who had joined their party overheard them talking about killing the president and how they would go about assassinating Senator Obama. The woman left the party and contacted authorities.

On August 24, 2008, in the early morning hours, Gartrell was arrested in Aurora, Colorado, when he was pulled over for driving erratically. He was found to be heavily armed with a stolen rifle fitted with a silencer, fake identification, and wigs, as well as the necessary equipment to make methamphetamines. Gartrell told the police that the weapons belonged to his cousin Adolf, and he agreed to lead the police to his cousin. Gartrell led them straight to the Hyatt. Adolf attempted to escape by jumping out of the hotel window. He fell from the sixth story to a second-story roof, then to the ground, breaking his ankle in the process and making him an easy catch. Adolf was wearing body armor at the time. Johnson was taken into custody without incident.

The three men were separated, and very quickly Johnson divulged that Adolf was planning to assassinate Senator Obama. Early in the investigation, it was stated that there was enough evidence to charge them with conspiring to assassinate, but ultimately they were only criminally charged for the weapons and drug violations.

Two other men, white supremacists from Tennessee, also plotted to kill the Democratic Party presidential nominee in the fall of 2008. Paul Schlesselman, eighteen, and Daniel Cowart, twenty, were skinheads who were brought together by a mutual friend. Their intent was to kill eighty-eight black Americans, the majority of them being children from a local black school, before killing Obama. Their plots included wild fantasies of driving alongside the president-elect's limousine and shooting it up, wearing white tuxedos and top hats during the attempt, and decorating their car with Nazi swastikas.

On October 22, 2008, the two drove to the Beech Grove Church of Christ in Brownsville, Tennessee, and fired a shot at the front door. No one was injured, as there was no one at the church at the time of the shooting. The two later bragged about shooting at the church, which had made the local news, and a female friend of theirs told her mother, who then notified the local sheriff. The two were arrested for conspiracy, and several weapons were confiscated. They admitted they were planning to assassinate Obama and although it was not believed their plan was fully developed, they were indicted by a grand jury for conspiring to assassinate the candidate.

CONCLUSION

The presidential assassination attempts detailed in this chapter were all believed to have been legitimate attempts on the president's life, but failed to achieve their aim and did not injure or harm the president due to various circumstances. The Baltimore plot failed because President Lincoln circumvented the city of Baltimore, where the assassination attempt was to occur. The other cases failed simply because the individuals involved lacked intelligence and chose to brag about their intent. Despite these failures, in each case it has been determined that the president's life was or was believed to have been the target of a potential attack. Although these attacks did not achieve their intended end, they all in some way changed the way in which the president is protected, ranging from the retention of the Pinkerton Detective Agency during the Civil War to the closing off of Pennsylvania Avenue in front of the White House. Every assassination attempt is now run through an internal agency review at the U.S. Secret Service, as its primary mission is to protect the life of the president.

Although this chapter is by no means an exhaustive list of would-be assassinations, it is an attempt to detail all of the known incidents that rise to the level of assassination attempts. There have been many cases of individuals scaling the fence outside of the White House, but their intent was not clear enough to detail them as would-be assassins. Many of these individuals were mentally ill, thrill seekers, and so on, without clear means or intent to assassinate the president. However, the list of presidential assassinations is yet not entirely complete within the pages of this book, for the two deaths of sitting presidents, Zachary Taylor and Warren G. Harding, have long been the subject of rumors that they occurred not by natural causes but rather by the hands of assassins. Although there is no definitive proof of these assertions, the next chapter explores the circumstances surrounding the deaths of these two presidents and assesses the possibility that they were assassinated.

12

Rumored Assassinations

INTRODUCTION

When it comes to the death of a sitting president, it is not surprising that rumors of conspiracies begin to circulate. Did the president really die as stated, or was there a cover-up of something more heinous? As we have seen in the case of President John F. Kennedy, even when a president was, in fact, assassinated, conspiracy theories abound. Of the eight U.S. presidents who have died in office, half died by assassination (Lincoln, Garfield, McKinley, and Kennedy). The others (Harrison, Taylor, Harding, and F. D. Roosevelt) died by natural causes, or so it was assumed. Harrison's death a month into office, caused by having caught pneumonia giving a long inauguration speech on a cold and wet day, left little room for speculation. The other three, however, were subject to debate. Rumors about Roosevelt's death centered on his affair with Lucy Rutherfurd,[1] who was with him at Warm Springs when he died; and although there has been some wild speculation that he was assassinated, these assertions generally have little credibility.[2] That leaves the "natural deaths" of Zachary Taylor and Warren G. Harding while in office as the twelfth and twenty-ninth presidents, respectively, to be explored. These two deaths have spawned a number of rumors of assassinations. It is to the circumstances of these deaths that this chapter now turns.

ZACHARY TAYLOR

Zachary Taylor was born in Barboursville, Virginia, on November 24, 1784,[3] the third of nine children of Colonel Richard Lee Taylor and Sarah Strother. His family had an interesting lineage. Zachary Taylor was related to James Madison (a second cousin) and Robert E. Lee (a third cousin, once removed), he was a descendent of King Edward I of England, and he was related to several passengers on the *Mayflower*.

When "Little Zach," as he was known, was still a young child, the family moved to Jefferson County, Kentucky, where grew up on a plantation called Springfield (today the site of the Zachary Taylor House). Little Zach was home-schooled and tutored in his early years, and he assisted in working the plantation. Little Zach, however, wanted to become a soldier like his father. By the age of twenty-four, he achieved that goal.

Zachary Taylor drew upon his relationship with his cousin James Madison in 1808 to secure a commission as a first lieutenant. He was assigned to the Seventh Infantry Regiment and ordered west. Over the next several years, he was assigned to a number of places, ranging from the Indiana territory down to New Orleans. He became ill in 1810 while in New Orleans and was sent home to convalesce. During this leave, he met Margaret Mackall Smith of Maryland, and they were married that June. Margaret, over the next sixteen years, would bear one son and five daughters, two of whom died in early childhood, the result of a malaria outbreak. Margaret also contracted malaria, but recovered, remaining a semi-invalid the rest of her life.

Taylor returned to his military duty and for his dedication was promoted to captain in November 1810. At the opening of the War of 1812, Taylor was assigned to command Fort Harrison, located on the Wabash River. Unbeknownst to Taylor, the British, along with about 500 American Indians, planned to attack the fort in early September of that year. The Indians attempted a ruse, showing a flag of truce and asking to be fed, but the next night, September 4, and for the next ten days, they attacked the fort. Taylor orchestrated the fort's defense, and only after eight days under siege was he able to send for help. The story of the fort's successful defense spread across the country; for his heroics at the Battle of Fort Harrison, the first land victory of the war, Taylor received the first brevet promotion to major ever awarded. The order was signed by his cousin, President James Madison.

Taylor continued his service in the military over the next several years, but with little recognition and little reward. He decided to resign his commission and return to his plantation. In 1816, Taylor accepted a commission as a major of a local regiment, where he split his time between the military and the plantation. In 1819, he was promoted to the rank of lieutenant colonel and remained in this dual role for over a decade.

In May 1832, with the beginning of the Black Hawk War, he was promoted to colonel and called to full-time service. He was assigned to Fort Armstrong in Illinois and was placed in command of regular troops, but he saw no action, for the war was over by August. He returned to his dual-status life. At this time, a young Jefferson Davis began courting Taylor's daughter Sarah. They were married, against Taylor's wishes, but three months after their wedding, Sarah contracted malaria and died. Interestingly, during the Mexican-American War, Taylor and Davis would cross paths again, but this time Taylor accepted Davis into the family, and Davis visited the Taylors frequently.

In 1835, during the Seminole War, Taylor was once again brought back to active duty. The war was slow to develop, and toward the end of 1837, around Christmas, Taylor requested permission to take the fight to a number of Seminole bands in his area. His soldiers became engaged, and Taylor's leadership led to victory in the Battle of Lake Okeechobee. Early the next year, he received a brevet promotion to brigadier general, and in May 1838, he was assigned as commanding general of all U.S. forces in Florida. But perhaps most honorable was the nickname his troops bestowed upon him, which would carry him into the White House: "Old Rough and Ready."

Although Taylor was already a national figure, the war that would ultimately move his name into presidential consideration was the Mexican-American War. As tensions between Mexico and America began to rise, President James Polk placed Taylor in command of the Corps of Observation at Fort Jesup on the Sabine River in order to protect Texas. Taylor was then moved to Corpus Christi, where he trained an army of over 3,500 men. Taylor reported a raid by Mexicans into American territory where they had crossed the Rio Grande River, and Polk went to Congress and received a declaration of war. Taylor then achieved minor victories at Palo Alto and Resaca de la Palma, and then two major victories: the Battle of Monterrey (September 21–23, 1846) and the Battle of Buena Vista (February 22–23, 1847). By the end of 1847, Taylor returned to the United States and heard the rumors he was being considered as a leading candidate for the presidential election of 1848.

In early 1848, Taylor declared himself to be a "good Whig" and would receive the nomination from that party. Millard Fillmore of New York was chosen to run as Taylor's vice president. Although Taylor ran on the Whig platform, politically he was largely an unknown quantity for he had never voiced many political views and most people did not know where he truly stood on the issues. His military heroics, agrarian roots, and homespun nature became his political assets. He managed to defeat the Democratic candidate, Lewis Cass, as well as the Free Soil candidate, Martin Van Buren. On March 5, 1849, Taylor was inaugurated as the twelfth president of the United States of America.

The Whigs, who had staked their economic platform on resurrecting the national bank, soon discovered that Taylor was against the idea of a national bank. They also learned that despite being a slave owner himself, Taylor was not very sympathetic to his fellow southerners when it came to this issue. For instance, southerners wanted California, New Mexico, and Deseret (Utah) to enter the Union as slave states. Taylor did not think slavery would be economically viable in these states and was against their admission as slave states. The Fugitive Slave Act was also being considered for passage during this time, which would mandate that northern states return escaped slaves to their southern owners. Taylor was also not in favor of the act.

While these debates continued to fester, there was an outbreak of cholera in Washington, D.C., in August 1849.[4] To avoid the illness, President Taylor traveled to Pennsylvania and New York. The official reason for the trip was for Taylor to familiarize himself with the issues of the North, having been a southerner all his life, which sounded reasonable. It also provided the president with a rest from the strain and tension associated with his position, for, as one visitor to the White House explained, Taylor seemed "put down considerable."[5]

The trip commenced on August 9, and the itinerary included many stops along the way. He was well received in Baltimore and Harrisburg, but became ill, suffering from diarrhea and vomiting.[6] Taylor attributed it to a change in the water. His personal physician, Dr. Wood (also his son-in-law), administered medicine, and the travels continued.

He traveled on to Pittsburgh and then Ohio, giving speeches, where he affirmed that although he was a slave holder himself, he would neither force a current slave state to abolish the practice nor allow any new state to enter into the Union as a slave state. These statements, a Taylor compromise, were well received. He next went to Waterford, Pennsylvania, to deliver a similar speech, but he again became violently sick with vomiting, diarrhea, a fever, and the shakes. His doctor ordered him to Erie, just north of Waterford, and then to bed. The concern became so severe that Dr. Wood called for Navy Surgeon William Maxwell Wood for consultation, and Margaret Taylor was notified and told to come to his bedside. The next day, however, he began to improve, and five days later he was up and about. Margaret had traveled as far as Baltimore, then was told to return to Washington, D.C. Taylor was deemed fit enough to continue his travels, but the illness had left him exhausted and weak, so Taylor returned to Washington, D.C. After a few weeks of rest, he was back to full strength and the illness was forgotten.

The next six months were tumultuous and arduous for Taylor. The debates over slavery continued to heat up, and he was faced with a number of foreign challenges, one of which led the United States to the brink of war, but Taylor managed to pull the country back. America was about to celebrate its seventy-fourth birthday on July 4, 1850. The celebration would, at least, break up the routine and the pressure.

The president was up and about early on July 4. Many witnesses claimed Taylor exhibited good health, but one of Taylor's biographers, Holman Hamilton, a contemporary of his, noted that he was "slightly under par."[7] Taylor may have been fatigued, some said, because he was facing a number of political disagreements with his cabinet and was considering the idea of replacing most of its members. He worried about the implications of this move and had had a fitful night of sleep.[8]

After breakfast he attended a school recital in honor of America's Independence. Either before or after the recital (Holman Hamilton's account is vague), Taylor "'may' have "munched green apples."[9] Then Taylor proceeded by carriage to what is today a completed monument to President Washington.

The major event of that day was a ceremony in which the cornerstone of the future monument would be laid. Senator Henry S. Foote was the main speaker, and Taylor is said to have either spent over two hours under the hot sun without a hat listening to the speeches, or sat beneath the shade of the trees on the grandstand, most likely with a hat, listening to the two-hour oration.[10] While there has been a great deal of debate over these two scenarios, what was not in debate was the fact that it was a typical Washington July day, hot and humid. Either scenario could have induced heat-related complications, but then again, Taylor was from the South, and had spent years in Florida and Mexico, so he was used to sultry weather. In fact, it apparently did not bother him at the time, for after the speech he decided to take a stroll around the Potomac flats.[11] A reporter from the *Philadelphia Bulletin* later reported that, in his opinion, Taylor was "to all appearances, sound in health and in excellent spirits."[12]

Taylor exhibited no signs of illness when he returned by carriage to the White House at approximately 4:00 P.M. He remarked to his personal physician, Dr. Alexander S. Witherspoon, that he was "very hungry."[13] Had he been a victim of the heat, this would have been unlikely. Taylor then set about eating his dinner.[14] Taylor relished cherries, and he is reported to have eaten a copious amount at dinner. Some biographers have noted that Taylor had dined with his personal physician, who advised him that eating too many cherries was imprudent.[15] According to Holman Hamilton, there are also many accounts that Taylor ate raw vegetables, cucumbers, cabbage, bread, and mush, and followed this up with either draughts of iced milk or water. The legend has it that he ate cherries, drank milk, and then died. Yet, cherries and milk do not usually cause death—otherwise, no one would eat cherries or drink milk. The exact cause of his illness is a source of debate, but at this point Taylor still showed no signs of illness. Then, about an hour after dinner, he became sick.[16]

At first it was nausea, which developed into diarrhea, and finally, like the previous year, he began vomiting. A fever quickly followed, and he began to experience the shakes. The doctors were summoned. Witherspoon was the first to arrive, and eventually four physicians would tend to Taylor: Drs. Witherspoon, Coolidge, Hall, and Wood. Initially Taylor was to be given calomel, but he refused. Later they gave him calomel (which contains a mercury compound), quinine, and opium, to which he no longer objected. They tried to make him as comfortable as possible, but Taylor was still suffering cramps and showing signs of fever as he sweated profusely and suffered chills.

The doctors conferred about the cause of Taylor's illness. The term *cholera morbus* was a catch-all phrase of the time for any type of inexplicable, sudden illness. It was unlikely that the cherries and milk were the cause. The Washington, D.C., water supply was a possible culprit, assuming the fruit had been washed in the water or Taylor had drunk copious amounts of water rather than milk. One sure way of knowing would be if there were reports of an outbreak in the city, and here there is another debate. While there were reports of a cholera epidemic sweeping parts of the country, it was generally accepted that there was no such outbreak that summer in Washington, D.C.[17] Yet it was also reported that other prominent people in the city, such as Clayton, Seward, Crawford, and Bliss, were also sick with similar symptoms at approximately the same time as Taylor.[18]

On July 5, Taylor was still faring poorly, but by the morning of July 6, he was beginning to show signs of improvement. He was more lucid that day and

engaged in some presidential correspondence, but remained in bed. That evening, however, his condition worsened and he suffered a good portion of the
night. Come Sunday he seemed to have improved, but throughout the day he
continued to have bouts of violent illness. The doctors continued to give him
calomel and quinine, and he sucked on ice cubes, but often even vomited those
liquids. It was becoming clear by that Sunday afternoon that the president
would probably not survive the illness. Although reports being released to the
public were often conflicting, for everyone inside the White House it was
obvious he would soon be dead.

He continued to suffer through Monday, July 8, and was in and out of delir-
ium. At one point, when he was more cogent, he predicted that "in two days I
shall be a dead man."[19] In fact, Taylor explained to one of the doctors, "I
should not be surprised if this were to terminate in my death. I did not expect
to encounter what has beset me since my elevation to the Presidency. God
knows I have endeavored to fulfill what I conceived to be an honest duty. But
I have been mistaken. My motives have been misconstrued, and my feelings
most grossly outraged."[20] He was clearly getting worse, and on Tuesday, despite news reports of his improvement, he began to vomit a green matter and
his pulse was dangerously slow. The doctors attempted to bleed him, most
likely hastening his already inevitable demise.

Word was sent to Congress, and Senator Andrew Butler of South Carolina,
while giving a pro-slavery speech, was interrupted by Senator Daniel Webster.
He stated, "I have a sorrowful message to deliver. A great misfortune threatens
the nation. The President of the United States, General Taylor, is dying and
may not survive the day."[21] The Senate was in shock. It adjourned and filed
out without taking a vote.

A number of the legislators made their way to the White House to pay their
respects to Taylor and his family. The family gathered and said their goodbyes.
The president lingered, in and out of consciousness, that evening, but even
Taylor knew he was close to death. When asked if he was comfortable, he
reportedly said, "Very," then uttered his final words:

[B]ut the storm in passing, has swept away the trunk. . . . I am about to die—I expect
the summons soon—I have endeavored to discharge all my official duties faithfully. I
regret nothing, but am sorry that I am about to leave my friends.[22]

Zachary Taylor died at 10:35 P.M. in the presence of his wife, Margaret; his
daughters, Ann and Betty Bliss; and their husbands. Jefferson Davis, widower
of Taylor's daughter Sarah, was there as well. By some accounts, Vice
President Millard Fillmore and several members of the House and Senate were
also present. [23]

Taylor was the first president to die in office while Congress was in session.
Word was passed to Taylor's cabinet, who then notified Vice President Millard
Fillmore that he was now the president of the United States. On the following

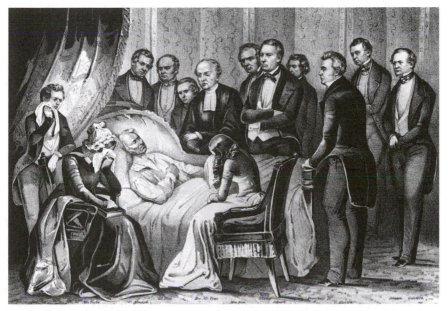

Figure 12.1. This lithograph depicts President Zachary Taylor on his deathbed, surrounded by friends and family members in the White House. Taylor died on July 9, 1850. Although there were rumors that he was assassinated by poison, there is no evidence to verify these allegations. (Courtesy of the Library of Congress.)

day, at noon in the House of Representatives, Fillmore was sworn in as the thirteenth president. He did not make a speech, but later delivered a message to Congress regarding Taylor's service to his country.

The president's body was packed in ice and prepared for the viewing. Margaret, visiting her husband's body, ordered that his body not be embalmed, and that all services would be closed casket. After the casket was in fact closed, she ordered it reopened several times before she allowed her husband to be taken away. As Taylor was only the second president to die in office (the first was William Henry Harrison), the funeral arrangements were elaborate. The president's body would lie in state in the East Room of the White House on July 12 and, after the funeral service on Saturday July 13, the body was escorted by a black hearse bearing eight white horses. Taylor's own horse, Old Whitey, would follow, with Taylor's boots placed backward in the stirrups, an old military tradition. General Winfield Scott supervised the two-mile procession to the temporary burial site, where the casket would remain until it was later moved to Kentucky and interred at Taylor's plantation in what became known as the Zachary Taylor Cemetery.

Pro-slavery Vice President Millard Fillmore became president. Within two months, a deal collectively known as the Compromise of 1850 was reached. California would be admitted as a free state, and the slave trade was abolished in the District of Columbia. New Mexico and Utah, however, would enter as slave states, and the passage of a very tough Fugitive Slave Law would force escaped slaves to journey to Canada in order to gain their freedom. This fast change in Taylor's policies by Fillmore brought the country ever closer to a civil war.

Rumors began to spread almost immediately that the president had been assassinated.[24] People speculated about the facts that Taylor had rejected his own party's viewpoints on slavery and that if he died, his own vice president, being adamantly pro-slavery, would take office and change Taylor's policies. When exactly that happened, it further fueled the notion that the president had been assassinated. Additional evidence—that there was no cholera outbreak in Washington, D.C., at the time of his death, and that cherries and milk were not known to be deadly—helped foment the rumors. The only thing that caused the rumors to die down was America's preoccupation with the slave issue and the possibility of a civil war.

The allegations, however, would again rear their head in the post–Civil War period. A *New York Times* article on August 29, 1881, for example, reported that Reverend Doctor A. Stewart Walsh, while preaching a sermon, spoke of the threats directed to Taylor by his own son-in-law, Jefferson Davis, that if Taylor did not sign two pro-slavery bills, the South would hold him personally responsible. Several days later he was dead, and there were allegations that he had been poisoned.[25] These types of rumors continued well into the twentieth century.

In 1991, while working on a book on Zachary Taylor, Clara Rising investigated the assassination theory. She suspected arsenic poisoning and spoke with a pathologist who confirmed that the circumstances surrounding his death were consistent with such poisoning. She obtained permission from a direct descendant to exhume Taylor's body. She presented her research to the coroner of Jefferson County, Dr. Richard Greathouse, who agreed to exhume the body and collect samples for tests. Ms. Rising agreed to pay for all costs. Permission was then sought from the Department of Veterans Affairs, which subsequently granted the request.[26] On June 17, 1991, the body of President Zachary Taylor was exhumed.

A number of samples were collected from the body of the president, including fingernails, hair, tissues, and bone scrapings. The specimens were sent to three different laboratories for testing. Less than two weeks later, the state of Kentucky's medical examiner, Dr. George Nichols, announced at a news conference that Taylor had not been poisoned. The media reported the nonstory, and the case appeared to be closed. Taylor had died from cherries and milk. Yet one historian decided this still did not make sense and decided to pursue the investigation even further.[27]

Historian Michael Parenti attempted to obtain a copy of the medical examiner's report, only to be eventually mailed a copy of the coroner's press statement. The statement offered the conclusion that Taylor had died from "gastroenteritis" and not from arsenic poisoning, for Taylor's arsenic level was "within the anticipated baseline concentration of that substance in human tissues."[28] However, after obtaining the lab results, Parenti found that the reported levels of arsenic found in

Taylor's hair and nail samples were five to fifteen times higher than today's normal range, countering the statement by the medical examiner. While it had been suggested the embalming fluid may have contributed to higher levels of arsenic found in the body, it is well known that Margaret did not want her husband's body embalmed. Parenti's investigation also speculated that the tests utilized whole-hair testing and that more refined tests use the root and only the first centimeter, yielding more accurate results and, in the case of arsenic poisoning, higher levels, suggesting that the tests used by the labs were inadequate.

The report of death by "gastroenteritis" is also questionable, as this is a general term for viruses and bacteria causing reactions due to food poisoning or allergies. The ability to take Taylor's symptoms and conclude such a cause of death is perhaps no different than the doctors during Taylor's time calling all stomach ailments cholera. In terms of this particular diagnosis, Parenti investigated the symptoms exhibited by Taylor and compared them with his attending physicians' reports of *cholera morbus* and found that it could not have been this particular disease because the symptoms were significantly different.

In the end, there is no definitive proof that Taylor was assassinated, nor would it appear that there is definitive proof that he was not. In the immediate aftermath of President Zachary Taylor's death, there was no autopsy performed, there was no examination of what he ate or drank, there was no inquiry or commission to investigate his death, and the media did not question much beyond the fact that he ate cherries, drank milk, and died. The modern investigation did not offer anything conclusive; it only raised more questions. Any notion that Zachary Taylor was in fact the first president to be assassinated remains a rumor.

WARREN G. HARDING

Warren Gamaliel Harding was born on November 2, 1865, just outside of Marion, Ohio (today called Blooming Grove, Ohio). His father, Dr. George Tyron Harding Sr., was a schoolteacher, and his mother, Phoebe Elizabeth (Dickerson) Harding, was a midwife who would later obtain a medical license. Warren was the oldest of eight children. In the late 1870s, Warren's father purchased a local newspaper, *The Argus,* in Caledonia, Ohio, and the family relocated to this small town. There, Warren came to learn the journalism trade, and when he attended Ohio Central College in Iberia, Ohio, he studied both the printing and newspaper trades while working at the *Union Register* in nearby Mount Gilead.

Upon graduation, Harding and some friends moved to Marion, Ohio, and purchased a failing paper, the *Marion Daily Star.* Harding and his friends had some success revamping the paper into a conservative and pro–Republican Party publication. The full-time management of the newspaper would take a toll on his health, and he suffered from both exhaustion and fatigue. He would spend many weeks in the coming years trying to recover at the Battle Creek Sanitarium.

During this same period, he met Florence Kling DeWolfe, the daughter of Amos Hall Kling, a local real estate magnate who had in the past opposed Harding and his newspaper. Florence was five years older than Harding, a divorcée, and the mother of a young son, but despite all of this (considering the times), they were married on July 8, 1891. Florence Harding helped her husband grow the newspaper and make it not only powerful but financially successful as well.

The newspaper gave Harding an enormous amount of exposure, and he was elected to the Ohio State Senate in 1899. He went on to be elected lieutenant governor of Ohio from 1903 to 1905. In 1910, he ran for governor, but lost to the incumbent, Judson Harmon, a Democrat.

In 1912, Harding made his move to the national stage by giving the nominating speech for President William Howard Taft at the Republican National Convention. He was encouraged to run for the U.S. Senate in 1914, and won. He served in the Senate until his inauguration as president of the United States on March 4, 1921. He had won the presidency as a "dark horse" candidate because of a serious deadlock within the Republican Party over who should be their candidate. Harding was a compromise candidate, and when asked if there was anything in his past that might prevent him from winning the presidency, he answered, "No."

In reality, Harding had a number of "negatives" that might have worked against him. He was, outside of Ohio, largely unknown. He had no real formal education to speak of—his college education was more geared toward a trade than to professions like those of previous presidents. He was a heavy drinker, despite the fact that Prohibition was in effect. And he had a longtime affair with Carrie Fulton Phillips, the wife of an old friend, and later (while in office) Nan Britton, with whom it was said he had fathered a child.[29]

Despite all of these issues, he ran a campaign that spoke of returning to normalcy, especially in the wake of World War I, and he managed to get a number of influential conservatives behind him, including business types such as Harvey Firestone and Hollywood stars like Douglas Fairbanks. It should also be noted that this was the first election in which women could vote, and he was well received by women voters. With 60 percent of the popular vote and 404 electoral votes,[30] Harding won by a landslide.

Harding's successes included the creation of both the Bureau of Veterans Affairs and the Bureau of the Budget, and the appointment of former President William Howard Taft as chief justice of the U.S. Supreme Court. But Harding's administration was marked heavily with scandal. Thomas Miller, the head of the Office of Alien Property, was convicted of accepting bribes; Charles Forbes, the head of the Bureau of Veterans Affairs, was convicted of fraud and bribery; and Harry Daugherty, the attorney general, resigned for accepting bribes. The worst of the scandals, however, was the Teapot Dome Scandal.

Teapot Dome refers to land in Wyoming that was owned by the federal government.[31] It was named for a rocky outcrop that looked like a teapot. What was critical about the land was that it was an oilfield that could make any owner quite wealthy. In 1921, the Navy Department owned the land as a naval reserve, but an executive order signed by President Harding transferred it to the Department of the Interior, run by Albert B. Fall. The following year, Fall leased the Teapot Dome oil fields to Harry F. Sinclair of Mammoth (Sinclair) Oil without a competitive bid. For doing this, Fall received over $400,000 in gifts from the oilman (equivalent to over $4 million in current dollars). The *Wall Street Journal* exposed the land lease on April 14, 1922, and Fall was indicted for conspiracy and accepting bribes in 1923. The day after the *Wall Street Journal* article appeared, the U.S. Senate initiated an investigation into the Teapot Dome Scandal. By the summer of 1923, the investigation was in full swing and the exposure began to wear on President Harding.

On June 20, 1923, a typically hot and humid Washington, D.C., afternoon, President Harding set out on what was to be a 1,500-mile, two-month journey to be known as the "Voyage of Understanding." This was a campaign largely to shore up his reputation and, in today's parlance, reinvent himself. He had to first undo the political damage he sustained from allowing the leases, and then establish a reputation as a president who put the Constitution first.[32] In many ways, it was really about escapism; it was a means for Harding to get away from all of his political troubles as well as seek some needed rest. He had told many close to him that he was not planning to run for reelection, and least not until he was able to return to the public's grace.[33]

The president was accompanied by sixty-five aides and guests, as well as ten members of the U.S. Secret Service. His train stopped in a number of cities and towns, including Martinsburg, West Virginia; Kansas City, Kansas; and Denver, Colorado. He explored Yellowstone National Park before making his way to Portland, Oregon, and Tacoma, Washington. At the latter, he boarded a ship for a 1,000-mile voyage to Alaska, toured there for approximately a week, and then sailed on to Vancouver before arriving in Seattle. In Seattle, Harding was scheduled to give the first of a series of speeches in major cities along the west coast. Sixty thousand citizens were waiting to hear his speech in the Seattle Stadium.[34]

Although Harding had thought getting away from Washington, D.C., would allow him some rest, the constant traveling was beginning to wear on him. He would, in the end, give eighty-five speeches in a period of six weeks.[35] He was greatly fatigued. As one Harding biographer noted, "[H]is slack face, the slightly green tinge to his cheeks, the way his jaws set in pain"[36] all were indicators to his aides that his health was beginning to fail. This was even more evident when he began to slur his words during the speech in Seattle, so much so that "Alaska" sounded like "Nebraska" and other words were simply indecipherable. He fumbled his speech, dropped the manuscript, and clutched at the lectern to steady himself. Herbert Hoover came to his aid, picked up the papers, handed the next pages to the president, and then sorted them out. Harding finished his speech, but was clearly showing signs of distress.

Later, he was supposed to attend a luncheon at the Press Club and give a speech. The event was changed to a dinner and Harding attended, spoke briefly, then sat down, clearly in a state of exhaustion. He was moved back to his train, put to bed, and the next events and speeches were quickly postponed. He then began suffering cramps and indigestion, which Dr. Charles Sawyer blamed on some of the crabmeat he had eaten earlier.[37] His events for the next two days were canceled.

Harding's aides debated how to proceed. One thing that came out from the discussion was that Harding was suffering from something far worse than indigestion. A number of doctors had examined Harding and found that he had an enlarged heart. They suspected he may have had a heart attack. It was decided that the train would go directly to San Francisco and that Dr. Ray Lyman Wilbur, the president of both Stanford University and the American Medical Association, would meet the train to treat the president.

The train arrived Sunday morning on July 29, 1923, and Harding reported that he was feeling better. Dr. Wilbur met the train along with Dr. Charles Minor Cooper, a renowned heart specialist. The president was encouraged to accept help dressing and to use a wheelchair to get to the waiting limousine. He refused both. A photographer who by chance was present snapped a photograph, which turned out to be the last one taken of Harding, showing "an aging, flabby-faced man with slack chin and puffy eyes, forcing himself into a half-smile as he squints in the sunshine."[38]

Harding was taken to the elaborate Palace Hotel on Market Street, where a suite was awaiting him. He went directly to bed. His closest aides, Herbert Hoover and Hubert Work, had rooms next to his, and his wife was across the hall. When Harding awoke, he was examined, and the doctors conferred with the president's aides. Any thoughts of giving a speech in San Francisco were quickly dismissed. Harding slept fitfully through the night, and in the morning it was clear to all that he had taken a turn for the worse. He now had a temperature of about 102° Fahrenheit, and his pulse was racing at 120 beats per minute. By that night, Harding was in trouble. Doctor Wilbur explained that "his acute illness came to a peak on Monday night with the rapid development of bronchial pneumonia."[39] His breathing was irregular, and he was greatly distressed. He slept fitfully again Monday night.

On Tuesday morning, the president claimed to feel better. He was more cheerful and conversant than he had been on Monday, and he talked about taking a vacation.[40] On Wednesday, he appeared even more improved as he sat up in bed, ate solid foods, and read the newspaper. His pulse was still racing at 100 beats per minute, but the fever had broken. Thursday was even better, and Harding began to talk about returning to Washington, D.C., on the coming Sunday. He felt he was "out of the woods," but still reported he was "so tired, so tired."[41]

On Thursday evening, after his wife had dinner with Attorney General Harry Daugherty, she entered Harding's room and read him an article from the *Saturday Evening Post*.[42] The article praised Harding for being a "calm man," and he was greatly pleased. Mrs. Harding left his room and returned to hers. When she left, he was still sitting up in bed, propped against several pillows with his eyes closed. It was then that his nurse, Ruth Powderly, having gone for a glass of water with which to give the president his nightly medicine, found him with his head slumped and lolling to the right, his face twitching and his mouth hanging open. She ran out of the room, first to Mrs. Harding's room and then to get the others by screaming, "Get Doctor Boone! Get Doctor Boone!" Mrs. Harding reached her husband first, while the nurse continued to call for help.[43]

Hoover and Work ran to Harding's room. Nurse Powderly stood in the doorway, and Mrs. Harding sat by her husband on the bed and sobbed his name. The president was dead at the age of fifty-eight. What they also found, after conferring with Nurse Powderly, was that the pillows had been removed from behind the president, Harding's body was lying flat, his body was wrapped in a white dressing gown, and his mouth had been closed. His body appeared to be at peace.

Dr. Sawyer arrived and examined the president. He believed that Harding had died from a cerebral hemorrhage. When Wilbur, Cooper, Work, and Boone arrived to examine the body, they disagreed, saying Harding had died from a heart attack.[44] They wanted to resolve the dispute by performing an autopsy, but Harding's wife would not allow an autopsy, nor did she want a death mask made of the president.[45] Lacking further evidence, the doctors debated and signed an agreement that Harding's "death was apparently due to some brain evolvement, probably an apoplexy."[46] As this information was being released to reporters, conflicting reports about how Harding had died, who was in the room when he died, and even the exact time of death were beginning to raise questions.[47]

Colonel Edmund Starling, head of the U.S. Secret Service, ordered his agents to clear the hotel, and he assigned San Francisco police officers to guard all of the entrances.[48] Once the hotel was cleared, the undertakers and an embalmer from N. Gray & Company arrived to prepare the body. Upon completion the next morning, Harding's body was placed in a brown metal coffin, then transferred to a hearse and taken to the waiting train. The body then traveled across the United States, and whenever it passed a town, throngs of people gathered to pay their respects.

Once the body arrived at Washington, D.C.'s Union Station, it was transferred to another hearse and taken to the East Room of the White House. Mrs. Harding spent time with her husband's body before the next morning, when a procession of dignitaries paid their respects. Later, a service was held before the body was moved to the U.S. Capitol, where, once again, the body lay in state while 35,000 filed by to pay their last respects.[49] The body was then taken to Marion, Ohio, where a final service was held. President Harding's body was eventually interred in a new mausoleum in 1931.

It did not take long for conspiracy theories to arise in regard to President Harding's death. This is not surprising, given the conflicting information about the circumstances at the time of death.[50] The exact time of death, who was in

Figure 12.2.   The body of President Warren G. Harding lies in state in the U.S. Capitol's Rotunda, after his death in California on August 2, 1923. Although there were rumors that he was assassinated by poison, there is no evidence to verify these allegations. (Courtesy of the Library of Congress.)

the room, and the actual cause all became sources of debate. The fact that Mrs. Harding wanted neither an autopsy performed nor a death mask made fueled speculation that she may have been involved in his death. Additionally, there was a growing awareness of President Harding's role in the Teapot Dome Scandal, his various affairs, and the possibility that he had fathered a child with Nan Britton (and Mrs. Harding had hired former Bureau of Investigation Agent Gaston B. Means to investigate this). All of this gave motive to Florence Harding possibly wanting her husband dead, whether simply for revenge or as a means of protecting his reputation.[51]

A series of strange events that followed the death of President Harding also contributed to the speculation about a conspiracy. First, it was said that over the next year and a half, Mrs. Harding worked diligently to destroy a number of papers that may have been damaging to her and her husband. Then, the following year, while Mrs. Harding was visiting Dr. Sawyer, he died of what was believed to be, ironically, a cerebral hemorrhage. Mrs. Harding was the last one to see him alive. Six months later, Mrs. Harding was dead.[52]

In 1927, Nan Britton published a book claiming that President Harding was the father of her child, fueling the motive portion of the conspiracy theory. Although a paternity suit was never brought, in a challenge between Britton and the author of a book that contested her assertions, Britton was unable to bring forth any evidence of paternity.[53]

In 1930, Gaston B. Means, the agent Florence Harding hired to investigate her husband's affair with Nan Britton, published his own tell-all book.[54] Means conveys a conversation he allegedly had with Mrs. Harding in which she explained that she had poisoned her husband, possibly in collusion with Dr. Sawyer. This was supported by the belief that Mrs. Harding and Dr. Sawyer were lovers, which was exacerbated in turn when it was learned that Mrs. Harding was the last person to see Dr. Sawyer before he died.

Means's story, however, was largely discredited, first and foremost by Means himself. After making a fair sum on the publication of the book, he repudiated his own assertions. Means was also renowned for fabricating stories to advance fraudulent schemes. The most serious of these was related to the Lindbergh Baby kidnapping. Means fabricated a story that he was in contact with the kidnappers and convinced Evalyn Walsh McLean, the owner of the Hope Diamond, to give him $100,000 in order to pay the ransom for the baby. Means was eventually arrested, tried, and convicted, but McLean never saw her money again. Means died in 1938 while imprisoned in the Fort Leavenworth penitentiary.

In the end, there are essentially four possible explanations for Harding's death. First, he died of natural causes, a heart attack and possibly a stroke. Knowing the way he lived his life, this would not be all too surprising. Second, he was a victim of negligent homicide because Doctor Sawyer was largely incompetent and the dispute between the doctors did little to save his life. Third, he committed suicide to escape his growing troubles; a key question is whether his wife or Dr. Sawyer had been complicit. Finally, he was murdered by his wife, possibly with the assistance of Dr. Sawyer. The evidence to support this, however, is mostly circumstantial or entirely fabricated by the likes of people such as Gaston Means.

So, which theory is correct? It would appear that based on the evidence available, there is little proof for any other than death by natural causes, no matter how strange some of the facts surrounding the case appear to be. At the least, there is not enough evidence to state President Harding was assassinated, and so that assertion remains in the category of rumor.

CONCLUSION

Almost from the very day that both Presidents Zachary Taylor and Warren G. Harding died, there have been rumors that they died by assassination and not of natural causes. In the case of Zachary Taylor, it has been speculated he was poisoned through a pro-slavery conspiracy. For Warren G. Harding, the speculation holds that he was poisoned by his wife. In both cases, the evidence of assassination is entirely circumstantial and there is little factual evidence to support the claims. Despite the lack of facts, the rumors continue to circulate, the stories retold, and the questions asked over and over. In the absence of new evidence, owing to the passage of time, we cannot establish that these two deaths were assassinations. For now, and possibly forever, they will remain simply "rumors of assassination."

Notes

PREFACE

1. See for instance Sifakis, Carl. (1991). *Encyclopedia of Assassinations*. New York: Facts on File.

2. McKinley, James. (1977). *Assassination in America*. New York: Harper & Row Publishers.

3. Clarke, James W. (1982). *American Assassins: The Darker Side of Politics*. Princeton, NJ: Princeton University Press.

CHAPTER 1: ANDREW JACKSON

1. This section is based on the following sources: Brands (2005); DeGregorio (1997); Graff (1997); Remini (1977); Remini (1981); Remini (1984); Schlesinger (1946); Van Deusen (1959).

2. Remini (1999).

3. Clarke (1982).

4. Clarke (1982), p. 195.

5. Clarke (1982).

6. Lawson (1915).

7. Lawson (1915), p. 539.

8. Lawson (1915).

9. Clarke (1982), p. 197.

10. Clarke (1982), p. 197.

11. Clarke (1982), p. 197.

12. Lawson (1915), p. 539.

13. Remini (1984), p. 227.

14. As quoted in Remini (1984), p. 227.

15. Barber (1991); Meacham (2008).

16. Melanson (2002).

17. Meacham (2008), p. 254.
18. Cole (1993), p. 221.
19. Sumner (1899).
20. Marquis (1938), p. 685; Remini (1984), p. 228.
21. Martineau (1838), p. 161.
22. Remini (1984), p. 228.
23. As quoted in Brands (2005), p. 503.
24. As quoted in Brands (2005), p. 503.
25. See for instance Meacham (2008).
26. Clarke (1982), p. 195; Cole (1993), p. 221.
27. Ward (1955), p. 114.
28. Remini (1984), p. 228.
29. Van Buren (1920/1973), p. 353.
30. Burstein (2003), p. 202.
31. Marquis (1938).
32. As cited in Remini (1984), p. 229.
33. As quoted in Brands (2005), p. 504.
34. As quoted in Brands (2005), p. 504.
35. As quoted in Brands (2005), p. 504.
36. As quoted in Brands (2005), p. 504.
37. As quoted in Brands (2005), p. 504.
38. As quoted in Brands (2005), p. 504.
39. As quoted in Brands (2005), p. 504.
40. Marquis (1938), p. 685.
41. Burstein (2003), p. 202.
42. Marquis (1938).
43. As cited in Remini (1984), p. 228.
44. Marquis (1938); Ward (1955).
45. Martineau (1838), p. 162.
46. As cited in Remini (1984), p. 229.
47. Meacham (2008); Sumner (1899).
48. Sumner (1899), p. 433.
49. As cited in Remini (1984), p. 229.
50. As cited in Remini (1984), p. 229.
51. As cited in Remini (1984), p. 229.
52. As cited in Remini (1984), p. 229.
53. Burstein (2003), p. 202.
54. As cited in Ward (1955), p. 115.
55. As cited in Remini (1984), p. 230.
56. Barber (1991).
57. Lawson (1915), p. 526.
58. Lawson (1915), p. 527.
59. Sumner (1899).
60. Clarke (1982), p. 194; Sifakis (1991), p. 84.
61. Jones (1996), p. 6; see also McKinley (1977).
62. Clarke (1982), p. 194.
63. Van Deusen (1959).
64. Melanson and Stevens (2002).

CHAPTER 2: ABRAHAM LINCOLN

1. Arnold (1893).
2. Donald (1995); Kaplan (2008), p. 44; Hanchet (1994), p. 9.
3. Arnold (1893); Bak (1998); Keneally (2003).
4. Keneally (2003); Hanchett (1994), p. 16; McGovern (2009), p. 23.
5. Arnold (1893); Keneally (2003).
6. McGovern (2009).
7. Arnold (1893).
8. Epstein (2008); Holzer (1999); Kaplan (2008).
9. Carwardine (2006).
10. Hanchett (1994); McGovern (2009).
11. Donald (1995); Kaplan (2008); Putnam (1909).
12. Kaplan (2008).
13. McGovern (2009).
14. Donald (1995).
15. Arnold (1893); Putnam (1909).
16. McGovern (2009), p. 38.
17. Bak (1998); Keneally (2003).
18. McGovern (2009).
19. Arnold (1893); Steers (2001).
20. McGovern (2009), p. 42.
21. McGovern (2009).
22. Epstein (2008).
23. Epstein (2008). Harrell (1997); Kaplan (2008).
24. Peterson (1994).
25. Harris (2004).
26. McGovern (2009).
27. Donald (1995). Harrell (1997); McGovern (2009).
28. McGovern (2009).
29. Peterson (1994).
30. Steers (2001).
31. Harris (2004).
32. Harris (2004); McGovern (2009).
33. Keneally (2003).
34. Bishop (1955), p. 105.
35. Bak (1998).
36. McGovern (2009).
37. McGovern (2009).
38. Peterson (1994).
39. Kaplan (2008).
40. Keneally (2003).
41. Steers (2001); Stern (1939); Weichmann (1975).
42. Bak (1998).
43. Donald (1995).
44. Bishop (1955).
45. Bak (1998), p. 48.
46. Kauffman (2004); Weichmann (1975).
47. Bak (1998).

48. Swanson and Weinberg (2001).

49. Bishop (1955); Oldroyd (1901); Reck (1987).

50. Bak (1998); Swanson and Weinberg (2001).

51. Harris (2004); Reck (1987).

52. Bishop (1955).

53. Bak (1998); Bishop (1955).

54. Steers (2001).

55. Epstein (2008); Kauffman (2004); Reck (1987).

56. Reck (1987).

57. Donald (1995); Goodrich (2005); Stern (1939).

58. Steers (2001).

59. "Sic Semper tyrannis" is the state motto of Virginia, which means "Thus always to tyrants". Some reports indicate that Booth yelled, "The South shall be free!" Yet others reported hearing Booth shout, "The South is avenged!" or even "Revenge for the South!" Still others indicated that he screamed, "I have done it!" Some in the audience that night claimed that he said nothing at all.

60. Epstein (2008).

61. Bak (1998); Kauffman (2004).

62. Epstein (2008); Reck (1987).

63. Peterson (1994); Oldroyd (1901); Reck (1987).

64. Donald (1995); Swanson and Weinberg (2001).

65. Donald (1995).

66. Peterson (1994).

67. Bak (1998).

68. Harris (2004), p. 225; McGovern (2009), p. 145; Peterson (1994), p. 4; Steers (2001), p. 14.

69. Arnold (1893); Goodrich (2005); Starkey (1976).

70. Steers (2001).

71. Bak (1998); Stern (1939).

72. Steers (2001); Swanson and Weinberg (2001).

73. Bak (1998); Oldroyd (1901).

74. Harris (2004); Peterson (1994).

75. McGovern (2009); Peterson (1994); Steers (2001).

76. Steers (2001).

77. Arnold (1893); Goodrich (2005).

78. Steers (2001).

79. Harris (2004); Steers (2001).

80. Peterson (1994).

81. Harris (2004).

82. Steers (2001).

83. Steers (2001).

84. Craughwell (2007).

85. Holzer (1999).

CHAPTER 3: JAMES A. GARFIELD

1. Jewell (2005).

2. McKelroy (1986).

3. Sifakis (2001).

4. McElroy (1986); Bundy (1880); Hoyt (1964).
5. This was also referred to as the Campbellite faith in Bundy (1880); Caldwell (1931).
6. Jewell (2005).
7. DeGregorio (1997); Rutkow (2006); Jewell (2005); Alger (1881).
8. McElroy (1986), p. 8.
9. Jewell (2005); Alger (1881).
10. McElroy (1986).
11. DeGregorio (1997); Jewell (2005); Rutkow (2006).
12. McElroy (1986).
13. Jewell (2005).
14. DeGregorio (1997).
15. Alger (1881); McElroy (1986).
16. Rutkow (2006).
17. DeGregorio (1997); Jewell (2005); St. George (1999); Alger (1881).
18. McElroy (1986).
19. McElroy (1986).
20. DeGregorio (1997).
21. McElroy (1986).
22. Caldwell (1931).
23. DeGregorio (1997).
24. McKinley (1977).
25. McCabe (1881).
26. McKinley (1977).
27. McElroy (1986).
28. Koenig (2000); McElroy (1986); McCabe (1881).
29. Ackerman (2003).
30. McKinley (1977); Ackerman (2003).
31. McKinley (1977).
32. Ackerman (2003); McKinley (1977).
33. Ackerman (2003).
34. McKinley (1977).
35. Ackerman (2003).
36. Ackerman (2003).
37. Ackerman (2003); Grant (2004).
38. Ackerman (2003).
39. Ackerman (2003); Grant (2004).
40. Ackerman (2003), p. 273.
41. Rutkow (2006).
42. McKinley (1977).
43. Rutkow (2006).
44. Taylor (1970).
45. Ackerman. (2003); Rutkow (2006).
46. Rutkow (2006).
47. Hoyt (1964).
48. DeGregorio (1997).
49. Rutkow (2006); Ackerman (2003).
50. Rutkow (2006); Ackerman (2003).
51. McCabe (1881); Hoyt (1964); Peskin (1978); McKinley (1977).
52. Peskin (1978).

53. Peskin (1978).

54. McKelroy (1986); McCabe (1881).

55. Rutkow (2006); Hoyt (1964).

56. Taylor (1970).

57. Rutkow (2006).

58. McElroy (1986).

59. Hoyt (1964).

60. Wicker (2003); McKelroy (1986); DeGregorio (1997).

61. Koenig (2000), p. 269; McKinley (1977), p. 42; Ackerman (2003), p. 378; Rutkow (2006), p. 83; St. George (1999), p. 37.

62. McCabe (1881); Peskin (1978).

63. Rutkow (2006), p. 2.

64. Rutkow (2006), p. 84; St. George (1999), p. 39.

65. DeGregorio (1997); Rutkow (2006); St. George (1999).

66. Ackerman (2003); Carroll and Graf, p. 380; Rutkow (2006), p. 84.

67. Ackerman (2003), p. 380; St. George (1999), p. 39; Rutkow (2006), pp. 2–3.

68. Rutkow (2006).

69. Ackerman (2003); St. George (1999).

70. McElroy (1986).

71. McElroy (1986).

72. Taylor (1970).

73. McElroy (1986).

74. Some reported Garfield's last words as "Swaim, can't you stop this (pain)? Oh, Swaim!" See DeGregorio (1997), p. 303.

75. Ackerman (2003).

76. Peskin (1978), p. 596; Rutkow (2006), p. 83.

77. Ackerman (2003), p. 379.

78. DeGregorio (1997), p. 302; Rutkow (2006), p. 89.

79. McElroy (1986).

80. Rutkow (2006), p. 90.

81. Hoyt (1964).

82. St. George, Judith (1999).

83. McKinley (1977), p. 50.

84. Sifakis (2001), p. 75.

85. Ackerman (2003).

86. Hoyt (1964).

87. McKinley (1977), p. 50.

88. Taylor (1970).

89. Sifakis (2001), p. 75.

90. DeGregorio (1997), p. 303; Jewell (2005), p. 162; Wicker (2003), p. 60.

91. Ackerman (2003).

92. Jewell (2005).

93. Caldwell (1931).

94. Rutkow (2006).

CHAPTER 4: WILLIAM MCKINLEY

1. Rauchway (2003); Wicker (2003).

2. DeGregorio (1997); Leech (1959); McElroy (1996).

3. McElroy (1996).
4. Gould (1980); Jewell (2005); Leech (1959).
5. DeGregorio (1997).
6. Fallows (1901); Leech (1959); McElroy (1996).
7. Fallows (1901); Leech (1959).
8. DeGregorio (1997).
9. Phillips (2003).
10. DeGregorio (1997); Jewell (2005).
11. DeGregorio (1997); Fallows (1901); Jewell (2005); Leech (1959); McElroy (1996).
12. McElroy (1996).
13. Jewell (2005); Young (2000); Phillips (2003); St. George (1999).
14. Jewell (2005).
15. McElroy (1996).
16. Fallows (1901).
17. Jewell (2005).
18. McElroy (1996).
19. Phillips (2003).
20. Phillips (2003).
21. McElroy (1996).
22. Jewell (2005).
23. Jewell (2005).
24. Jewell (2005); St. George (1999).
25. DeGregorio (1997); Young (2000).
26. McElroy (1996).
27. McElroy (1996).
28. McElroy (1996).
29. McElroy (1996).
30. DeGregorio (1997); Rauchway (2003).
31. Sifakis (2001).
32. Leech (1959).
33. Rauchway (2003).
34. Leech (1959); McElroy (1996).
35. McElroy (1996).
36. McElroy (1996).
37. McElroy (1996).
38. McElroy (1996).
39. DeGregorio (1997).
40. Leech (1959), p. 587.
41. Leech (1959).
42. Leech (1959); St. George (1999).
43. Leech (1959).
44. St. George (1999).
45. St. George (1999).
46. Fallows (1901).
47. Rauchway (2003), p. 386.
48. DeGregorio (1997).
49. Fallows (1901), p. 15.
50. DeGregorio (1997), p. 367; Leech (1959), p. 595.

51. Fallows (1901), p. 14; St. George (1999), p. 62.
52. McElroy (1996), p. 161.
53. McElroy (1996).
54. Fallows (1901), p. 20; St. George (1999), p. 72.
55. Fallows (1901).
56. McElroy (1996).
57. Fallows (1901).
58. Leech (1959); St. George (1999).
59. Fallows (1901).
60. Fallows (1901).
61. Fallows (1901), p. 23; Leech (1959), p. 599.
62. McElroy (1996).
63. DeGregorio (1997).
64. Young (2000), p. 71.
65. McElroy (1996).
66. Fallows (1901).
67. McElroy (1996).
68. DeGregorio (1997).
69. McElroy (1996).
70. Fallows (1901).
71. Fallows (1901); Leech (1959).
72. DeGregorio (1997), p. 368.
73. Fallows (1901).
74. McElroy (1996); Wicker (2003).
75. Fallows (1901).
76. Rauchway (2003).
77. Fallows (1901), p. 444.
78. DeGregorio (1997).
79. McElroy (1996), p. 183; Wicker (2003), p. 60.
80. Sifakis (2001), p. 136.
81. Rauchway (2003).
82. McKinley (1977).
83. Young (2000).
84. McElroy (1996).

CHAPTER 5: THEODORE ROOSEVELT

1. This section is based on the following sources: Brands (1997); Dalton (2002); Miller (1992); Morris (1979); Morris (2001).
2. Bishop (1920).
3. Bishop (1920).
4. Bishop (1920), p. 334.
5. Brands (1997).
6. Dalton (2002), p. 403.
7. Chace (2004), p. 229.
8. Clarke (1982); McKinley (1977).
9. Clarke (1982); McKinley (1977).
10. Clarke (1982), p. 218.

11. Clarke (1982).
12. McKinley (1977).
13. Clarke (1982); McKinley (1977).
14. Jeffers (1994).
15. Clarke (1982), p. 219; McKinley (1977), p. 58.
16. McKinley (1977).
17. Clarke (1982); McKinley (1977).
18. McKinley (1977), p. 59.
19. McKinley (1977), p. 59.
20. Morris (2001).
21. Millard (2005), p. 265.
22. Morris (2001), p. 8.
23. McKinley (1977); Netzley (2000).
24. Morris (1979), p. 128.
25. Morris (2001), p. 266.
26. Morris (1979), p. xx.
27. Melanson and Stevens (2002), p. 31.
28. Melanson and Stevens (2002), p. 31.
29. Melanson and Stevens (2002).
30. Clarke (1982).
31. It should be noted that early and contemporary sources claim the hotel as "Hotel Gilpatric" while later and more current sources cite it as "Hotel Gilpatrick." The authors use the current spelling. See also Leach (1921); McKinley (1977).
32. Chace (2004).
33. Chace (2004); Miller (1992).
34. Remey, Cochems, and Bloodgood (1912).
35. Remey, Cochems, and Bloodgood (1912).
36. Clarke (1982); Dalton (2002), p. 404.
37. Chace (2004), p. 230.
38. Remey, Cochems, and Bloodgood (1912).
39. Remey, Cochems, and Bloodgood (1912), p. 6. It should be noted that a number of other sources state that the crowd began yelling, "Lynch him! Lynch him!" (See for instance Bishop [1920], p. 337). The authors abide by the writing of Remey, Cochems, and Bloodgood because they were actually there at the assassination attempt in front of the Hotel Gilpatrick.
40. Bishop (1920), p. 337; Chace (2004), p. 230; Miller (1992), p. 530.
41. Chace (2004), p. 231.
42. Remey, Cochems, and Bloodgood (1912), p. 6.
43. Clarke (1982).
44. Chace (2004), p. 231.
45. Bishop (1920), p. 337.
46. Bishop (1920), p. 337; Chace (2004), p. 231.
47. Leach (1921).
48. Chace (2004), p. 231; Thayer (1919).
49. Bishop (1920), p. 337; Chace (2004), p. 231.
50. Bishop (1920), p. 337–338.
51. Clarke (1982), p. 215; Leach (1921); Remey, Cochems, and Bloodgood (1912), p. 6.

52. Clarke (1982), p. 215; Leach (1921).

53. Bishop (1920), p. 338.

54. McCullough (1981); McKinley (1977); O'Toole (2006), p. 78; Remey, Cochems, and Bloodgood (1912).

55. Bishop (1920), p. 340.

56. Bishop (1920), p. 340.

57. Bishop (1920), p. 338; Millard (2005), p. 10; Miller (1992), p. 530.

58. Bishop (1920), p. 338.

59. Clarke (1982), p. 215.

60. Leach (1921).

61. Roosevelt (1967).

62. Chace (2004), p. 232.

63. Remey, Cochems, and Bloodgood (1912).

64. Bishop (1920), p. 338.

65. Remey, Cochems, and Bloodgood (1912).

66. Jones (1996); Melanson and Stevens (2002).

67. Sifakis (2001), p. 165.

68. Bishop (1920), p. 341.

69. Remey, Cochems, and Bloodgood (1912).

70. Remey, Cochems, and Bloodgood (1912), p. 34.

71. Bishop (1920), p. 341.

72. Clarke (1982), p. 216.

73. Clarke (1982), p. 220–221.

74. Clarke (1982), p. 221; Sifakis (1991), p. 165.

75. Sifakis (1991), p. 165.

76. McKinley (1977).

77. Clarke (1982).

78. Roosevelt (1967).

79. Chace (2004), p. 233; Roosevelt (1967).

80. Dalton (2002), p. 405.

81. Dalton (2002); Roosevelt (1967).

82. Caroli (1998).

83. Remey, Cochems, and Bloodgood (1912).

84. Bishop (1920), p. 338–339.

85. Bishop (1920), p. 339.

86. Bishop (1920), p. 339.

87. Chace (2004), p. 234–235.

88. Bishop (1920), p. 340; Remey, Cochems, and Bloodgood (1912), p. 27.

89. Remey, Cochems, and Bloodgood (1912).

90. Dalton (2002), p. 405.

91. Dalton (2002), p. 405.

92. Millard (2005).

93. Dalton (2002), p. 406.

94. For a full treatment of Roosevelt's journey through the Amazon and an excellent read, the authors highly recommend Millard (2005).

95. Bishop (1920), p. 343.

96. Bishop (1920), p. 344.

97. Jeffers (1994), p. 211.

98. Jeffers (1994), p. 211–212.
99. Jeffers (1994), p. 212.
100. Bishop (1920), p. 343.
101. Bishop (1920), p. 344.
102. Bishop (1920), p. 345.
103. Millard (2005).
104. Melanson and Stevens (2002).

CHAPTER 6: FRANKLIN D. ROOSEVELT

1. St. George (1999).
2. Smith (2007).
3. Alsop (1982).
4. Bremer (1971).
5. Bremer (1971); Smith (2007).
6. Sullivan (2000).
7. Bremer (1971); Smith (2007).
8. DeGregorio (1997); Smith (2007).
9. Black (2003); Jenkins (2003); Smith (2007); Sullivan.
10. Black (2003).
11. Jenkins (2003).
12. Bremer (1971); Jenkins (2003); Smith (2007).
13. Bremer (1971); Smith (2007).
14. Black (2003).
15. Black (2003); Smith (2007).
16. Smith (2007).
17. Bremer (1971).
18. Jewell (2005); Smith (2007).
19. Jenkins (2003).
20. Alsop (1982); Smith (2007).
21. Jenkins (2003), p. 54.
22. Bremer (1971).
23. DeGregorio (1997).
24. Bremer (1971).
25. McKinley (1977).
26. Alter (2006); Grant (2004), p. 163; St. George (1999).
27. Smith (2007).
28. St. George (1999).
29. Black (2003), p. 264.
30. Wicker (2003).
31. Alsop (1982); Alter (2006); McKinley (1977); Sifakis (2001); Wicker (2003).
32. Alter (2006).
33. Alter (2006), p. 170; St. George (1999).
34. Alter (2006).
35. Smith (2007).
36. Black (2003).
37. McKinley (1977).
38. McKinley (1977).

39. DeGregorio (1997), p. 494.
40. Black (2003).
41. Alter (2006).
42. Alter (2006).
43. Smith (2007), p. 297.
44. Alter (2006), p. 170.
45. Black (2003).
46. Smith (2007), p. 298.
47. Black (2003).
48. Black (2003), p. 263.
49. Smith (2007); Sullivan (2000).
50. Jewell (2005); Wicker (2003).
51. Alter (2006), p. 176.
52. Federal Bureau of Investigation (2002).
53. Federal Bureau of Investigation (2002).
54. Federal Bureau of Investigation (2002).
55. Federal Bureau of Investigation (2002).
56. Picchi (2003).
57. Federal Bureau of Investigation (2002).
58. Federal Bureau of Investigation (2002).
59. Alter (2006), p. 176.
60. Alter (2006), p. 176.
61. Alter (2006), p. 176.
62. Alter (2006); Black (2003); Grant (2004); Wicker (2003).
63. Alter (2006), p. 176.
64. Alter (2006).
65. Smith (2007), p. 297.
66. Black (2003).
67. McKinley (1977).
68. Federal Bureau of Investigation (2002).
69. Black (2003).
70. DeGregorio (1997); Jenkins (2003).
71. Alsop (1982), p. 7.

CHAPTER 7: HARRY S TRUMAN

1. Hunter and Bainbridge, Jr. (2005), p. 220.
2. DeGregorio (1997); Ferrell (1984).
3. Ferrell (1984); Jewell (2005).
4. DeGregorio (1997); McCullough (1992).
5. Ferrell (1984).
6. DeGregorio (1997); Ferrell (1984); Jewell (2005); McCullough (1992); Truman (1973).
7. McCullough (1992).
8. McCullough (1992).
9. DeGregorio (1997); Ferrell (1984); Jewell (2005).
10. DeGregorio (1997); Jewell (2005); McCullough (1992).
11. Truman (1973).

12. McCullough (1992).
13. McCullough (1992).
14. Ferrell (1984).
15. Ferrell (1984); Truman (1973).
16. Jewell (2005).
17. Ferrell (1984).
18. Dallek (2008); McCullough (1992).
19. McCullough (1992).
20. Truman (1973).
21. McCullough (1992); Truman (1973).
22. Truman (1973).
23. Ferrell (1984).
24. Ferrell (1984); McCullough (1992).
25. McCullough (1992).
26. DeGregorio (1997); McCullough (1992).
27. Ferrell (1984).
28. McCullough (1992).
29. Jewell (2005).
30. Dallek (2008); Ferrell (1984); McCullough (1992), pp. 394–396; Truman (1973).
31. Ferrell (1984); Truman (1973).
32. Dallek (2008); Ferrell (1984); Truman (1973).
33. Botting (1985).
34. Dallek (2008); DeGregorio (1997).
35. Ferrell (1984).
36. Ferrell (1984), p. 163.
37. DeGregorio (1997).
38. Dallek (2008).
39. Truman (1973).
40. Hunter and Bainbridge, Jr. (2005).
41. Hunter and Bainbridge, Jr. (2005).
42. Grant (2004); Hunter and Bainbridge, Jr. (2005).
43. DeGregorio (1997); McCullough (1992); St. George (1999).
44. Truman (1973).
45. Dallek (2008); McCullough (1992).
46. McCullough (1992).
47. Grant (2004).
48. Hunter and Bainbridge, Jr. (2005).
49. Hunter and Bainbridge, Jr. (2005).
50. Hunter and Bainbridge, Jr. (2005); Truman (1973).
51. Hunter and Bainbridge, Jr. (2005).
52. Hunter and Bainbridge, Jr. (2005).
53. Hunter and Bainbridge, Jr. (2005).
54. Grant (2004); St. George (1999); Truman (1973).
55. McCullough (1992).
56. Hunter and Bainbridge, Jr. (2005); McCullough (1992).
57. Sifakis (2001); St. George (1999).
58. Hunter and Bainbridge, Jr. (2005).
59. Sifakis (2001).

60. McCullough (1992).
61. Truman (1973).
62. McCullough (1992).
63. Hunter and Bainbridge, Jr. (2005).
64. Hunter and Bainbridge, Jr. (2005).
65. Hunter and Bainbridge, Jr. (2005); McCullough (1992).
66. McCullough (1992); Truman (1973); Wicker (2003).
67. Hunter and Bainbridge, Jr. (2005).
68. Hunter and Bainbridge, Jr. (2005); McCullough (1992).
69. Hunter and Bainbridge, Jr. (2005).
70. McCullough (1992); St. George (1999); Truman (1973).
71. McCullough (1992), p. 811.
72. Truman (1973).
73. McCullough (1992), p. 811.
74. McCullough (1992).
75. McCullough (1992).
76. Hunter and Bainbridge, Jr. (2005).
77. McCullough (1992).
78. Hunter and Bainbridge, Jr. (2005).
79. McCullough (1992).
80. St. George (1999).
81. Hunter and Bainbridge, Jr. (2005).
82. Hunter and Bainbridge, Jr. (2005); McCullough (1992).
83. Sifakis (2001).
84. Truman (1973).
85. Truman (1973).
86. DeGregorio (1997), p. 522.

CHAPTER 8: JOHN F. KENNEDY

1. Jewell (2005).
2. St. George (1999).
3. Rubin (2005).
4. DeGregorio (1997), p. 551.
5. DeGregorio (1997).
6. Wicker (2003).
7. Jewell (2005).
8. DeGregorio (1997); Jones (2008).
9. Rubin (2005).
10. Rubin (2005); St. George (1999).
11. DeGregorio (1997).
12. Jewell (2005).
13. Gardner (2000).
14. Bugliosi (2007); Groden (1995); Pietrusza (1997).
15. Bugliosi (2007); Posner (1993).
16. Pietrusza (1997).
17. Groden (1995).
18. Groden (1995).

19. Bugliosi (2007).
20. Posner (1993).
21. Bugliosi (2007); Groden (1995); Wicker (2003).
22. McKinley (1977).
23. Hosty (1996); Posner (1993).
24. Pietrusza (1997); Posner (1993).
25. Groden (1995).
26. Posner (1993).
27. Pietrusza (1997); Wicker (2003).
28. Pietrusza (1997).
29. Groden (1995).
30. Bugliosi (2007).
31. Manchester (1963).
32. Gardner (2000).
33. Pietrusza (1997).
34. Hosty (1996); Grant (2004); McKinley (1977).
35. McKinley (1977).
36. Wicker (2003).
37. Bishop (1968).
38. DeGregorio (1997); Grant (2004).
39. Bishop (1968), p. 133; Manchester (1963), p. 153; Pietrusza (1997), p. 19; St. George (1999), p. 84.
40. Posner (1993).
41. Wicker (2003).
42. St. George (1999).
43. Bugliosi (2007), p. 40; Bishop (1968), p. 133.
44. DeGregorio (1997), p. 559; Pietrusza (1997), p. 21.
45. Bugliosi (2007); St. George (1999).
46. Posner (1993); Pietrusza (1997).
47. Pietrusza (1997).
48. St. George (1999).
49. Posner (1993).
50. St. George (1999).
51. DeGregorio (1997); Posner (1993).
52. Pietrusza (1997).
53. Grant (2004).
54. St. George (1999).
55. Wicker (2003).
56. St. George (1999).
57. Pietrusza (1997).
58. Bugliosi (2007); Groden (1995); Hurt (1985); Kurtz (1982).
59. Posner (1993).
60. Bugliosi (2007).
61. Posner (1993), p. 3.
62. Groden (1995).
63. Wicker (2003).
64. Pietrusza (1997).
65. Pietrusza (1997).

66. Wicker (2003).
67. Posner (1993), p. 397; Pietrusza (1997), p. 38.
68. Pietrusza (1997), p. 38.
69. St. George (1999); Wicker (2003).
70. Bugliosi (2007); Hosty (1996).
71. Groden (1995).
72. Hosty (1996).
73. David (1997); Posner (1993).
74. Posner (1993).
75. Ford and Stiles (1965), p. 25.
76. Hurt (1985).
77. McKinley (1977).
78. Thompson (1967).
79. Garrison (1988).
80. Brown (1995); Jewell (2005); Lifton (1980); Lane (1992); Wicker (2003).
81. Pietruza (1997).
82. Bugliosi (2007).
83. DeGregorio (1997).
84. Sifakis (2001).
85. Garrison (1988).
86. Belin (1988).
87. DeGregorio (1997).
88. DeGregorio (1997).
89. Sifakis (2001).
90. Belin (1988).
91. Hurt (1985).

CHAPTER 9: GERALD R. FORD

1. Brinkley (2007); DeGregorio (1997); Jewell (2005).
2. Collins (1990); Gould (2000).
3. DeGregorio (1997).
4. Collins (1990); DeGregorio (1997).
5. Jewell (2005).
6. Collins (1990); Jewell (2005).
7. Jewell (2005).
8. Collins (1990); DeGregorio (1997); Jewell (2005).
9. Collins (1990).
10. Jewell (2005).
11. Gould (2000).
12. Collins (1990).
13. Gould (2000); Werth (2006).
14. Gould (2000).
15. Collins (1990).
16. Gould (2000).
17. Brinkley (2007).
18. DeGregorio (1997).
19. DeGregorio (1997); Jewell (2005).

20. Jewell (2005).
21. Bravin (1997).
22. Bravin (1997).
23. Sifakis (2001).
24. Bravin (1997).
25. Bravin (1997).
26. Bravin (1997).
27. St. George (1999).
28. St. George (1999), p. 121.
29. Bravin (1997); DeGregorio (1997).
30. Bravin (1997).
31. Bravin (1997).
32. Bravin (1997).
33. Bravin (1997).
34. Bravin (1997).
35. Bravin (1997).
36. Bravin (1997).
37. Bravin (1997).
38. Sifakis (2001).
39. Bravin (1997), p. 8.
40. Bravin (1997).
41. Bravin (1997), p. 9; Sifakis (2001), p. 63.
42. DeFrank (2007).
43. St. George (1999), p. 120.
44. St. George (1999).
45. Bravin (1997).
46. Sifakis (2001).
47. Bravin (1997).
48. Bravin (1997).
49. Bravin (1997).
50. Bravin (1997).
51. Bravin (1997).
52. Bravin (1997).
53. Bravin (1997).
54. Bravin (1997).
55. Jewell (2005).
56. Collins (1990).
57. DeFrank (2007).
58. Bravin (1997).
59. St. George (1999).
60. Bravin (1997).
61. Bravin (1997); Spieler (2009).
62. Spieler (2009).
63. Spieler (2009).
64. Spieler (2009).
65. Spieler (2009).
66. Spieler (2009).
67. Bravin (1997); Sifakis (2001).

68. Spieler (2009).
69. St. George (1999).
70. Jewell (2005).
71. Collins (1990).
72. Sifakis (2001).
73. Spieler (2009), p. 153.
74. DeFrank (2007).
75. Bravin (1997), p. 284.
76. Spieler (2009).
77. DeFrank (2007).
78. Collins (1990); Jewell (2005).
79. Brinkley (2007).
80. Spieler (2009), pp. 156–57.
81. Spieler (2009).
82. Bravin (1997), p. 284.
83. Bravin (1997).
84. Bravin (1997), p. 285.
85. Spieler (2009).
86. Spieler (2009).
87. Bravin (1997).
88. Bravin (1997).

CHAPTER 10: RONALD REAGAN

1. Abrams (1992); Jones (1996); McCarthy and Smith (1985); Melanson and Stevens (2002); Reagan (1990).
2. The biography of Ronald Reagan is largely based on the following sources: Brinkley (1997); Cannon, (1991); DeGregorio (2002); Dugger (1983); Edwards (1981); Kengor (2006); Morris (1999); Reeves (2005).
3. Reagan (1990).
4. Reagan (1990).
5. Brinkley (1997).
6. Morris (1999).
7. Dugger (1983); Edwards (1981).
8. Brinkley (1997).
9. Cannon (1991).
10. DeGregorio (2002).
11. Reagan (1981).
12. Abrams (1992).
13. Brinkley (2007), p. 12.
14. Clarke (1990); Edwards (1981).
15. Abrams (1992), p. 20.
16. Abrams (1992); Jones (1996).
17. Abrams (1992).
18. Abrams (1992), p. 23.
19. Abrams (1992).
20. McCarthy and Smith (1985).
21. Jones (1996), p. 117.

22. Jones (1996), p. 118.

23. Abrams (1992); Jones (1996); McCarthy and Smith (1985); Melanso and Stevens (2002); Reagan (1990).

24. Edwards (1981).

25. McCarthy and Smith (1985).

26. Brinkley (2007); Jones (1996).

27. McCarthy and Smith (1985); Reeves (2005).

28. Reagan (1990), p. 259; Reeves (2005), p. 34.

29. Abrams (1992); McCarthy and Smith (1985); Melanson and Stevens (2002).

30. Jones (1996).

31. Jones (1996).

32. Melanson and Stevens (2002).

33. Abrams (1992), p. 54.

34. Edwards (1981), p. 262.

35. McCarthy and Smith (1985).

36. McCarthy and Smith (1985).

37. McCarthy and Smith (1985).

38. Abrams (1992), p. 55.

39. Melanson and Stevens (2002), p. 120.

40. Abrams (1992), p. 57.

41. Abrams (1992), p. 57.

42. Abrams (1992), p. 58.

43. Reeves (2005), p. 35.

44. Abrams (1992), p. 60; Jones (1996), p. 123; Edwards (1981), p. 263.

45. Reagan (1990).

46. Morris (1999).

47. Abrams (1992), p. 62.

48. Reagan (1990); Reeves (2005).

49. Jones (1996), p. 123.

50. Reagan (2007), p. 12.

51. McCarthy and Smith (1985).

52. Bonnie, Jeffries, and Low (2008).

53. Taylor (1982).

54. Village of Orland Park Police Department (2009).

55. Reagan (1990), p. 262.

56. Dugger (1983); Simon and Aaronson (1988).

57. Jones (1996), p. 125.

58. Jones (1996), p. 126.

59. U.S. Department of the Treasury (1981).

60. McCarthy and Smith (1985).

61. Melanson and Stevens (2002).

62. Abrams (1992).

63. Cannon (1991).

CHAPTER 11: OTHER ASSASSINATION ATTEMPTS

1. Kline (2008).

2. Cuthbert (1949).

3. Kline (2008).
4. Kline (2008), p. 268.
5. Cuthbert (1949).
6. Kline (2008).
7. Nash (2004).
8. Anderson (1996); Schlesinger (2002).
9. Nash (2004), p. 185.
10. Schlesinger (2002).
11. Nash (2004), p. 185.
12. McKinely (1977); Melanson and Stevens (2002).
13. Clarke (1982); McKinely (1977).
14. Clarke (1982).
15. Clarke (1982).
16. Clarke (1982); Sifakis (2001).
17. Clarke (1982).
18. Melanson and Stevens (2002).
19. Melanson and Stevens (2002), p. 107.
20. Clarke (1982), p. 128; Melanson and Stevens (2002), p. 107.
21. Clarke (1982); Sifakis (2001).
22. Clarke (1982).
23. Melanson and Stevens (2002), p. 108.
24. Sifakis (2001).
25. Melanson and Stevens (2002), p. 109.
26. Clarke (1982), p. 128; Melanson and Stevens (2002), p. 108.
27. Melanson and Stevens (2002), p. 108.
28. Preston (1987).
29. See chapter 11, endnote No. 21 in 9/11 Commission (2004).
30. *Time* (1979).
31. One of the authors, Willard M. Oliver, was a second lieutenant at the time of the Persian Gulf War and served as second platoon leader in the 304th Military Police Company, which was mobilized out of Bluefield, West Virginia.
32. Office of the Inspector General (1997).
33. Office of the Inspector General (1997).
34. Office of the Inspector General (1997).
35. Ibrahim (1993).
36. Ibrahim (1993).
37. Von Drehle and Smith (1993).
38. Melanson and Stevens (2002).
39. U.S. Department of Treasury (1995).
40. Pear (1994).
41. U.S. Department of Treasury (1995), p. 29.
42. U.S Department of Treasury (1995).
43. Melanson and Stevens (2002).
44. This section is drawn largely from the U.S Department of Treasury (1995).
45. U.S. Department of Treasury (1995), p. 32.
46. Melanson and Stevens (2002).
47. U.S. Department of Treasury (1995). At the time, the Secret Service was part of the Treasury Department. It is now part of the Department of Homeland Security.

48. ABC News (2001).

49. *New York Times* (2001).

50. Sullivan (2001).

51. The National Commission on Terrorist Attacks Upon the United States (9/11 Commission) (2004).

52. Federal Bureau of Investigation (2006).

CHAPTER 12: RUMORED ASSASSINATIONS

1. Persico (2008).

2. Hanson (2000).

3. The biographical sketch of Zachary Taylor is based on the following references: Bauer (1985); Eisenhower (2008); Hamilton (1966); Howard (1892); Smith (1988).

4. Bauer (1985).

5. Bauer (1985), p. 268.

6. Bauer (1985).

7. Hamilton (1966), p. 388.

8. Smith (1988).

9. Hamilton (1966), p. 388.

10. Hamilton (1966); Howard (1892); Parenti (1999).

11. Howard (1892).

12. Parenti (1998), p. 151.

13. Parenti (1998), p. 151.

14. Bauer (1985).

15. Howard (1892).

16. Hamilton (1966); Howard (1892).

17. Bauer (1985).

18. Eisenhower (2008); Smith (1988).

19. Bauer (1985), p. 315.

20. Parenti (1998), p. 153.

21. Bauer (1985), p. 316.

22. Eisenhower (2008), p. 134; Smith (1988), p. 157.

23. Howard (1892).

24. Parenti (1999); Parenti (1998).

25. *New York Times* (1881)

26. Marriott (1991); Rising (2007).

27. Parenti (1999); Parenti (1998).

28. Parenti (1998), p. 144.

29. Anthony (1998).

30. Trani and Wilson (1977).

31. The section on the Teapot Dome Scandal is based on McCartney (2008); Noggle (1962).

32. McCartney (2008).

33. Trani and Wilson (1977).

34. Russell (1968); Trani and Wilson (1977).

35. Sinclair (1965).

36. Russell (1968), p. 589.

37. Sinclair (1965).

38. Russell (1968), p. 590.
39. Russell (1968), p. 590.
40. Trani and Wilson (1977).
41. Russell (1968), p. 591.
42. Russell (1968); Trani and Wilson (1977).
43. Wood (1932).
44. Starling (1946).
45. Anthony (1998); Russell (1968); Sinclair (1965).
46. Russell (1968), p. 592.
47. Anthony (1998).
48. Starling (1946).
49. Trani and Wilson (1977).
50. Anthony (1998).
51. Anthony (1998); Britton (1927).
52. Anthony (1998).
53. *Britton v. Klunk*, 1931, Toledo, Ohio.
54. Means (1930).

Bibliography

ABC News. (2001). "Alleged White House Gunman Said Troubled." *ABC News*. http://www.abc-news.com (accessed June 19, 2009).

Abrams, Herbert L. (1992). *"The President Has Been Shot": Confusion, Disability, and the 25th Amendment in the Aftermath of the Attempted Assassination of Ronald Reagan*. New York: Norton.

Ackerman, Kenneth D. (2003). *Dark Horse*. New York: Carroll and Graf.

Alger, Horatio, Jr. (1881). *From Canal Boy to President*. Philadelphia: David McKay.

Alsop, Joseph. (1982). *F.D.R.: A Centenary Remembrance*. New York: Viking.

Alter, Jonathan. (2006). *The Defining Moment*. New York: Simon & Schuster.

Anderson, Christopher P. (1996). *Jack and Jackie: Portrait of an American Marriage*. Darby, PA: Diane Publishing.

Anthony, Carl Sferrazza. (1998). *Florence Harding: The First Lady, the Jazz Age, and the Death of America's Most Scandalous President*. New York: William Morrow.

Arnold, Isaac N. (1893). *The Life of Abraham Lincoln*. Chicago: A. C. McClurg.

Bak, Richard. (1998). *The Day Lincoln Was Shot*. Dallas: Taylor Publishing.

Barber, James G. (1991). *Andrew Jackson: A Portrait Study*. Seattle: University of Washington Press.

Bauer, K. Jack. (1985). *Zachary Taylor: Soldier, Planter, Statesmen of the Old Southwest*. Baton Rouge: Louisiana State University Press.

Belin, David W. (1988). *Final Disclosure*. New York: Charles Scribner's Sons.

Bishop, Jim. (1955). *The Day Lincoln Was Shot*. New York: Harper & Row.

Bishop, Jim. (1968). *The Day Kennedy Was Shot*. New York: Funk and Wagnalls.

Bishop, Joseph Bucklin. (1920). *Theodore Roosevelt and His Time*, Vol. 2. New York: Charles Scribner's Sons.

Black, Conrad. (2003). *Franklin Delano Roosevelt: Champion of Freedom*. New York: Public Affairs.

Bonnie, Richard C., John C. Jeffries, and Peter W. Low. (2008). *A Case Study in the Insanity Defense: The Trial of John W. Hinckley, Jr*. Mineola, NY: Foundation Press.

Botting, Douglas. (1985). *From the Ruins of the Reich*. New York: New American Library.

Brands, H. W. (1997). *T.R.: The Last Romantic*. New York: Basic Books.

Brands, H. W. (2005). *Andrew Jackson: His Life and Times*. New York: Doubleday.

Bravin, Jess. (1997). *Squeaky: The Life and Times of Lynette Alice Fromme*. New York: Buzz Books.

Bremer, Howard F. (1971). *Franklin Delano Roosevelt, 1882–1945*. Dobbs Ferry, NY: Oceana Publications.

Brinkley, Alan. (1997). "Ronald Reagan." In *The Presidents: A Reference History*, 2nd ed. ed. H. F. Graff, pp. 569–588. New York: MacMillan Library Reference.

Brinkley, Douglas. (2007a). *Gerald R. Ford*. New York: Times Books.

Brinkley, Douglas. (2007b). *The Reagan Diaries*. New York: HarperCollins.

Britton v. Klunk. (1931). Toledo, OH.

Britton, Nan. (1927). *The President's Daughter*. New York: Elizabeth Ann Guild.

Brown, Walt. (1995). *Treachery in Dallas*. New York: Carroll and Graf.

Bugliosi, Vincent. (2007). *Reclaiming History: The Assassination of President John F. Kennedy*. New York: Norton.

Bundy, J. M. (1880). *The Life and Public Services of General James A. Garfield*. New York: A. S. Barnes.

Burstein, Andrew. (2003). *The Passions of Andrew Jackson*. New York: Alfred A. Knopf.

Caldwell, Robert Granville. (1931). *James A. Garfield: Party Chieftain*. New York: Dodd, Mead.

Cannon, Lou. (1991). *President Reagan: The Role of a Lifetime*. New York: Touchstone.

Caroli, Betty Boyd. (1998). *The Roosevelt Women*. New York: Basic Books.

Carwardine, Richard. (2006). *Lincoln: A Life of Purpose and Power*. New York: Alfred A. Knopf.

Chace, James. (2004). *1912: Wilson, Taft and Debs: The Election That Changed the Country*. New York: Simon & Schuster.

Clarke, James W. (1982). *American Assassins: The Darker Side of Politics*. Princeton, NJ: Princeton University Press.

Clarke, James W. (1990). *On Being Mad or Merely Angry: John W. Hinckley, Jr. and Other Dangerous People*. Princeton, NJ: Princeton University Press.

Cole, Donald B. (1993). *The Presidency of Andrew Jackson*. Lawrence: University Press of Kansas.

Collins, David R. (1990). *Gerald R. Ford*. Ada, OK: Garrett.

Craughwell, Thomas J. (2007). *Stealing Lincoln's Body*. Cambridge, MA: Belknap.

Cuthbert, Norma B. (1949). *Lincoln and the Baltimore Plot, 1861: From Pinkerton Records and Related Papers*. San Marino, CA: Huntington Library.

Dallek, Robert. (2008). *Harry S. Truman*. New York: Times Books.

Dalton, Kathleen. (2002). *Theodore Roosevelt: A Strenuous Life*. New York: Alfred A. Knopf.

Davis, John H. (1989). *Mafia Kingfish: Carlos Marcello and the Assassination of John F. Kennedy*. New York: McGraw-Hill.

DeFrank, Thomas M. (2007). *Write It When I'm Gone*. New York: G. P. Putnam's Sons.

DeGregorio, William A. (2002). *The Complete Book of U.S. Presidents*. New York: Gramercy Books.

Donald, David Herbert. (1995). *Lincoln*. New York: Simon & Schuster.

Dugger, Ronnie. (1983). *On Reagan: The Man and His Presidency*. New York: McGraw-Hill.

Edwards, Lee. (1981). *Ronald Reagan: A Political Biography*. Houston, TX: Nordland.

Eisenhower, John S. D. (2008). *Zachary Taylor*. New York: Times Books.

Epstein, Daniel Mark. (2008). *The Lincolns: Portrait of a Marriage*. New York: William Morrow.

Fallows, Samuel. (1901). *Life of William McKinley: Our Martyred President*. Chicago: Regan.

Federal Bureau of Investigation. (2002). *Franklin D. Roosevelt (Assassination Attempt)*. Washington, DC: U.S. Department of Justice.

Federal Bureau of Investigation. (2006). "The Case of the Failed Hand Grenade Attack." *FBI Homepage*. http://www.fbi.gov/page2/jan06/grenadeattack011106.htm (accessed March 25, 2010).

Ferrell, Robert H. (1984). *Truman: A Centenary Remembrance*. New York: Viking Press.

Fetzer, James H. (2003). *The Great Zapruder Film Hoax*. Chicago: Catfeet Press.

Ford, Gerald R. (1979). *A Time to Heal: The Autobiography of Gerald R. Ford*. New York: Harper & Row.

Ford, Gerald, and John R. Stiles. (1965). *Portrait of the Assassin*. New York: Simon & Schuster.

Gardner, Joseph L., rev. Louis L. Gould. (2000). "John Fitzgerald Kennedy: Inspiring a Generation." In *American Heritage Illustrated History of the Presidents*, ed. Michael Beschloss. New York: Crown.

Garrison, Jim. (1988). *On the Trail of the Assassins*. New York: Sheridan Square Press.

Goodrich, Thomas. (2005). *The Darkest Dawn: Lincoln, Booth, and the Great American Tragedy*. Bloomington: Indiana University Press.

Gould, Lewis L. (1980). *The Presidency of William McKinley*. Lawrence: Regents Press of Kansas.

Gould, Lewis L. (2000). "Gerald Rudolph Ford: A Time for Healing." In *American Heritage Illustrated History of the Presidents*, ed. Michael Beschloss. New York: Crown.

Graff, Henry F. (1997). *The Presidents: A Reference History*, 2nd ed. New York: Gramercy.

Grant, R. G. (2004). *Assassinations*. New York: Readers' Digest Association.

Groden, Robert J. (1995). *The Search for Lee Harvey Oswald*. New York: Penguin.

Guttridge, Leonard F., and Ray A. Neff. (2003). *Dark Union*. Hoboken, NJ: John Wiley.

Hamilton, Holman. (1966). *Zachary Taylor: Soldier in the White House*. Hamden, CT: Archon Books.

Hanchet, William. (1994). *Out of the Wilderness*. Urbana: University of Illinois Press.

Hanson, Bill. (2000). *Closely Guarded Secrets: The Assassination of F.D.R., Japan's Atomic Bomb, the Massacre at Port Chicago*. Philadelphia: Xlibris.

Harrell, Carolyn L. (1997). *When the Bells Tolled for Lincoln: Southern Reaction to the Assassination*. Macon, GA: Mercer University Press.

Harris, William C. (2004). *Lincoln's Last Months*. Cambridge, MA: Harvard University Press.

Hesseltine, William B. (1960). *Lincoln's Plan of Reconstruction*. Tuscaloosa, AL: Confederate Publishing.

Higgins, Eva. (1989). *William McKinley*. Canton, OH: Daring.

Holzer, Harold. (1999). *Lincoln as I Knew Him*. Chapel Hill, NC: Algonquin.

Hosty, James P., Jr. (1996). *Assignment: Oswald*. New York: Arcade.

Howard, Oliver Otis. (1892). *General Taylor*. New York: D. Appleton.

Hoyt, Edwin P. (1964). *James A. Garfield*. Chicago: Reilly and Lee.

Hunter, Stephen, and John Bainbridge, Jr. (2005). *American Gunfight: The Plot to Kill Harry Truman*. New York: Simon & Schuster.

Hurt, Henry. (1985). *Reasonable Doubt*. New York: Holt, Rinehart and Winston.

Ibrahim, Youssef M. (1993). "Suspects' Haste a Puzzle in Kuwait Trial." *New York Times*, June 13, p. A1.

Jacobs, David, rev. Lewis L. Gould. (2000). "Harry S. Truman: The Buck Stopped Here." In *American Heritage Illustrated History of the Presidents*, ed. Michael Beschloss. New York: Crown.

Jeffers, H. Paul. (1994). *Commissioner Roosevelt: The Story of Theodore Roosevelt and the New York City Police, 1895–1897*. New York: John Wiley.

Jenkins, Roy. (2003). *Franklin Delano Roosevelt*. New York: Times Books.

Jewell, Elizabeth. (2005). *U.S. Presidents Factbook*. New York: Random House.

Jones, Howard. (2008). *The Bay of Pigs*. New York: Oxford University Press.

Jones, Rebecca C. (1996). *The President Has Been Shot! True Stories of the Attacks on Ten U.S. Presidents*. New York: Troll Books.

Kaplan, Fred. (2008). *Lincoln: The Biography of a Writer*. New York: HarperCollins.

Kauffman, Michael W. (2004) *American Brutus: John Wilkes Booth and the Lincoln Conspiracies*. New York: Random House.

Keneally, Thomas. (2003). *Abraham Lincoln*. New York: Viking.

Kengor, Paul. (2006). *The Crusader: Ronald Reagan and the Fall of Communism*. New York: Regan.

Kline, Michael J. (2008). *The Baltimore Plot: The First Conspiracy to Assassinate Abraham Lincoln*. Yardley, PA: Westholme.

Koenig, Louis W. (2000). "James Abram Garfield: The Preacher." In *American Heritage Illustrated History of the Presidents*, ed. Michael Beschloss, pp. 262–269. New York: Crown.

Kunhardt, Dorothy M., and Philip B. Kunhardt, Jr. (1965). *Twenty Days*. New York: Harper & Row.

Kurtz, Michael. (1982). *Crime of the Century*. Knoxville: University of Tennessee Press.

Lane, Mark. (1992). *Rush to Judgement*. New York: Thunder Mouth Press.

Larson, Kate Clifford. (2008). *The Assassin's Accomplice: Mary Surratt and the Plot to Kill Abraham Lincoln*. New York: Basic Books.

Lawson, John Davison. (1915). *American State Trials*. Cambridge, MA: Harvard University Press.

Leach, Eugene W. (1921). "Attempted Assassination of Theodore Roosevelt." *Racine Journal*, August 13. Available on-line at http://www.wisconsinhistory.org/wlhba/articleView.asp?pg=1&id=14014 (accessed November 2009).

Leech, Margaret. (1959). *In the Days of McKinley*. New York: Harper and Brothers.

Leonard, Elizabeth D. (2004). *Lincoln's Avengers*. New York: Norton.

Lifton, David S. (1980). *Best Evidence*. New York: MacMillan.

Mailer, Norman. (1995). *Oswald's Tale*. New York: Random House.

Manchester, William. (1963). *The Death of a President*. New York: Harper & Row.

Marquis, James. (1938). *The Life of Andrew Jackson*. Indianapolis, IN: Bobbs-Merrill.

Marriott, Michel. (1991). "President Zachary Taylor's Body to Be Tested for Signs of Arsenic." *New York Times*, June 15. http://www.nytimes.com (accessed March 25, 2010).

Martineau, Harriet. (1838). *Retrospect of Western Travel*. London: Saunders and Otley.

McCabe, James Dabney. (1881). *Our Martyred President*. Cleveland, OH: Hamilton.

McCarthy, Dennis V. N., and Philip W. Smith. (1985). *Protecting the President*. New York: Dell.

McCartney, Laton. (2008). *The Teapot Dome Scandal: How Big Oil Bought the Harding White House and Tried to Steal the Country*. New York: Random House.

McCullough, David. (1981). *Mornings on Horseback*. New York: Simon & Schuster.

McCullough, David. (1992). *Truman*. New York: Simon & Schuster.

McElroy, Richard L. (1986). *James A. Garfield: A Pictorial History*. Canton, OH: Daring.

McElroy, Richard L. (1996). *William McKinley and Our America*. Canton, OH: Stark County Historical Society.

McGovern, George. (2009). *Abraham Lincoln*. New York: Henry Holt.

McKinley, James. (1977). *Assassination in America*. New York: Harper & Row.

McLauglin, Emmett. (1963). *An Inquiry into the Assassination of Abraham Lincoln*. New York: Lyle Stewart.

Meacham, Jon. (2008). *American Lion: Andrew Jackson in the White House*. New York: Random House.

Means, Gaston B. (1930). *The Strange Death of President Harding*. New York: Guild.

Melanson, Philip H., and Peter F. Stevens. (2002). *Secret Service: The Hidden History of an Enigmatic Agency*. New York: Carroll & Graf.

Millard, Candice. (2005). *Theodore Roosevelt's Darkest Journey: The River of Doubt*. New York: Broadway Books.

Miller, Nathan. (1992). *Theodore Roosevelt: A Life*. New York: Quill.

Morris, Edmund. (1979). *The Rise of Theodore Roosevelt*. New York: Modern Library.

Morris, Edmund. (1999). *Dutch: A Memoir of Ronald Reagan*. New York: Random House.

Morris, Edmund. (2001). *Theodore Rex*. New York: Modern Library.

Nash, Jay Robert. (2004). *The Great Pictorial History of World Crime*. Lanham, MD: Scarecrow Press.

Netzley, Patricia D. (2000). *Presidential Assassins*. San Diego, CA: Lucent Books.

New York Times. (1881). "Assassination of President: The Rev. Dr. Walsh Asserts That Zachary Taylor Was Murdered." *New York Times*, August 29. http://www.nytimes.com (accessed March 25, 2010).

New York Times. (2001). "National Briefing, Washington: Guilty Plea by Gunman." *New York Times*, June 21, p. A1.

9/11 Commission. (2004). *The 9/11 Commission Report*. New York: Norton.

Noggle, Burl. (1962). *Teapot Dome: Oil and Politics in the 1920s*. Baton Rouge: Louisiana State University Press.

Oates, Stephen B. (1977). *With Malice Toward None: The Life of Abraham Lincoln*. New York: Harper & Row.

Office of the Inspector General. (1997). *The FBI Laboratory: An Investigation into Laboratory Practices and Alleged Misconduct in Explosives-Related and Other Cases*. Washington, DC: U.S. Department of Justice, Section D.

Oldroyd, Osborn H. (1901). *The Assassination of Abraham Lincoln*. Washington, DC: Oldroyd.

O'Toole, Patricia. (2006). "The War of 1912." *Time*, July 3.

Ownsbey, Betty. (1993). *Alias "Paine": Lewis Thornton Powell, the Mystery Man of the Lincoln Conspiracy*. Jefferson, NC: McFarland.

Parenti, Michael. (1998). "The Strange Death of President Zachary Taylor: A Case Study in the Manufacture of Mainstream History." *New Political Science* 20: pp. 141–158.

Parenti, Michael. (1999). *History as Mystery*. San Francisco: City Lights.

Pear, Robert. (1994). "Friends Depict Loner with Unraveling Life." *New York Times*, September 13, p. A1.

Persico, Joseph E. (2008). *Franklin and Lucy: President Roosevelt, Mrs. Rutherfurd, and the Other Remarkable Women in His Life*. New York: Random House.

Peskin, Allan. (1978). *Garfield*. Kent, OH: Kent State University Press.

Peterson, Merrill D. (1994). *Lincoln in American Memory*. New York: Oxford University Press.

Phillips, Kevin. (2003). *William McKinley*. New York: Times Books.

Picchi, Blaise. (2003). *The Five Weeks of Giuseppe Zangara: The Man Who Would Assassinate FDR*. Chicago: Academy of Chicago.

Pietrusza, David. (1997). *John F. Kennedy*. San Diego, CA: Lucent Books.

Posner, Gerald. (1993). *Case Closed: Lee Harvey Oswald and the Assassination of JFK*. New York: Random House.

Preston, Edmund. (1987). *Troubled Passage: The Federal Aviation During the Nixon-Ford Term, 1973–1977*. Washington, DC: Government Printing Office.

Putnam, George Haven. (1909). *Abraham Lincoln*. New York: G. P. Putnam's Sons.

Rauchway, Eric. (2003). *Murdering McKinley*. New York: Hill and Wang.

Reagan, Ronald. (1981). "First Inaugural Address." In *Public Papers of the Presidents of the United States*. Washington, DC: Government Printing Office.

Reagan, Ronald. (1990). *Ronald Reagan: An American Life*. New York: Simon & Schuster.

Reck, W. Emerson. (1987). *A. Lincoln: His Last 24 Hours*. Columbia: University of South Carolina Press.

Reeves, Richard. (2005). *President Reagan: The Triumph of Imagination*. New York: Simon & Schuster.

Remey, Oliver, Henry Cochems, and Wheeler Bloodgood. (1912). *The Attempted Assassination of Ex-President Theodore Roosevelt*. Milwaukee, WI: Remey.

Remini, Robert V. (1977). *Andrew Jackson: The Course of American Empire, 1767–1821, Vol. 1*. New York: Harper & Row.

Remini, Robert V. (1981). *Andrew Jackson: The Course of American Freedom, 1822–1832, Vol. 2*. New York: Harper & Row.

Remini, Robert V. (1984). *Andrew Jackson: The Course of American Democracy, 1833–1845, Vol. 3*. New York: Harper & Row.

Rising, Clara. (2007). *The Taylor File: The Mysterious Death of a President*. Philadelphia: Xlibris.

Roosevelt, Nicholas. (1967). *Theodore Roosevelt: The Man as I Knew Him*. New York: Dodd, Mead.

Roscoe, Theodore. (1959). *The Web of Conspiracy*. Englewood Cliffs, NJ: Prentice Hall.

Rubin, Gretchen Craft. (2005). *Forty Ways to Look at JFK*. New York: Ballantine.

Russell, Francis. (1968). *The Shadow of Blooming Grove: Warren G. Harding and His Times*. New York: McGraw-Hill.

Russell, Francis. (1969). *President Harding: His Life and Times, 1865–1923*. London: Eyre & Spottiswoode.

Rutkow, Ira. (2006). *James A. Garfield*. New York: Times Books.

Schlesinger, Arthur M., Jr. (1946). *The Age of Jackson*. Boston: Little, Brown

Schlesinger, Arthur M., Jr. (2002). *A Thousand Days: John F. Kennedy in the White House*. New York: Houghton Mifflin Harcourt.

Sifakis, Carl. (2001). *Encyclopedia of Assassinations*. New York: Checkmark.

Simon, Rita J., and David E. Aaronson. (1988). *The Insanity Defense: A Critical Assessment of Law and Policy in the Post-Hinckley Era*. Westport, CT: Praeger Publishers.

Sinclair, Andrew. (1965). *The Available Man: The Life behind the Masks of Warren Gamaliel Harding*. New York: MacMillan.

Smith, Elbert B. (1988). *The Presidencies of Zachary Taylor & Millard Fillmore*. Lawrence: University Press of Kansas.

Smith, Jean Edward. (2007). *F.D.R.* New York: Random House.

Spieler, Geri. (2009). *Taking Aim at the President*. New York: Palgrave MacMillan.

St. George, Judith. (1999). *In the Line of Fire*. New York: Holiday House.

Starkey, Larry. (1976). *Wilkes Booth Came to Washington*. New York: Random House.

Starling, Edmund W. (1946). *Starling of the White House*. New York: Simon & Schuster.

Steers, Edward, Jr. (2001). *Blood on the Moon: The Assassination of Abraham Lincoln*. Lexington: University Press of Kentucky.

Stern, Philip Van Doren. (1939). *The Man Who Killed Lincoln*. New York: Random House.

Sullivan, Shay. (2001). "Possible Longboat Terrorist Incident." *Longboat Observer*, September 26, p. A1.

Sullivan, Wilson, rev. Lewis L. Gould. (2000). "Franklin Delano Roosevelt: New Dealer and Global Warrior." In *American Heritage Illustrated History of the Presidents*, ed. Michael Beschloss. New York: Crown.

Sumner, William Graham. (1899). *Andrew Jackson*. Boston: Houghton, Mifflin.

Swanson, James L. (2006). *Manhunt: The Twelve-Day Chase for Lincoln's Killer*. New York: Morrow.

Swanson James L., and Daniel R. Weinberg. (2001). *Lincoln's Assassins: Their Trial and Execution*. New York: William Morrow.

Taylor, John M. (1970). *Garfield of Ohio: The Available Man*. New York: Norton.

Taylor, Stuart, Jr. (1982). "Hinckley Hails 'Historical' Shooting to Win Love." *New York Times*, July 9.

Thayer, William Roscoe. (1919). *Theodore Roosevelt: An Intimate Biography*. London: Constable.

Thompson, Josiah. (1967). *Six Seconds in Dallas*. New York: Bernard Geis.

Tidwell, William A., James O. Hall, and David Winfred Gaddy. (1989). *Come Retribution: The Confederate Secret Service and the Assassination of Lincoln*. Jackson: University Press of Mississippi.

Time. (1979). "Skid Row Plot." *Time*, May 21.

Trani, Eugene P., and David L. Wilson. (1977). *The Presidency of Warren G. Harding*. Lawrence: Regents Press of Kansas.

Truman, Margaret. (1973). *Harry S. Truman*. New York: William Morrow.

U.S. Department of the Treasury. (1981). *Management Review on the Performance of the U.S. Department of the Treasury in Connection with the March 30, 1981, Assassination Attempt on President Ronald Reagan*. Washington, DC: Department of the Treasury.

U.S. Department of the Treasury. (1995). *Public Report of the White House Security Review*. Washington, DC: U.S. Treasury Department.

Van Buren, Martin. (1920/1973). *Autobiography*. New York: Da Capo.

Village of Orland Park Police Department. (2009). http://www.orland-park.il.us/ (accessed August 17, 2009).

Von Drehle, David, and R. Jeffrey Smith. (1993). "U.S. Strikes Iraq for Plot to Kill Bush." *New York Times*, June 27, p. A1.

Ward, John William. (1955). *Andrew Jackson: Symbol for an Age*. New York: Oxford University Press.

Weichmann, Louis J. (1975). *A True History of the Assassination of Abraham Lincoln and the Conspiracy of 1865*. New York: Vintage.

Werth, Barry. (2006). *31 Days*. New York: Doubleday.

Wicker, Tom. (2003). *Four Days in November*. New York: St. Martin's.

William, Graham. (1899). *Andrew Jackson*. Boston: Houghton, Mifflin, and Wings.

Wood, Clement. (1932). *Warren Gamaliel Harding: An American Comedy*. New York: William Faro.

Young, Donald, rev. John Milton Cooper, Jr. (2000). "William McKinley: Bridge to a New Century." In *American Heritage Illustrated History of the Presidents*, ed. Michael Beschloss. New York: Crown.

Index

About the Authors

WILLARD M. OLIVER is a professor of criminal justice in the College of Criminal Justice, Sam Houston State University. His research interests revolve around federal crime-control policy and are particularly focused on the office of the president. He is the author of *The Law & Order Presidency* and coauthor of *The Public Policy of Crime & Criminal Justice*.

NANCY E. MARION is a professor of political science and fellow at the Bliss Institute of Applied Politics at the University of Akron. Her research interests revolve around the interplay of politics and criminal justice. She has published many books and articles that describe and analyze how political actors affect, and are affected by, criminal-justice policies.